Islam and Political Legitimacy

Islam and Political Legitimacy explores one of the most challenging issues facing the Muslim world: the Islamisation of political power. It presents a comparative analysis of Muslim societies in West, South, Central and South East Asia and highlights the immediacy of the challenge for the political leadership in those societies. *Islam and Political Legitimacy* contends that the growing reliance on Islam for justifying power across the Muslim world, even in states that have had a strained relationship with Islam, has contributed to the evolution of Islam from a social and cultural factor to an entrenched political force.

The geographic breadth of *Islam and Political Legitimacy* offers readers a nuanced appraisal of political Islam that transcends parochial eccentricities. Contributors to this volume examine the evolving relationship between Islam and political power in Bangladesh, Indonesia, Iran, Malaysia, Pakistan, Saudi Arabia and Uzbekistan. Researchers and students of political Islam and the growth of radicalism in the Muslim world will find *Islam and Political Legitimacy* of special interest. This is a welcome addition to the rich literature on the politics of the contemporary Muslim world.

Shahram Akbarzadeh is a Senior Lecturer in Global Politics at the School of Political and Social Inquiry, Monash University, Australia. His research interests focus on the politics of Central Asia, Islamic radicalism and the Middle East. He is co-editor of *Global Change, Peace and Security*. Among his latest publications are *Muslim Communities in Australia* (with Abdullah Saeed) and the *Historical Dictionary of Tajikistan* (with Kamoludin Abdullaev).

Abdullah Saeed is Associate Professor and Head of the Islamic Studies Programme at the Melbourne Institute of Asian Languages and Societies, the University of Melbourne. Among his recent publications are *Islamic Banking and Interest, Freedom of Religion, Apostasy and Islam* and *Islam in Australia*.

Islam and Political Legitimacy

**Edited by Shahram Akbarzadeh
and Abdullah Saeed**

LONDON AND NEW YORK

First published 2003
by Routledge
2 Park Square, Milton Park, Abingdon, Oxon, OX14 4RN

Simultaneously published in the USA and Canada
by Routledge
270 Madison Ave, New York NY 10016

Routledge is an imprint of the Taylor & Francis Group

Transferred to Digital Printing 2007

Editorial Matter © 2003 Shahram Akbarzadeh and Abdullah Saeed
Individual chapters © the authors

Typeset in Times by
Keystroke, Jacaranda Lodge, Wolverhampton

All rights reserved. No part of this book may be reprinted or reproduced or utilised in any form or by any electronic, mechanical, or other means, now known or hereafter invented, including photocopying and recording, or in any information storage or retrieval system, without permission in writing from the publishers.

British Library Cataloguing in Publication Data
A catalogue record for this book is available from the British Library

Library of Congress Cataloguing in Publication Data
  Islam and political legitimacy / edited by Shahram Akbarzadeh & Abdullah Saeed.
    p. cm.
  Includes bibliographical references and index.
  1. Islam and politics. 2. Islam and state. 3. Religion and politics.
  4. Islamic countries—Politics and government. I. Akbarzadeh, Shahram. II. Saeed, Abdullah.

BP173.7 .I837 2003
320.5′5′0917671—dc21

                                      2002036960

ISBN10: 0–415–31428–3 (hbk)
ISBN10: 0–415–44437–3 (pbk)

ISBN13: 978–0–415–31428–2 (hbk)
ISBN13: 978–0–415–44437–8 (pbk)

Contents

List of contributors vii
Acknowledgements xi

1 Islam and politics 1
SHAHRAM AKBARZADEH AND ABDULLAH SAEED

2 The official ulema and religious legitimacy of the modern nation state 14
ABDULLAH SAEED

3 Saudi Arabia: re-reading politics and religion in the wake of September 11 29
LARBI SADIKI

4 The politics of reform in the Islamic Republic of Iran 50
FARIDEH FARHI

5 Pakistan and the struggle for 'real' Islam 70
SAMINA YASMEEN

6 The Islamic dilemma in Uzbekistan 88
SHAHRAM AKBARZADEH

7 Failure of the 'welfare state': Islamic resurgence and political legitimacy in Bangladesh 102
TAJ I. HASHMI

8	**Islam and political legitimacy in Malaysia** OSMAN BAKAR	**127**
9	**Divided majority: limits of Indonesian political Islam** GREG FEALY	**150**
10	**State legitimacy** SHAHRAM AKBARZADEH	**169**
	Bibliography	175
	Index	183

Contributors

Shahram Akbarzadeh is a Senior Lecturer in the School of Political and Social Inquiry, Monash University, Australia. His research interests include Islam and globalisation and political Islam in Central Asia. He is currently writing on the democratisation process in Uzbekistan. Among his latest publications are a co-edited book (with Abdullah Saeed) on *Muslim Communities in Australia* (University of New South Wales, 2001) and a co-authored book with Kamoludin Abdullaev, *Historical Dictionary of Tajikistan* (Scarecrow Press, 2002). He edits the internationally refereed journal *Global Change, Peace & Security*, published by Taylor & Francis in the United Kingdom.

Osman Bakar holds a PhD in Islam from Temple University, Philadelphia, and is currently Visiting Professor and Malaysia Chair of Islam in Southeast Asia at Georgetown University's School of Foreign Service, Washington, DC. A former Professor of Philosophy of Science and Deputy Vice-Chancellor (Academic) at the University of Malaya, Kuala Lumpur, he has written a dozen books and more than 100 articles on various aspects of Islamic thought and civilisation, both classical and contemporary, including Southeast Asian Islam. Some of his works have been translated into various languages, including Arabic, Persian, Turkish, Urdu, Indonesian, Chinese and Spanish. Among his works are *Classification of Knowledge in Islam, Islam and Civilisational Dialogue* and *Sufism in the Malay-Indonesian World*.

Farideh Farhi graduated from the University of Colorado, Boulder, with an MA (1980) and PhD in Political Science (1986). She has taught comparative politics at the University of Colorado, Boulder, the University of Hawaii at Manoa (where she was an Associate Professor until 1994), the University of Tehran and Shahid Beheshti University (Tehran). She was a research associate at the Institute for Political and International Studies (Tehran) between 1993 and 1998. She is currently an independent researcher and lives in Honolulu. Among her publications are *States and Urban-Based Revolutions: Iran and Nicaragua* (University of Illinois Press, 1990). Her publications on comparative analysis of revolutions and Iranian politics and foreign policy have also appeared in *Comparative Political Studies, Theory and Society, Journal of Developing Societies, Iranian Journal of International Affairs*, and *International Journal of Politics, Culture and Society*.

Greg Fealy is Research Fellow and Lecturer in Indonesian politics held jointly in the Research School of Pacific and Asian Studies and the Faculty of Asian Studies, The Australian National University. His doctoral research was on the political history of Indonesia's largest Islamic organisation, Nahdlatul Ulama, and he has co-edited *Nahdlatul Ulama, Traditional Islam and Modernity in Indonesia* (Monash Asia Institute, 1996) with Greg Barton. More recently he has published articles on contemporary trends in Indonesian Islamic politics as well as on issues of terrorism, democratisation and separatism. His current research focuses on campus neo-revivalist groups in Indonesia.

Taj I. Hashmi holds a PhD in Modern South Asian History, the University of Western Australia. He is currently a Research Associate at York Centre for Asian Research, York University, Canada, and has taught history and anthropology at universities in Australia, Bangladesh, Canada and Singapore. He is presently working on two projects: 'South Asian Islam: Reforms, Resurgence and Militancy' and 'Revisiting Culture of Poverty: Case Studies from South Asia'. His latest publications include *Women and Islam in Bangladesh: Beyond Subjection and Tyranny* (Macmillan, 2000), *Islam, Muslims and the Modern State* (Macmillan, 1994), *Pakistan as a Peasant Utopia* (Westview Press, 1992) and *Colonial Bengal* (in Bengali), (Papyrus, 1985).

Larbi Sadiki teaches democracy, democratisation and Human Rights in the Middle East and the Arab World in the Department of Politics, the University of Exeter, England. His research interests focus on Islamism in relation to questions of democracy and democratisation, areas he published on in journals such as *Political Studies, International Journal of Middle East Studies, British Journal of Middle Eastern Studies, Arab Studies Quarterly, Third World Quarterly, Orient, Australian Journal of International Affairs* and *Democratization*.

Abdullah Saeed is Associate Professor and Head of the Arabic and Islamic Studies Programme of the Melbourne Institute of Asian Languages and Societies, the University of Melbourne, Australia. He holds a BA in Arabic and Islamic Studies from Saudi Arabia, a PhD in Islamic Studies and a

Masters Degree in Applied Linguistics both from the University of Melbourne. His teaching and research interests include modern Islamic thought with particular reference to areas such as Qur'anic hermeneutics, Islamic finance, pluralism, human rights as well as Islam in Australia. His recent monographs include, *Islamic Banking and Interest* (E.J. Brill, 1996, 1999), *Muslim Communities in Australia* (co-edited; University of New South Wales, 2001), *Islam in Australia* (Allen & Unwin, 2003), *Freedom of Religion, Apostasy and Islam* (co-authored; Ashgate) and *Approaches to Qur'an in Indonesia* (edited; Oxford University Press), both forthcoming.

Samina Yasmeen is a Senior Lecturer in International Politics in the Department of Political Science, the University of Western Australia (UWA), Perth. Before joining the University, she conducted post-doctoral research on US Military relations with Pakistan at the Strategic and Defence Studies Centre, the Australian National University, Canberra. She has also worked as Executive Director of the Indian Ocean Centre for Peace Studies at UWA and Curtin Universities (1995), a Research Specialist in Defence at the Legislative Research Service of the Australian Parliament (1985) and Senior Research fellow in a UNESCO-funded project at the Ministry of Education, the Government of Pakistan (1966–9). She is a specialist in political and strategic developments in South Asia, and the role of Islam in world politics. She has published extensively in referred journals and contributes annually on Australia–India relations to *The Asia–Australia Survey* edited by Bishop and McNamara since 1993. She is currently directing a large ARC grant project on women and citizenship which, among other issues, focuses on the views of Indian and Pakistani immigrant women on being Australian citizens.

Acknowledgements

The editors would like to acknowledge the generous support provided for this project by the Melbourne Institute of Asian Languages and Societies, the University of Melbourne, the 'Politics, Religion and Culture in an Age of Terrorism' initiative at the School of Political and Social Inquiry, Monash University and the Monash University Research Fund.

1 Islam and politics

Shahram Akbarzadeh and Abdullah Saeed

The September 11 attacks by al-Qaeda struck at the heart of the United States and brought Islamic radicalism to the international spotlight. The subsequent moblisation of public opinion and security forces in the United States and its allies in the 'war on terror' have ensured Islamic radicalism prominence on the security and foreign policy agenda. The apparent shift in the strategic thinking of the United States suggests that meeting the threat posed by Islamic militancy is no longer a secondary consideration but a top priority. However, for many Muslim states this is not a qualitatively new challenge. They have faced an ever-growing Islamic opposition in the past decades. Islamic militancy has led to regime change in Iran (1979), the assassination of the Egyptian President Anwar al-Sadat (1981), a wave of political violence and assassinations in Algeria, Taliban successes in Afghanistan (1996), the on-going Kashmiri Islamic mobilisation and guerilla war that has impacted on the domestic politics of Pakistan and challenged India, on-going separatist pressures in Aceh and inter-communal violence in Indonesia (2000–1).

Muslim states, therefore, are not surprised by the political potency of the militant Islamic threat, although the sheer magnitude of the September 11 attacks was shockingly unprecedented. They have borne the brunt of this growing tide of radicalism and agitation and have been the primary targets of the Islamic revolutionary zeal. This challenge and the altered political conditions have forced state leaders to re-evaluate their image and symbols of power. In recognition of its emotive and familiar message, Islam has been systematically incorporated in the (explicit or implicit) frame of reference of the state to offset the increasingly plausible challenge to the legitimacy of the political leadership. This dynamic of challenge and response has made politics in many Muslim societies a volatile, sometimes violent, affair, the boundaries of which are not predetermined or confined to institutions. Symbols and informal aspects of politics serve an important role in advancing or detracting from the legitimacy of the political elite, a feature that has not escaped the attention of the latter. Except in the case of Iran and Saudi Arabia, where institutional Islamisation is the norm, the leadership in other Muslim states have moved in earnest to claim Islamic symbolism, while endeavouring to contain the over-flow effects into institutional politics. It is this dynamism that engages the authors in this volume.

The challenge of political Islam (i.e. presenting Islam as the guiding principle, even the blueprint, for government, which may also be called Islamism) to secular modes of government and the legitimacy of 'irreligious' rule is essentially a new and modern phenomenon, although it is presented by its exponents as a continuation of a long tradition in Islamic political thought. This challenge, which is somewhat pejoratively called fundamentalism, traces its ideological roots to early Hadith against 'quietism'. The challenge rests on the assumption that Islam and politics are inseparable, pointing to the early history of Islam when Prophet Muhammad acted as ruler and spiritual leader in Medina and the subsequent four Caliphs (*khulafa rashidun*) whose religious and political roles were entwined. This assumption is then incorporated in the political philosophy of just and Islamic government which provides an ideological framework for political activism. Accordingly political power is only just and legitimate if it operates on Divine Law (shari'a) and serves the cause of Islam. This is because temporal rule is not seen as possessing its own source of authority, independent of the Divine Law. Any attempt to rule independent of the shari'a is, therefore, considered illegitimate.

Ann K.S. Lambton identifies two prophetic sayings as the ideological justifications for Islamic activism: 'there is no (duty of) obedience in sin' and 'do not obey a creature against his creator'.[1] These sayings helped provide the theological justification for the Shi'a and Khawarij rebellions in the first Islamic century. But this activist interpretation of Islam soon gave way to a more complacent and pragmatic version, whereby Muslim jurists offered their allegiance to temporal rulers and decreed obedience as a Qur'anic obligation: 'obey God, obey the prophet and those in authority among you'.[2] This injunction and a realistic apprehension about the prospects of social discord provided the justification for a large body of jurisprudence literature recommending obedience to those in authority, even if they appear sinful. Al-Mawardi, writing about appropriate relations between Muslims and Seljuq rulers (whose adherence to Islam was seen as questionable) in the mid-eleventh century, proclaimed:

> Listen to them and obey them in everything that is comfortable to the truth. If they are good, it will be to your benefit and theirs, and if they do evil it will be to your benefit but harmful to them.[3]

Al-Mawardi's views came to be highly influential in Islamic political thought. Al-Ghazali, writing a half-century later, expounded on al-Mawardi's theme, declaring that 'necessity makes lawful what is forbidden'. The search for the 'unattainable' perfect Islamic model, al-Ghazali implied, took Muslims beyond the realm of possibilities and promised conflict and social mayhem. Al-Ghazali understood the limits of politics as the 'art of the possible' and was clearly apprehensive of the grave dangers in striving for unrealistic goals. In an observation that is remarkably relevant to Islamic militants striving to depose what they consider to be un-Islamic governments in modern times, he continued:

> ... which is to be preferred, anarchy and the stoppage of social life for lack of properly constituted authority, or acknowledgement of the existing power, whatever it be? Of these two alternatives, the jurist cannot but choose the latter.[4]

Faced with the advancing Mongol armies Ibn Taymiyya gave voice to this tradition:

> It is obvious that the [affairs of the] people cannot be in a sound state except with rulers, and even if somebody from among unjust kings becomes ruler, this would be better than there being none. As it is said: 'Sixty years with an unjust ruler are better than one night without a ruler'. And it is related of [the fourth Caliph] Ali, May God Be Satisfied with Him, to have said that: 'The people have no option but to have a rulership [*imara*], whether pious or sinful'. People asked him: 'We understand the pious, but why bother for the sinful?' He said: '[Because,] thanks to it, highways are kept secure, canonical penalties are applied, holy war is fought against the enemy, and spoils are collected'.[5]

This judgment formed the core of Islamic political thought well into the twentieth century, when the more radical interpretations of Islam became salient. Dubbed 'quietism' by its critics, this perspective carried an important caveat: obedience is justified, indeed required of Muslims, if the ruler does not actively work against Islam. In other words, so long as the ruler protected life and limb of the Muslims and allowed their practice of Islam, there was no cause to question the legitimacy of his rule, even if the ruler was not personally regarded as a devout Muslim or versed in the shari'a. This caveat was effectively met by all rulers until the dawn of secularism in the Muslim world in the twentieth century.

The *de facto* separation of temporal and religious leadership which began to emerge in the early Abbasid period (750 AD onwards) and formalised under subsequent caliphs, was a reflection of the duality of *din* and *dawla* (religion and government). But this effective separation was by no means absolute. On the contrary the temporal ruler and the ulema were in a mutually dependent relationship, whereby each relied on the other, one for its physical protection and the other for its authority to rule. Temporal rulers needed the air of legitimacy that Islamic scholars could offer by virtue of their position as interpreters of Divine Law and the latter needed the physical protection and social order in which Islam could flourish that the former was capable of securing. *Din* and *dawla* were not the same, but two sides of the same coin.

The advent of secularism in the Muslim world and the push to divorce Islam from politics put enormous strain on the dialectical relationship that had sustained Muslim polities. The European experience of secular rule was regarded as a model by state-builders in the twentieth century, who tried to emulate Europe by relegating Islam to the private domain. Atatürk in Turkey and Reza Shah in Iran were the most systematic and vehement supporters of the Islam/state separation. The new states no longer sought formal legitimacy in Islam but looked for other sources of authority. Socialism, nationalism and paternalism were seen as alternatives to Islam, although none seemed comprehensive and broad enough to replace Islam's all-encompassing and pervasive nature. For that reason the political elite, even the most ardent exponents of secularism, have found it often difficult to purge Islam and its symbols of authority from the state.

Moves to decouple *din* and *dawla* have caused a significant crisis of authority in the Muslim world in the twentieth century. The revolutionary interpretation of Islam in modern times, espoused by political Islam, is a response to a model of development that excludes indigenous traditions and large segments of the population, now called citizens in the parlance of modern statehood. But such radicalism is not content with the restoration of *din* and *dawla* inter-dependent duality. It seeks their unity, idealised in the model of the Muhammadan Medina.

Three developments have contributed to the potency and popularity of Islamic militancy: military defeat in the hands of Israel, inroads by western cultural values, and the failure of the welfare state model. The creation of the state of Israel despite fierce Arab opposition and the consequent Arab-Israeli wars which delivered defeat after defeat to Arab armies were stark reminders of the chronic weakness of Arab states. The plight of the Palestinians, taken-up in a number of international fora, and the inability of Arab leaders to turn international sympathy into a concrete plan of action to force an Israeli withdrawal from Palestinian lands helped radicalise sections of those societies. The cause of Palestinian statehood and control over Jerusalem galvanised Muslim masses, a factor that has gained additional weight since the 1987 Palestinian intifada. The sense of indignation and disillusionment with the political elite is not confined to Arab societies. All Muslim societies are hurting, even as far as Indonesia and Malaysia where the Muslim student movements have aligned themselves with the Palestinian cause.

Coupled with this sense of powerlessness against Israel and its international backer (the United States) and indignation with the political elite for their inability or unwillingness to pursue the Palestinian cause, was deep resentment at the way Muslim societies were at the receiving end of a cultural onslaught. Indigenous cultures seemed to be 'contaminated' and undermined by Western-originated values of individualism, excessive consumerism and permissiveness. The adoption of Western dress for women, dancing and watching Hollywood movies came to epitomise the pervasive nature of Western culture in Muslim societies. That cinemas and nightclubs, as well as banks and official buildings, are often targeted in urban riots attest to their 'alien' image for many Muslims. As in the case of military defeats, the political elite is held responsible for its inability to hold back, or complacency in, this cultural encroachment.

This backlash against the political elite has occurred against the backdrop of state failure to deliver development and prosperity. The promise of social development and wealth were central to the underlying logic of modern territorial states in the Muslim world. The opening of universities and polytechnics were presented as an important step in promoting social mobility. But Muslim states have, by and large, failed to deliver the promised development package for a combination of reasons, among them lack of long-term planning, corruption in the form of patronage, disproportionate investment in security forces, and a population explosion. The development model of the welfare state caused a profound social revolution. It uprooted peasants who flooded urban centres in search of work, leading to the spread of shanty-towns in the periphery of urban areas. It produced an ever-growing body of aspiring university graduates who found the job market too rigid and inflexible to cope with their employment needs. In an ironic twist, advances in the health system contributed to a population explosion that exerted extra pressure on the limited resources of the state. Muslim states were unable to meet the expectations they had fostered. As in many other third world societies, such unfulfilled expectations are a source of grave social strife.

The combination of the above three factors helped alienate Muslim societies from their political elite. The response of political Islam to this pervading sense of alienation and powerlessness has been to blame state leaders for decades of corruption and imitation of the West (dubbed Westoxification). Muslim societies have lost their direction, argued Islamists, and the only way to restore the self-respect of the Muslims was to return to the essential principles of Islam as expounded in the shari'a. This meant rejecting laws, made by temporal leaders, and the institutions they foster, as illegitimate – insisting on the supremacy of the revealed 'word of God'.

Political Islam presents an unambiguous challenge to the political elite and its temporal source of authority.

The message of political Islam had particular appeal to aspiring members of the middle class. University students, merchants and professionals were especially drawn to the ideals of purity and social justice.[6] Some of the most vocal and authoritative exponents of political Islam have been trained in modern/secular institutions. Hasan al-Banna (1906–49) and Sayyid Qutb (1906–66) who acted as leaders of the Muslim Brotherhood were both trained as 'teachers in modern subjects'.[7] Mawlana Abul Ala Mawdudi (1903–79) who founded the Jamaat-i Islami and helped define the qualities of an Islamic state in South Asia was a journalist by profession. In that respect the resurgent Islamic radicalism is a modern phenomenon.

Political Islam is far removed from traditional Islam; it is not concerned with describing and sanctioning social realities, the way traditional Islam is resigned to the social and political *status quo*, but searches for ways to change the conditions which it deems unjust and illegitimate. This approach sets the radical vision of political Islam on a collision course with the established Islamic institutions which often act as a bastion of conservatism, justifying the status quo and rejecting political activism. The ulema's attitude to power is generally defined by the dictum of 'any order is better than no order', even if the ruler does not abide by the principles of Islam. Even Ayatollah Khomeini (d. 1989), the late leader of the Islamic revolution in Iran and perhaps the most influential practitioner of political Islam, adhered to this doctrine before the experience of exile radicalised his views. This overriding concern with social order, as opposed to social justice, has informed relations between the ulema and political power and has led them to dismiss Islamic militants as misguided and at best 'deficient in their knowledge of Islam'.[8] In a classic response to the challenge posed by Islamic activism, Mufti Abdurashid qori Bahromov of Uzbekistan rejected the politicisation of Islam as un-Islamic and linked the spread of Islamic radicalism to the absence of religious education, promising to 'fight illiteracy with enlightenment'.[9] This is of course a double-edged sword. On the one hand broader public education in Islam is designed to promote the 'true' and 'authentic' version of Islam which justifies the status quo and is resigned to the existing order. On the other, such religious training would inevitably make Muslims more familiar with classical Islamic teachings and text, and would consequently expose them to the scriptural and puritan interpretations of Islam that have mobilised many activists.

The political elite's response to this dilemma in Muslim societies has followed the same pattern: allow some religious freedom and education for Islam but control its content as tightly as possible. In Egypt Anwar al-Sadat sensed the growth of a backlash to his rule and tried to appease his Islamic critics by wrapping key government policies in an Islamic cloak. He even oversaw the 1980 constitutional amendment which made Islam the 'religion of the state' and shari'a the 'main source of legislation'. In Pakistan, a state which emerged as a fulfilment of Muslim aspirations for self-rule in South Asia, the popularly elected Prime Minister Zulfikar Ali Bhutto endorsed the return of Islam to the discourse of power and politics by talking about 'Islamic socialism'. Despite their differences, General Zia ul-Haq reinforced this trend by embarking on a project of Islamisation in Pakistan. The Bangladesh experience resembles that of Pakistan in that military leaders took up the mantle of Islam to disarm their critics and improve their public standing. An added factor for General Zia ur-Rahman was his concern with India's influence in Bangladesh and the need for transparent and salient distinctions in the mind of Bangladeshis about the borders of the nation. Reverting to Islam was as much about short-term political expediency as about the more complex process of nation-building. President Islam Karimov has faced a similar challenge in steering Uzbekistan away from its Soviet past and consolidating the ideal of the Uzbek nation: a cohesive and orderly community that practices traditional Islam and is respectful toward authority. To that effect the Uzbek government has become an ardent sponsor of 'true' Islam.

In Indonesia, the most populous Muslim state and perhaps the most internally diverse society, Islam occupies a critical place. It is the cement that helps keep distinct island communities together. But the unifying qualities of Indonesian Islam were carefully moulded into 'cultural Islam' to thwart radical interpretations. Abdurahman Wahid represented cultural Islam. He promoted the separation of Islam and power when, as president, he refrained from making any move to Islamise the state. Political Islam has not had much success in this milieu until recently. The situation in Malaysia is not fundamentally different. In spite of sizable non-Muslim minority groups, the Malay political leadership has linked the state with Islam. The constitution gives Islam the status of official religion, and Prime Minister Mahathir Muhammad has been careful to maintain at least a semblance of cooperation with Islamic actors, evident most significantly in the 1983 co-option of Anwar Ibrahim, an intellectual Islamist.

What the above cases have in common is that the political elite, faced with growing opposition from Islamists, finds it expedient to co-opt Islam as its modus operandi, in some cases even incorporating it in the constitution. The case of Iran and Saudi Arabia points to a different experience, although it may be argued that the dynamics of relations between political elite and Islam are very similar to other Muslim societies. In the Islamic Republic of Iran, political legitimacy is coupled with the principle of the *velayat-e faqih*, the guardianship of the jurisconsult, which superimposes the *vali-ye faqih*, now the spiritual leader Seyyed Ali Khamenei, over the state and constitution.

Box 1.1 Constitutional excerpts pertaining to Islam

Bangladesh

Article 2A: The state religion of the Republic is Islam, but other religions may be practised in peace and harmony in the Republic.
(http://www.bangladeshgov.org/pmo/constitution/consti2.htm#2A)

Egypt

Article 2: Islam is the religion of the State. Arabic is its official language, and the principal source of legislation is Islamic Jurisprudence (shari'a).
(http://www.newafrica.com/egypt/constitution.asp)

Iran

Article 1: The form of government of Iran is that of an Islamic Republic, endorsed by the people of Iran on the basis of their longstanding belief in the sovereignty of truth and Quranic justice, in the referendum of 29 and 30 March 1979, through the affirmative vote of a majority of 98.2 per cent of eligible voters, held after the victorious Islamic Revolution led by Imam Khumayni.

Article 2: The Islamic Republic is a system based on belief in:

1 the One God (as stated in the phrase 'There is no God except Allah'), His exclusive sovereignty and right to legislate, and the necessity of submission to His commands;
2 Divine revelation and its fundamental role in setting forth the laws;
3 the return to God in the Hereafter, and the constructive role of this belief in the course of man's ascent towards God;
4 the justice of God in creation and legislation.

Article 12: The official religion of Iran is Islam and the Twelver Ja'fari school, and this principle will remain eternally immutable.
(http://www.uni-wuerzburg.de/law/ir00000_.html)

Malaysia

Article 3.1: Islam is the religion of the Federation; but other religions may be practised in peace and harmony in any part of the Federation.
(http://www.eur.nl/frg/iacl/armenia/constitu/constit/malaysia/malays-e.htm)

Pakistan

Preamble: Whereas sovereignty over the entire Universe belongs to Almighty Allah alone, and the authority to be exercised by the people of Pakistan within the limits prescribed by Him is a sacred trust.

Article 2: Islam shall be the State religion of Pakistan.
(http://www.pakistani.org/pakistan/constitution)

Islam, represented by the ulema, is entwined with political leadership. Similarly in the Kingdom of Saudi Arabia, the House of Saud claims custodianship of Islam and its most holy place. It follows strict Islamic rules and promotes Islamic education. In both cases, Islam is their *raison d'être* and the most damaging challenge to their legitimacy would be to question the Islamicity of the state.

In their search for political legitimacy, the leadership has promoted a favourable interpretation of Islam by the ulema as 'true' and 'authentic'. The ulema's jurisdiction in interpreting and promoting 'true' Islam has helped create an Islamic orthodoxy which is endorsed by the state and followed by the people. That interpretation relies on state patronage and as Abdullah Saeed argues, tends to render the 'official' ulema dependent on the political elite. This often translates into state 'supervision' of the ulema and the network of mosques through various government agencies, such as the Ministry of Religious Affairs, in order to ensure that 'Islamic orthodoxy' and its message of respect for authority is the primary voice on the pulpit. Other radical interpretations of Islam are rejected as misguided or heretical. This alignment between the ulema and the political elite, or their merger in the case of Iran and Saudi Arabia, is crucial in bestowing upon the state a somewhat divine authority.

The importance of ulema to the state is not lost to radical Islamists who have identified the official ulema and its 'orthodoxy' as an important bulwark to be pushed aside on the path to their ideal Islamic state. The ulema's ability to speak in the name of Islam and reach a wide audience that accepts its authority makes it a formidable challenger to revolutionary interpretations of Islam. The ulema can discredit the more radical interpretations as mere fallacy, even heresy, which leaves no appeal venue for the Islamic militants to dispute that decree. The ulema's quasi-monopolist hold on defending and promoting 'true' Islam, has resulted in an equally monopolist approach by Islamists in defining and 'reviving' the essence of Islam and its revolutionary message. They reject the official ulema and their version of Islam as subservient to the state and not worthy of the name. Consequently, Islam itself has become a contested territory where two opposite camps wrestle for the ultimate supremacy of their interpretation.

Islamists also reject attempts by the political elite to sponsor Islam as hypocritical, a charge that may be difficult to refute. But transparent hypocrisy may be the least of the problems for the state. As the political elite gradually incorporates Islam and its lexicon in official affairs, it welcomes by default Islam's politicisation and sets itself up for judgment by increasingly Islamic criteria. The more the leadership feels threatened and challenged, the more it attempts to present itself in an Islamic cloak to fend off criticisms of 'betrayal'. The promotion of state-sanctioned Islam is designed to convince the masses that the political leadership is in tune with the cultural and spiritual mood of the nation, and that it is fulfilling its role as guardian and protector of the nation to promote and defend the nation's value system which is encapsulated in Islam. In this respect, Islam has become a pillar of legitimacy for the state. This is a desperate response to genuine and widespread social anxiety regarding the future of Muslim societies in an increasingly integrated world. The new policy on Islam is not a blanket invitation; the political elite has been careful to mould and monitor Islam's message. But state control cannot be absolute. By soliciting approval from Islam, the leadership tacitly acknowledges that its actions can be judged according to Islamic measures, and that approval could be withheld.

It is the prospect of the latter that concerns the political elite. For once Islam and its teachings, even in the most benign form possible, have been elevated onto the political plane, Islam becomes an undeniably political force – a force that may not be tamed by the state, or the official ulema. The politicisation of Islam is even more evident in the Saudi Kingdom and Iran as both rely on their interpretation of Islam to justify the merger of Islam and state institutions. Other forms of legitimacy are secondary to the legitimacy derived from Islam. As a consequence of this overwhelming reliance on Islam, these two are much more sensitive than other Muslim states to threats to their monopoly over Islam and actively portray dissent (social or political) as un-Islamic. This policy places clear parameters on politics and, as Larbi Sadiki argues, the Saudi opposition has consciously avoided any hint that might question the unity of Islam and the state, instead confining itself to challenging the 'legitimacy of the rulers'.

Similarly, Islam is the primary source of legitimacy in Iran and is recognised as such by the two main factions. But the merger of the state and Islam, Farideh Farhi maintains, has paradoxically had a secularising effect on the latter by making it responsible for the 'organisation of the present temporal world'. This process has imposed on Islam secular constraints linked to public opinion. As a consequence a strong trend has gathered momentum among Iranian intellectuals and youth to formalise this relationship and recognise the importance of popular support for political legitimacy. This perspective, represented by the 'moderates' and President Muhammad Khatami, is not new and may be traced to the early days of the Islamic Republic and the drafting of its constitution which embodies two contradictory principles: *Velayat-e faqih* (i.e. the sovereignty of the jurisprudent) vs. the republic (the sovereignty of the people). The obvious tension between the sovereignty of God and the people has also marked the politics of Pakistan since its inception. Samina Yasmeen's account of the political development in that state sheds light on the pivotal and inescapable liberal Islam/political Islam dynamism. Even though Pakistan was created for Muslims, it was not conceived as an Islamic state by its founders. This conception, however, has come under severe strain as a result of a growing challenge to the more liberal/cultural interpretations of Islam and the Pakistani elite's desire to utilise Islam to further its domestic and regional objectives in Kashmir and Afghanistan.

Uzbekistan is new to the Muslim world, but has experienced the full force of political Islam and faces similar challenges that confront other Muslim societies. The Uzbek society has gone through rapid Islamisation in the aftermath of the Soviet collapse, with the tacit approval of the state. But as the more radical Islamic groups have emerged to question the legitimacy of the leadership and its sincerity in promoting Islam, the elite has been forced to draw a distinction between 'true' Islam and the 'alien' Wahabbi brand. Championing 'true' Islam, that is engrained in Uzbek identity and submissive to authority, the political elite is creating a new yardstick for measuring its performance. But by virtue of granting Islam, even in its most pacifist form, a measure of authority in politics, Shahram Akbarzadeh argues, the leadership is contributing to the politicisation of Islam.

Islam's political expediency is a familiar motif in the case of Bangladesh. Taj Hashmi, however, goes beyond this analysis and presents a holistic picture as to the significant social and economic changes that have impacted on the political culture of that state. Hashmi argues that the rush of displaced rural populations who have strong ties with Islam and the ulema, to cities in search of employment and the failure of the welfare model of development to provide for the economically disenfranchised, is contributing to the influence of political Islam. The failure of the welfare state has made Islam an alternative in the eyes of many. This trend is unlikely to subside in the near future as Bangladesh's economic involvement in the global economy subjects it to greater pressures for economic rationalism, resulting in the withdrawal of the state from social services.

In Malaysia, although Islam has been very close to the political establishment since the inception of that state, the presence of a large non-Muslim minority has also made it a problematic issue. Osman Bakar points to the Chinese support for a 'republican' model of governance, encapsulated in the slogan of 'Malaysian Malaysia' – a model that has not found resonance amongst the more religiously minded Malays. Instead some Islamic intellectuals represented in the influential Malaysian Muslim Youth Movement have pushed for a greater Islamisation of the state and its financial institutions as a response to economic malaise. But this is not the only Islamic voice. An alternative Islamic perspective on the importance of dialogue and tolerance between religions and within Islam is increasingly finding adherence among Malay intellectuals. The political implications of 'pluralist' Islam are very significant and go far beyond race relations. They question the authority of any Islamic group to represent Islam in its totality and, in a similar vein as the case of the moderate intellectuals in Iran, refute the monopolisation of Islam. Political legitimacy from this perspective, therefore, is not so much judged by the Islamisation of state institutions, but by the way the leadership facilitates genuine dialogue and cross-fertilisation.

Greg Fealy's detailed account of Islamic diversity in Indonesia highlights similar tensions between political and cultural Islam. In a fascinating look at Abdurraham Wahid, the best known proponent of cultural Islam and one-time president of Indonesia, Fealy links his interpretation of Islam with the 'quietist' tradition. Allegiance is accordingly offered the political leadership so far as it does not openly violate the life and religion of Muslims. This politically complacent approach made Nahdlatul Ulama, Indonesia's largest Islamic organisation led by Wahid, a functional quasi-opposition movement for President Soeharto. The momentous upheaval that brought Wahid to power, however, kindled hopes of a break with the past pattern of acquiescence to secular rule for the more radically minded Islamists. But much to their disappointment and to the surprise of many observers, Wahid did not make any move that could be interpreted as institutionalising an Islamic state. This odd arrangement whereby an Islamic scholar and activist presided over a secular state, was perhaps the ultimate test for cultural Islam and its apolitical worldview. Wahid's deliberate refusal to merge Islam and his government policies deprived him from the aura of Islamic legitimacy and contributed to the alienation of other Islamic groups in the legislature, the

People's Consultative Assembly. Consequently, this episode in Indonesian history has widened the gap between cultural and political Islam.

Muslim societies are experiencing rapid social, economic and political changes, partly as a result of external pressures and the responses that such pressures generate. Throughout this process Islam has remained a constant factor, either as a force for quietism and political stability or an inspiration for revolt and upheaval. But nothing in Islam predisposes it to either cause. The most frequent reason steering Islam in this or that direction is the behaviour of the political elite and its approach to Islam. The contemporary strategy to utilise the immense potential of Islam for political purposes, whether by avowed Islamic political leaders or by hitherto secular figures, sanctions the saliency of Islam in the public sphere and imparts new impetus to the politicisation of Islam. It is this paradoxical relationship that is the focus of contributors to the present volume.

Notes

1 Ann K. S. Lambton, *State and Government in Medieval Islam* (Oxford: Oxford University Press, 1981), p. 14.
2 Ibid., p. 20.
3 Ibid., p. 86.
4 Reuben Levy, *Sociology of Islam*, vol. 1 (London: Williams & Norgate, 1933), p. 306.
5 As quoted in Hamid Enayat, *Modern Islamic Political Thought* (London: Macmillan Press, 1982), p. 12.
6 In this regard, it is pertinent to remember that most of the perpetrators of the September 11, 2001 attacks on the United States had tertiary education in secular sciences.
7 John L. Esposito, *The Islamic Threat, Myth or Reality?* (Oxford: Oxford University Press, 1992), p. 127.
8 Esposito, *The Islamic Threat, Myth or Reality?*, p. 98.
9 Uzbek Television Channel 1 (27 January 2000), reproduced in *Uzbekistan Daily Digest*, www.EurasiaNet.org (28 January 2000).

2 The official ulema and religious legitimacy of the modern nation state

Abdullah Saeed

This chapter largely focuses on the 'official' ulema in the Muslim world in the modern period. It argues that given the status of the official ulema vis-à-vis political authority, these ulema are not often in a position to provide any substantial degree of religious legitimacy to a modern nation state. It focuses on the ulema within the Sunni Islam and does not attempt to cover shi'a ulema. The discussion is not related to a particular country or region but attempts to look at countries with a Muslim majority. Despite the shortcomings inherent in such an approach, I believe, it is possible to make meaningful comments on the institution of the ulema that would be valid for many Muslim majority countries. This is due to the similarities associated with the institution and the social and political roles of the ulema in these countries.

In this chapter the term ulema is used rather broadly to refer to anyone formally trained in Islamic religious disciplines such as law (*fiqh*), theology (*kalam*), exegesis (*tafsir*), traditions of the Prophet (hadith) and other associated sub-disciplines, and are recognised as having a high degree of competence to deal with matters of religion. Two types of ulema exist: the official ulema and the non-official (independent) ulema. The official ulema are usually part of the state bureaucracy and are generally dependent on the state. The non-official ulema are usually outside the state bureaucracy. Today, the latter are relatively few in most Muslim countries. They depend on their own sources of income and retain their independence,[1] much like the independent ulema of the early Islamic period who avoided rulers and their favours.[2]

It is widely believed that the ulema as a group tend to provide 'religious' legitimacy for many of the Muslim states today. As they are seen as 'guardians' of religion, what they bestow seems to satisfy the yearning of many Muslim states for a form of religious legitimacy. However, it could be argued that, throughout history, it is the ulema, in particular, the 'official' ulema, as a class who often have been dependent on, and sought their legitimacy from the rulers. More importantly, in the modern period, the nation state has significantly curtailed the power and influence of ulema in general by, among other devices, bureaucratising them and controlling the activities of the ulema, and by appropriating many of the functions the ulema historically had enjoyed.

In the past, as today, in Muslim societies the degree of respect for the ulema often depended on their distance from politics. Where the ulema became part of the ruling elite, collaborating with them, seeking their favour, the ulema lost the respect of the populace. Many prominent ulema of the classical period openly shunned the rulers as well their gifts and favours, and remained at arms length from politics. Such ulema were respected by both the rulers and the masses alike.[3] While some ulema retained their independence in this way during the pre-modern period, encroachments of the nation state into all aspects of life including functions of the ulema made it increasingly difficult for many of them today to remain independent. One could argue that, today, a large number of the ulema are thus closely connected, even part of, state bureaucracy in one way or another. While some may be reluctant to embrace the policies of the state wholeheartedly, it is difficult for them to shield themselves from state influence.

Separation of religion and politics[4]

A careful look at the actual practice of the Prophet, and at the laws he implemented in the first Islamic polis, or more accurately 'emirate' in Medina, reveals that he was quite pragmatic in conducting community affairs. In his scheme, there was no distinction between a religious domain and a political domain. Just as the separation of the religious from the political is problematic, it is equally problematic to consider *everything* the Prophet did as leader of the emirate as somehow 'religious'. Law, for instance, was needed to govern the community and he provided what was necessary at the time. When the community needed a particular law, he adopted it, often determined by the social and political considerations that pertained at the time. When the time required that those laws should be changed, he did change them. Even in the case of the Qur'an, it was the societal need that often determined which laws were introduced and implemented. In this sense, both the Prophet and the revelation reflected an acute awareness of what was necessary; what constituted the pragmatic reality of the social domain. In this environment, there was no particular clerical class to determine how the emirate should be run. The Prophet was not just a religious figure, he was also a political figure, judge, administrator, and military leader. There was no separation between his functions as a political leader and his functions as a religious leader. This continued with the Prophet's immediate successors (*al-khulafa' al-rashidun*).

During the time of the Prophet and the first two caliphs, the Islamic caliphate relied heavily on the participation of members of the *umma*. No one dominated the political stage, and members of the *umma* participated according to their skills and abilities. Even in decision-making, there was significant consultation with people without this being confined to a particular tribe, clan or class. However, during the period of the third caliph, Uthman (r. 644–56 AD), this began to change. In the later part of Uthman's reign, certain prominent families of the Meccan aristocracy, notably the Umayyads and their supporters, became dominant in senior positions such as governors throughout the caliphate territories.

This increasing concentration of power within one family, the Umayyads, led to certain tensions among Muslims, and resulted in revolt and ultimately the assassination of the caliph Uthman. Ali (d. 661 AD), the fourth caliph, functioned in a turbulent period in which division arose between the party of Ali and the party of the Umayyads, led by Mu'awiya (d. 680 AD), the then governor of Syria. With the success of Mu'awiya and the emergence of the Umayyad dynastic rule in 661, leadership changed from the participatory approach of the Rashidun caliphs (632–61 AD) to a somewhat autocratic one. Furthermore, the Umayyads revived pre-Islamic tribalism in their attempt to control the populace. Thus, old hatreds re-emerged: tribe against tribe, northern Arabs against southern Arabs. Poets revitalised pre-Islamic conflicts and tribal allegiances. In this climate the Umayyad caliph in Damascus took advantage of the deteriorating situation to strengthen his own political position.

Despite the shift to a more autocratic system of government, the centralisation tendencies shown by the Umayyads, particularly evident in the reign of Abd al-Malik b. Marwan (r. 685–705 AD), the arabisation of the administration and further bureaucratisation did not clearly separate the spheres of religion and politics. But gradually, during the Abbasid period, such a separation became evident. Confirming this, the Indian Muslim thinker Abu al-Hasan al-Nadawi says that 'the separation between religion and politics occurred in practice'.[5]

From the early Abbasid period onwards, a clear distinction began to emerge between two domains: the domain of religion and the domain of politics. The increasingly smaller domain of religion was controlled to some extent by the official ulema. The domain of politics (*siyasa*) was controlled by the rulers (actual or *de facto*) who were not ulema, a separation that continued in some respects until the modern period. Several factors appear to have led to this gradual separation.

Islamic disciplines

In the seventh and eighth centuries AD, the development of Islamic disciplines as represented by *fiqh*, hadith, *tafsir* and *kalam*, as well as Arabic literature and linguistics, were to provide the intellectual basis for this distinction between 'religious' and 'non-religious' domains of life.[6] Circulation of works in these areas and the emergence of specialists enabled the spread of teachings and writings that increasingly came to be seen as 'religious'. These religious disciplines were seen as opposed to the 'non-religious' disciplines like philosophy, mathematics and physical sciences in the wake of the translation movement launched by the early Abbasids. Religious disciplines came to be revered and held in high esteem whereas non-religious disciplines came to be seen with some degree of suspicion, most notably after the tenth and eleventh centuries AD.

Notions of divine rule

From the beginning, the Abbasids utilised a number of religious myths, notably an image of the family of the Prophet toppling the Umayyads and bringing about the revolution. Having succeeded in this aim in 750 AD, they needed to highlight their 'religious' credentials. They were assisted by ideas of divine rule inherited from the Sassanids whose rule held sway in the eastern provinces of the caliphate prior to the Islamic conquests of the seventh century. Coupled with this was the exploitation of existing Shia ideas on the Imamate. From the Shi'a point of view, the imam is divinely appointed. One could also argue that the Shi'a concept of the imam and the Abbasid concept of divine rule by the caliph are closely related. Once the Abbasids had achieved their political objective of bringing down the Umayyads, they increasingly utilised the idea of divine rule justifying and legitimising their own authority. With their coming to power, the Abbasids effectively changed the caliphate to one in which a caliph officially became the imam, head of Muslims by *religious* sanction, an emphasis that had not existed before in that form. They took upon themselves titles such as 'Ruler in the Name of God', 'Shadow of God on Earth,' 'the Caliph of God', 'One Who Rules in the Name of God', or the 'Representative of God'.

Despite this, the caliph was not expected to come from the ulema class,[7] although in some cases caliphs were considered ulema, such as Abd al-Malik b. Marwan (d. 705 AD) and Umar b. Abd al-Aziz (d. 720 AD). Theoreticians of Islamic governance like al-Mawardi did not consider that the caliph must be a scholar of religion (*'alim*),[8] though he refers to the need for caliphs having 'knowledge which equips them for *ijtihad* in unforseen matters and for arriving at relevant judgements'.[9] This seems to be a theoretical position which, in practice, was not given much weight as the rulers relied on official ulema in this area. Therefore, the idea that the Islamic caliphate is a theocracy run by a religious elite is quite incorrect.[10]

Law as a function of power

Despite the prevalence of political and military conflicts among Muslims in the seventh century AD (the first century of Islam), there were those who chose to concentrate on the intellectual and academic arena. Students flocked to prominent Companions such as Ibn Abbas in Mecca and Abd Allah b. Mas'ud in Iraq in order to study the Qur'an and learn about the ways in which the Prophet had led the community. When these prominent Companions died, their students continued with their study. Such ulema were often outside the control of the political authorities and managed to work independently for a relatively long period. But by the middle of the eighth century AD, the development of law, until now primarily in the hands of independent ulema rather than bureaucrat ulema, came to a certain extent to be under the influence of the Abbasid caliph. As the caliphate expanded, there was a need for a more systematic approach to the construction of law and the administration of justice. To meet this need, the early Abbasid caliphs intended to produce a legal framework to serve as the basis of legislation applicable throughout the entire caliphate. Hitherto, independent ulema had been encouraged to join an expanding judiciary as civil servants. While many ulema, including the Hanafi imam Abu Yusuf, complied, others refused to, fearing both loss of independence and the pressure of capricious rulers.

With the development of law now allied to the domain of politics, the office of *qadi* (judge) also became much more formalised and the *qadi* became a trained official of the state. Formal courts were established and gradually the rulers began to establish educational institutions for training administrators and judges to take on the role of bureaucrats. For instance, during the Fatimid rule in Egypt, the state established an important religious seminary, al-Azhar, as a means of spreading their brand of orthodoxy based on Shi'ism. It also aimed to supply the state with graduates in law and theology as state bureaucrats. Al-Azhar thus became closely aligned with the state, then based on the idea of divine dynastic rule. Within Sunni Islam also such institutions existed. One of the most well-known institutions is Nizamiyya in Baghdad, founded by the Seljuq vizier Nizam al-Mulk (d. 1092 AD). From the tenth century AD onwards, such institutions, supported by their rulers, were established for the purpose of providing the state with graduates in law as well as other bureaucrats, and of promoting the ruling brand of orthodoxy.[11] This connection between the political authorities and education in the areas of law and theology continued to a certain extent up to the modern period. The state, by linking itself to the educational institutions, at times found a way to control both them and their leaders (ulema). Many ulema, by virtue of being state employees in such institutions became state functionaries.

Theology as an expression of political hegemony

A key development during the Abbasid period was the caliph's attempt to dominate the theological arena, the first attempt of which occurred during the reign of the caliph al-Ma'mun (d. 833 AD). He sought to impose belief in the 'creation of the Qur'an' (*khalq al-qur'an*). Al-Ma'mun and his successors, al-Mu'tasim (d. 842 AD) and al-Wathiq (d. 847 AD) were backed by Mu'tazili theologians who promoted this belief. However, such imposition of theological beliefs was finally counter-productive. It led to a strong reaction on the part of leading ulema such as Ahmad b. Hanbal (d. 855 AD), operating from outside the system. This encroachment into the domain of dogma in fact triggered a lasting revolt against the rationalistic tendencies of the Mu'tazili theologians. Despite this failure, in ideological experimentation some later Abbasid caliphs again promoted theological positions, but these supported more mainstream Sunni views. The Abbasid caliph, al-Qadir (d. 1031 AD), to whom the famous Qadiri creed is attributed, is yet another example of such an attempt in the name of the supreme religious authority, the imam.

Ulema's own legitimation of the political authority

One of the main ways in which the ulema, both official and non-official, protected the interests of the political authority was by adopting a position that argued that the ruler (whether caliph or sultan) must be obeyed. This position gave strong legitimacy to the ruler's actions (be he just or unjust). More importantly, it discouraged the mobilisation of the community in rebellion or protest against injustice. This is consistent with the idea that the institution of the caliphate was a 'divine' one and, as such, the ruler was to be obeyed. One very important reason which motivated the ulema in taking up this position was that they were anxious to avoid chaos (*fitna*) that had existed among Muslims in the first century of Islam, for example between Mu'awiya and Ali, between Umayyads and Kharijites, and the Umayyads and Zubayrids. Such chaos led to innumerable wars and bloodshed. By adopting this 'quietist' position, the ulema hoped to avoid chaos within the *umma*.

The concept of obedience to the ruler has some basis in the Qur'an: 'Obey God and obey the Prophet and those invested with command among you' (4:59). This is a general statement which does not suggest total and unconditional obedience to a ruler. A more accurate representation of the

Qur'anic instruction would have been the first caliph Abu Bakr's interpretation. This specified obedience only to the extent that he followed Qur'anic and prophetic guidelines in discharging his duties. However, this was in practice ignored by the ulema as unworkable.

One of the very early discussions on this issue was by Ibn al-Muqaffa' (d. 756 AD), a Persian convert to Islam. In addressing the Abbasid caliph, Abu Ja'far al-Mansur, Ibn al-Muqaffa' declares obedience to the caliph to be an obligation. He goes on to say that the caliph (or, as he calls him, the imam) should command obedience in all matters related to rule and administration as well as in all matters religious. The caliph, according to Ibn al-Muqaffa', has the right to issue what he considers to be appropriate in his caliphate.[12] For al-Mawardi (d. 974 AD), 'it is incumbent upon the whole of the *umma* to hand over all matters of public interest to him [imam, caliph] without any remonstrance or opposition on their part.'[13] The only case in which the caliph was not to be obeyed was if he openly ordered Muslims to reject Islam or to deny God, or if he prohibited them from fulfilling the essential religious obligations.

For the ulema, the fact that there was a political authority provided some basis for the orderly functioning of society, as order was preferable, regardless of how it was achieved. However the ruler comes to power, whether by legitimate or illegitimate means, that ruler was to be obeyed. Perhaps those supporting this view realised that the ulema themselves did not have the political influence to object to the existing authority, and it was in their interest to accept and affirm the status quo.

Breakdown of caliphal authority

Until the early Abbasid period, the two forms of authority (political and religious) were conjoined in one person. However, from the tenth century AD onwards, the caliph increasingly became a mere figurehead. His power was gradually diffused into the 'religious' sphere by powerful warlords and sultans who, for all practical purposes, had usurped the power of the caliph. The new sultans and the warlords became the de facto rulers who held real political power, while the Abbasid caliph functioned merely as the symbolic head of the religious domain. Successive warlords, military figures and dynasties too, in fact, such as the Buyids (932–1062 AD) and Seljuqs (1038–1194 AD), although ruling in the name of the caliph, exploited the office of the caliph for the purpose of their own legitimacy. Slowly the convergent domains of political power and religious authority hardened into distinct and separate spheres. The caliph retained an aura of religious authority: his name was mentioned in the Friday *khutba* (sermon) and in all religious ceremonies, but the caliphate was changed from one that united religious and political worlds into one in which the caliph's authority was downgraded. It was still religious but now subservient to the political realm.

By the early years of the tenth century, the breakdown of caliphal authority was complete. The now powerless Abbasid caliphs recognised the 'existence of a supreme governing authority besides the caliph, exercising effective political and military power, and leaving the caliph only as formal head of the state and the faith and representative of the religious unity of Islam.'[14] The two forms of authority, religious and political, came to be so clearly differentiated and separated that during the Seljuq domination during the Abbasid period, when the caliph attempted to exercise political power, the Seljuq sultan protested against what he regarded as an infringement of the political authority's prerogatives. The caliph, he said, 'should busy himself with his duties as imam, as leader in prayer, which is the best and most glorious of tasks, and is the protection of the rulers of the world; he should leave the business of government to the sultans, to whom it was entrusted'.[15]

Ulema: role, status and legitimacy in the modern period

During the pre-modern period, the social status and position of the ulema appears to have been based on several interrelated factors. As scholars, judges and muftis they developed law. As judges (*qadis*) they administered justice and as administrators of *awqaf* (endowments), they often had substantial economic independence. The ulema also controlled the training of students, basing this on a model in which religious disciplines were given priority. The influence of religion in all aspects of life in the society thus confirmed the social role of ulema. By contrast, in the modern period the nation state has, to a large extent, appropriated many of the key functions previously held by the ulema. Measures have been taken in modern nation states to curtail the power and influence of the ulema. As a result, the social status and prestige formerly enjoyed by them has shrunk, and with it, their power.

Part of this marginalisation is of their own making. One example is their training. Educational curricula today for Islamic disciplines in Islamic seminaries, generally speaking, do not seem to prepare the ulema to deal effectively with the needs of a modern society. Their studies are often seen as outdated and irrelevant. Those who enrol in Islamic studies disciplines in Muslim societies are often seen as people without access to, or ability to undertake, the study of more 'prestigious' disciplines, such as medicine, engineering and the sciences. Their only form of education may have been that of the *madrasa*, where only 'religious' education was available. The disadvantaged or marginalised accessing the free but inadequate education in a traditional *madrasa* often move on to a seminary, itself marginalised, which prepares students to be 'religious leaders' who can issue fatwa, lead the prayer in mosques and teach Qur'an/religious education classes. The lucky ones may find a job in the bureaucracy of a department of 'religious affairs'. But irrespective of career prospects, these ulema are often seen to be ill-equipped to deal with the more complex issues of modern life.

The following highlights some of the measures the modern state takes in order to minimise the role and influence of the ulema.

Marginalisation of Islamic law

In the few nation states where Islamic law is implemented, the official ulema enjoy a relatively important role, for instance in Saudi Arabia and Iran. But in countries where the legal system has been changed or secularised, that role is limited and the ulema's importance is minimal. The primary role given to the ulema in most of the modern nation states in the legal system is in effect related to administering Islamic family law, which, in part, is still enforced in these states. Issues such as marriage, divorce, inheritance and, in some cases, child custody fall within the scope of family law. Several Muslim states such as Malaysia have adopted a system of shari'a courts with a strictly limited jurisdiction to family law. Where such courts do not exist, the ulema are subordinate to the civil law, but have some leeway to administer Islamic family law. Given this marginalisation, their role is often confined to areas such as officiating at marriages and administering the so-called Islamic affairs. This covers mosque management, leading the prayer, celebration of important religious festivals, teaching of religious education in schools, and the issuing of fatwa requested by the state, within the guidelines set by the state.

Bureaucratisation

Many Muslim states today employ a hierarchical system with regard to official ulema. The country may be divided into several regions, each region with its ulema at the local level. These ulema are led by a local council or a leading *'alim* who is also a state bureaucrat. At the national level, the ulema are usually led by a national council headed by the chief *'alim* or *mufti*. At the helm of the hierarchy often is the Minister for Religious Affairs. As a group, the official ulema are part of the state bureaucracy and subject to the official policy. This impacts on their role and limits what they can or cannot do, how they approach religious issues, and taboo topics they should avoid, in particular those related to politics and policy.

Regulating training

Today many Muslim states have nationalised the training of ulema or control this training at state level. One way of doing this is by establishing state-funded ulema training centres whose courses are recognised by the state, and whose graduates may become imams, religious education teachers at state schools, or masters of religious ceremonies. The state often sets the curricula and the method of training in line with its ideological, religious or political orientation. Graduates are trained to follow government policy, and are expected to be compliant. Where the state does not establish training centres, it often compels private providers to follow its line by recognising or not recognising a particular private institution or its qualifications. Non-recognition prevents graduates from pursuing any profession within the state bureaucracy, leaving the graduate often unemployed. In some cases, the state requires private providers of religious education to change their curricula to accommodate the state's interests and only then recognises their validity.

Control of mosques

A strategy to minimise the influence of the ulema is also related to the nationalisation of mosques. In many Muslim states, the management of the mosques has been entirely taken over by government, thus removing an important political base from the ulema. When the state manages the mosques, it controls mosque building and the appointment of the imam. Vocal opponents of the state are thus unlikely to be appointed as imams. This minimises political problems such as a congregation being encouraged to act in certain ways by means of religious talks, study circles and Friday sermons. Despite these restrictions, mosques seem to represent a formidable challenge to state authorities. They cannot close them down nor bring under state control activities such as indirect education of the masses. The mosque remains a place of inspiration for the people, a network for activists and a meeting point for dissidents. Opponents of the political authorities frequently take advantage of such community locales.

Religious education in schools

A further way to restrict the influence of the ulema is by prescribing what can be taught in public schools and other educational institutions. For instance, religious education teachers may be asked to adhere to the religious education syllabus or textbooks developed by the Ministry of Education of the state. No other textbooks may be used, and even in explaining the lessons, teachers may have to confine themselves to the information provided in the textbook.

This may include simple facts, basic beliefs, how to perform various rituals, the basic value system of Islam, and 'facts' about Islamic history. Discussion, analysis and critical reflection may not only be discouraged but may not be practised at all.

Control of awqaf

Up until the modern period, many non-official ulema often enjoyed a relatively high degree of economic independence by relying on endowments (*awqaf*) that supported their educational and religious activities. In the modern period, the nation state has often encroached upon this area, officially appropriating the management of endowments. This leaves the ulema again dependent on the state and obliged to provide services they once supplied whilst economically independent.

State legitimacy

The recognition the state gives to the ulema may be of sufficient significance for them to maintain their support to the state. Whether the state actually provides a relatively broad role for the ulema in the state bureaucracy in societies, such as in the case of Saudi Arabia, or not, as is the case in Indonesia, the official ulema often utilise their role in giving a veneer of 'Islamicity' to the state. The ulema may do this by highlighting the Islamic credentials of the state, or by issuing fatwas in support of activities undertaken by the state or of a particular policy or law. For instance, if the state wishes to crush a particular religious or political opponent, the official ulema may issue a fatwa stating that the views of the opponent are heretical, giving the state a free hand in dealing with the problem. This tactic is not entirely new in the modern period; it is a tradition that goes way back to early Islamic history when the official ulema declared even some leading non-official ulema as heretics. At times such dissidents may not be against the state as such, but against the official ulema themselves, challenging their views on a particular subject. By collaborating with the state, the official ulema are well placed to strengthen their position; by eliminating dissidents they dislodge any threat to their own legitimacy and existence.

Despite this, it is difficult to talk about the ulema providing a substantial degree of legitimacy to the state. A state like Saudi Arabia may argue that its legitimacy derives from religion because of its implementation of Islamic law, its protection of holy sites, or its global support of Islam. In other words, the state somehow acts as guardian of Islam and Islamic activities. Most nation states do not claim this role or the legitimacy. In Saudi Arabia, one could say that the official ulema do, to a certain extent, lend some legitimacy to the state, but in most other states that is not the case, although they may use certain Islamic symbols that may provide some degree of religious legitimacy, without recourse to official ulema.

Whether the state is officially 'Islamic' or 'secular', it usually reminds the Muslim populace that the state protects their religious interests. Examples of such interests include the preservation of certain aspects of Islamic family law, the building of new mosques and the preservation of old ones, the management of institutions like mosques and Islamic schools, the provision of Qur'an-teaching classes, the celebration of Ramadan, Eid and other religious festivals and the allocation of specific times for religious radio and television programs. Much of the 'Islamic' activity undertaken by the state falls into these categories and can often be symbolic. As long as the state is engaged in these activities, it will be seen to be playing its role in protecting the interests of the Muslim community.

The rise of activism and the challenge to official ulema

The politicisation of Islam in the modern period has led to the official ulema being challenged by an influential group of activists (Islamists). These activists are particularly keen to project an alternative program to expand the scope of what Islam means and its role in society. Those who belong to this category of Muslims are reacting to a situation in which the role of Islam in society, as they see it, is constantly being eroded. In their view, the roots of this erosion lie largely in the colonial period. In the post-independence period, in their view, the modern state continued with various colonial projects, including the marginalisation of Islamic law, and relinquishing public space to what these Muslims consider to be non-Islamic priorities.

These activists not only challenge the state that is seen to be eroding the role of Islam in society. They also challenge the official ulema whom they see as the mouthpiece of government. The roots of this challenge lie in the so-called Islamic 'awakening' (*al-sahwa al-islamiyya*) of the early twentieth century. Notable movements associated with this include the Muslim Brotherhood of Egypt and the Jama'at Islami of Pakistan. They have similar approaches to social change: an ideology that emphasises a more activist Islam that challenges the existing authorities, whether state or religious. They are determined to change Muslim societies from within. Any obstacle to the change they argue for may become the target of their challenge.

Most significantly, more militant groups of activists have emerged from these movements. The militant activists often declare that the nation state as it exists in the Muslim world is illegitimate. Their argument is that, for a state to be legitimate, it has to derive its authority or legitimacy from God, that is, from revealed religion, rather than from the people. God's sovereignty should be supreme in the state, in which case the state should enforce and implement Islamic law, not, as they say, 'man-made law'. Since none of the states covered in this book, except for Saudi Arabia and Iran, follow this ideal, such nation states are not seen as legitimate states and they are under challenge by militant activists.

The Islamists, both in their moderate and militant forms, have portrayed the official ulema negatively. Hasan al-Banna, the founder of the Muslim Brotherhood, contrasts the early non-official ulema who challenged the caliphs, rulers and governors without any fear, and the official ulema of today who endeavour to come closer to the authorities, accept their favours and collude with them.[16] The founder of Jamaat-i Islami, Mawdudi's early views on ulema (before the establishment of Pakistan) were highly negative as well. He regarded the ulema as an impediment to the success of his *da'wa*.[17] Referring to Mawdudi's views on the ulema, Seyyed Vali Reza Nasr in his extensive study on Mawdudi says:

> His discourse on the Islamic state deliberately sidestepped the ulema, depicting them as an anachronistic institution that has no place in a reformed and rationalised Islamic order . . . Mawdudi derided the ulema for their moribund scholastic style, servile political attitudes, and ignorance of the modern world.[18]

Sayyid Qutb is perhaps more critical of official ulema than many other Islamists. His criticism comes throughout his works. He criticises the very idea of 'men of religion' (*rijal al-din*) who take from religion a profession.[19] He considers these professional 'men of religion' as people corrupting the Qur'anic message, twisting its meanings to suit their needs, and attributing to God what He did not reveal.[20] He describes the 'professional men of religion' as those who sold their souls not to God or nation but to Satan.[21] He considers them in a sarcastic tone as people who do not live in the real world, who want to solve the problems of the world by issuing meaningless fatwas and speeches.[22] According to him, these 'men of religion' are 'the least able creatures of God who can represent what Islam stands for'.[23]

These Islamists argue that the official ulema have no legitimacy or authority because they are compliant and implement the interests of the ruling elite. The Islamists want not compliant ulema but ulema who will challenge the state and force it to give Islam a more prominent role in society. The state thus has to defend itself. Such counter-attacks on behalf of the state are usually undertaken not by the political authorities, but by the official ulema. Since the challenges are argued on the basis of Islamic logic, terminology and idiom, those who counter that must also use Islamic terms, ideas, concepts and idiom. It is here that the state exploits the utility of official ulema in countering the discourse of the Islamist opponents. In fact, the states covered in this book have often used the official ulema as a tool or as a buffer between them and the Islamists of one sort or another. The official ulema seek to counter the arguments of the Islamists by declaring that they fail to understand orthodox doctrines, and by insisting that the Islamists are engaged in activities that are not in line with 'true' Islam.

Conclusion

In the history of Islam, the official ulema, have not often been in a position to give religious legitimacy to the state, be it a caliphate, sultanate, emirate, or a modern nation state, largely as a result of the political authority's (*ulu al-amr*) pre-eminent role in the state where the ulema are subject to this authority. From the beginning, the ulema themselves depended for their legitimacy on the state, which gave them recognition and prestige by employing them in the state bureaucracy, and supporting them financially. In turn, the official ulema recognised their limitations and, tacitly or otherwise, recognised that the power really lay with the political authorities. The state was clearly aware of the danger posed by an independent class of ulema. It usually succeeded in controlling them by employing a number of tactics. Despite this, a substantial number of ulema remained independent in the pre-modern period and were anxious to dissociate themselves from rulers.

In the pre-modern period such independence was possible, largely because the state had less control in remote or rural areas and because the independent ulema had their own economic resources through endowments or personal wealth. However, this has changed significantly in the modern era. The modern nation states, due primarily to new communication technologies and sophisticated systems of governance and control, have largely succeeded in bringing the ulema under state control and reducing their independence. The situation of the official ulema today, in the sense of their own legitimacy, is perhaps worse than at any time in Islamic history. One can therefore argue then that it is a myth that the ulema today bestow substantial religious legitimacy on the modern nation state.

Notes

1 For a brief discussion on different types of ulema and their relationship to the state, see Abu al-Hasan 'Ali al-Husayni al-Nadawi, *Madha Khasira al-Alam bi Inhitat al-Muslimin* (Beirut: Dar al-Kitab al-Arabi, 1984), p. 133.
2 See for some details, Sayyid Qutb, *al-'Adala al-Ijtima'iyya fi al-Islam* (Cairo: Dar al-Shuruq, 1983), p. 140.
3 al-Nadawi, *Madha Khasira al-'Alam*, pp. 234–7.

4 See for a brief discussion on this, Jurji Zaydan, *History of Islamic Civilisation*, Trans. D. S. Margoliouth (New Delhi: Kitab Bhavan, 1981), pp. 248–50.
5 al-Nadawi, *Madha Khasira al-'Alam*, p. 133.
6 See for example, W. Montgomery Watt, *The Formative Period of Islamic Thought* (Oxford: Oneworld, 1998), pp. 253–71.
7 Bernard Lewis, *The Middle East: 2000 Years of History from the Rise of Christianity to the Present Day* (London: Phoenix, 1997), p. 138.
8 See for instance, the discussion on 'contract of imamate' in Abu'l –Hasan al-Mawardi, *al-Ahkam as-Sultaniyyah (The Laws of Islamic Governance)*, Trans. Asadullah Yate (London: Ta-Ha Publishers, 1996), pp. 10–36.
9 al-Mawardi, *al-Ahkam as-Sultaniyyah*, p. 12.
10 Bernard Lewis, *The Middle East*, p. 138.
11 Albert Hourani, *A History of Arab Peoples* (London: Faber and Faber, 1991), p. 163.
12 Ibn al-Muqaffa', 'Risalat al-Sahaba' (Beirut: Dar al-Kitab), n.d., pp. 195ff.
13 al-Mawardi, *al-Ahkam as-Sultaniyya*, p. 27.
14 Bernard Lewis, *The Middle East*, p. 81.
15 Bernard Lewis, *The Middle East*, p. 148.
16 Hasan al-Banna, *Majmu'at Rasa'il al-Imam al-Shahid Hasan al-Banna* (Cairo: Dar al-Tawzi' wa al-Nashr al-Islamiyya, 1992), p. 288.
17 Seyyed Vali Reza Nasr, *Mawdudi and the Making of Islamic Revivalism* (Oxford: Oxford University Press, 1996), p. 115.
18 Nasr, *Mawdudi and the Making of Islamic Revivalism*, p. 115.
19 Sayyid Qutb, *Fi Zilal al-Qur'an* (Cairo and Beirut: Dar al-Shuruq, 1992), vol. 1, p. 418.
20 Qutb, *Fi Zilal al-Qur'an*, vol. 1, p. 419.
21 Sayyid Qutb, *Ma'rakat al-Islam wa al-Ra'smaliyya* (Cairo and Beirut: Dar al-Shuruq, 1993), p. 6.
22 Qutb, *Ma'rakat al-Islam wa al-Ra'smaliyya*, pp. 6–16. See also, p. 37, pp. 58–9.
23 Qutb, *Ma'rakat al-Islam wa al-Ra'smaliyya*, pp. 63–5.

3 Saudi Arabia
Re-reading politics and religion in the wake of September 11

Larbi Sadiki

In the wake of the September 11 attacks on New York and Washington, no Arab and Muslim country drew as much security, media and academic attention as did Saudi Arabia. The exception was the Taliban's Afghanistan, which shared the spotlight with the Saudi Monarchy. The fact that most of the hijackers who crashed the planes on the Twin Towers and on the Pentagon were Saudi nationals came as a surprise not only to 'Saudi-ologists', but also to the Saudis themselves. The tragic events refocused attention on the oil-rich Arab country, forcing rethinking along a number of lines of inquiry. For this author, the most obvious and at the same time most academic question is whether the Saudi House would have survived the September 11 attacks had they been directed at Riyadh instead of New York or Washington. Hypothetical questions do not lend themselves to easy answers, but what is certain is that the Royal House would not have spared any firepower at its disposal to safeguard the position of its members and the Saudi Kingdom. Nor would have the US and its Western and Middle Eastern allies hesitated to fight on behalf of the Saudis. The Kuwaiti precedent is sufficiently illustrative of the point made here. So is a more relevant precedent: the 1979 takeover of the Grand Mosque by Saudi extremists, which was defused both violently and legally. Another intriguing aspect of the largely Saudi nationals-led attacks is the extent to which this brand of hideously violent militancy is a statement by Saudis against both their rulers and their rulers' protectors. It is not out of place to assume that the perpetrators of the violence visited upon New York and Washington on September 11 were motivated by local concerns (Saudi first, and Arab/Muslim second). This is in spite of the fact that their attacks seemed to signal a new wave of 'global terrorism' – thinking locally and acting globally. To lend credence to this line of investigation the whole question of the Royal House's political legitimacy must be placed under close scrutiny. If the September 11 events are to be read as an oppositional political behaviour, deploying a very bloody strategy, then questions must be asked about how political legitimacy is implicated in such happenings. This in turn leads to questions about the nature of politics and religion, noting from the outset that secularism has not hitherto featured as a political value that is either represented or contested in the Kingdom's top-down or bottom-up political discourses. Secularism is simply not an arena of contention or contestation as it is in other Middle Eastern states (such as Turkey, Algeria, Egypt, Tunisia or Syria). No reference will therefore be made to it in the ensuing analysis.

Specifically, two broad lines of inquiry guide the analysis. The first regards the nature or the brand of Islam adopted in Saudi Arabia and how it is implicated in statecraft. Despite the historical confusion of religion and politics in the Saudi Kingdom, Islam is increasingly becoming polycentric. Voices of challenge or opposition from below to 'official' Islam are emerging. The sources of these voices are identified and analysed, highlighting how the state has sought to control or influence Islamic responses from below. In the main, however, the dynamics of the relationship between Islam and the Saudi State generally remains intact. Wahhabi Islam is bound up with the Kingdom's *raison d'être*. But some adjustments have been made to shore up the House of Saud's political legitimacy, namely, by creating the long-awaited Majlis al-Shura (Consultative Council) in the early 1990s. Whether the Consultative Council and the emerging voices of Islam from below bode well for religious and political freedoms is not clear at the moment. This may become clearer in twenty years hence when a new political class made up of Saudis from both the Royal House (e.g. reform-minded princes, such as Talal bin Walid, who is not averse to elections) and from society (e.g. non-princely caste).

But one caveat exists. It is regarding the tendency of students of Arab and Muslim societies to 'Orientalise'.[1] When writing about Arab or Muslim countries, it is always tempting to proceed from the assumption that Islam is the master signifier of identity and that its place in polity and ideology is a given. Nowhere is that temptation stronger than in an essay that considers not only the nexus of politics and religion in Saudi Arabia, but also how these two shape and re-shape political legitimacy. In any case, such a temptation is doubly problematic. To resist it is to deny that the conflation of politics and religion in Saudi Arabia is empirically admissible. To give in to it is to engage in reductionism. For no critical exploration of the relation of state and politics in Saudi Arabia can be thorough without implicating equally important dynamics, which directly impact on the question of political legitimacy. Such dynamics include the political economy and its hydrocarbon basis, the absence of affinity between economic and political development, and external relations, namely the nature of the ruling house's alliance with the US and the resulting Pax-Americana that originated in the early 1990s. All of these factors cannot obviously be placed in separate boxes as though they do not intertwine. In order to capture the crisis of political legitimacy, the analysis below will therefore adopt an approach that stresses the interplay of the factors mentioned above rather than a mono-dimensional understanding of the question of legitimacy in Saudi Arabia. Such a multi-dimensional enquiry seems all the more timely given that the September 11 attacks have rekindled preoccupation with recurring research questions. These questions concern not only political legitimacy, but also the very viability of a Saudi state that continues to be averse to power sharing, institutionalisation, rulers' accountability, and greater equity. Autonomy from foreign powers is an additional thorny issue.

Islam, politics and the Saudi state

Narration of modern Saudi history is set against a backdrop of a warring, feuding and atomized tribal milieu. It is not surprising then that Islam is accorded a central place in such a narration. There are two reasons for this. One is that the pre-modern Saudi bedouin and tribal milieu lacked a unifying *asabiyya* (solidaristic affinity), with tribal kinship standing as a major obstacle against the minimum *esprit de corps* required for state building. In Khaldunian terms, *asabiyya* in that milieu was predominantly disintegrative. The other is that Islam, in its Wahhabi[2] brand, provided the only unifying force, that is, the type of integrative *asabiyya*, Ibn Khaldun views as instrumental for dynastic rule and state-making to be produced and reproduced.[3] Narrators of Saudi history implicate two figures in the birth of the Saudi state. These two figures shared more than their common first name: Muhammad. Muhammad ibn Abd al-Wahhab (1703–92) and Muhammad ibn Saud (1735–65) also shared in the glory of being the founding fathers of the Saudi state. The former, a religious reformer, laid down the Wahhabi teachings, which became the foundational and legitimising ideological framework, political and religious, of that state. The latter was once an *Amir* (Prince) of al-Dar'iyya[4] whose conversion to Wahhabism marked a key political event that was to shape the destiny and eventual birth of the modern Saudi state a hundred and fifty years later.[5]

The birth of the Saudi state owes then a great deal to the unity of the 'pen' and the 'sword'. The Wahhabi Ikhwan (brethren)[6] combined force with the charismatic Abd al-Aziz ibn Saud (1880–1953), whose swordsmen and political skill prevailed over all rival clans, culminating in the founding of the modern Saudi Kingdom in the 1930s.[7] But the most noticeable absence from all narration of Saudi Arabia's modern history is the state. The state owes its birth to an alliance of religion and politics. Nowhere do we find an indigenous concept of the state. The usual emblems of statehood – a national anthem, a flag, and an official name for the state – do not constitute a state. They simply provide symbols. The crossed swords and the *shahada* (the Islamic vow or declaration of belief: I declare that there is no God but Allah and that Muhammad is His Messenger) on the green Saudi flag are merely symbols of statehood. As symbols they capture a great deal of the foundational values of the Saudi state: its *raison d'être* is grounded in the inextricable link, mutuality and affinity between religion and politics.[8] It is therefore no exaggeration to suggest that the Saudi state is superimposed on a stateless society. The following reasons justify this view:

- Unlike the evolution of the state in the Maghrib (especially Tunisia) or in the Mashriq (especially Egypt), the Saudi state is without a historical tradition.
- There is no tradition of scholarly discourse of the concept of the state. The Saudi state cannot be considered a continuation of the state that the Prophet founded in the seventh-century Medina. Such a tradition is found elsewhere in the Mashriq and Maghrib.
- Despite having the emblems of modern statehood, the Saudi state lacks institutional development, approximating a private dynasty more than a modern state. It is true that huge financial outlays from the oil revenue have been used to develop mass education, public housing, etc. But the fact remains that the Royal House keeps a large share of revenue from rentier transactions. The Saudi state is a 'clan state'.
- Thus it cannot be said that the Saudi state has a solid tradition of acting legally and rationally, that is, fully and always to serve the 'general will' or to act in the name of public authority.[9] Personalist practices, preferences and interests give the Saudi state a strongly patrimonial character.

To an extent then the fusion of religion and politics in the founding of the Saudi state has served to defuse two potentially contested and contestable areas: the legality of the state and the legitimacy of the power holders. When the Qur'an is the constitution, when Islamic law is the law of the land, when Western-modelled institutions (e.g. parliaments, parties, etc.) are noted for their absence, and when the learned scholars of the Wahhabi creed continue to underwrite political power, the message is that the state's *raison d'être* and 'Godly' values are self-evident.[10] A human authority cannot question them even if the mortals who administer over the interpreting of the Qur'an into moral, legal or political values, and moral principles as well as their political masters happen to err. But the fact of religion and politics being wedded within the Saudi state calls for further elaboration. It is not religion that controls the state. Rather, it is the obverse that is true. Because the king amasses almost absolute power in his hands, his prerogative is without bounds. Theoretically, the shari'a (Islamic law) reigns supreme. But the prerogative of the king empowers him not only to control the clerical 'caste', by fiscal means, but also to appoint them in the first place. It is inconceivable that the king would entrust religious affairs to hostile scholars. Conversely, scholars tied to power structures through patronage-clientelism do rarely place their status and the privileges attached to it in jeopardy in the pursuit of their own political agendas or that of an opposition. It is the prerogative of the king to hire and fire his 'public servants' according to his preference and interest that captures the essence of his absolutism. The work by Aburish provides empirical evidence in support of this viewpoint. The examples abound and Khashoggi and Yamani are only two of the best known.[11] The religious bureaucracy is appointed as dictated by the king's interests and preferences, just the same as the technocrats who carry out the day-to-day running of temporal affairs. The royal house's recent appointment of al-Haram mosque's Imam (Mecca), Shaykh Salih bin Abdullah al-Humayd, to the Consultative Council's Presidency is further evidence of the fusion of religion and politics in the Saudi state. After September 11 the royal house is more than ever before in need of the religious establishment's underwriting of political power.

Tension between the religious and the political

Two important caveats need elaboration. To argue that Wahhabi orthodoxy and politics are inextricably linked is not to say that there is no tension whatsoever between religion and politics. It is true that such a tension does not often derive from the state top clerics. There is, however, no shortage of popular clerics and emerging Islamist activists on the opposite side of the state and its clerical clients. Just as the state deploys Wahhabi orthodoxy for the underwriting of political power, centrifugal forces are increasingly using their own brand of Islam to challenge and oppose the state. In other words, the state is disallowed monopoly over the use of religion to its own ends. More importantly, if the state can use religion for legitimising purposes, there is nothing stopping society from using it to contest the rulers' legitimacy or at least attempt to de-legitimise their policy orientations and preferences. The second caveat regards the tendency to single out religion as the source of contests and counter contests. To an extent religion is an arena which is susceptible to contests within Saudi society, involving religious scholars and non-scholars who tend to use religion to justify and defend their own stances and discourses. Despite the fact that religion seems to permeate most contests within Saudi society and polity, the nature of power, the running of the economy, military alliances and overall morality are hotly debated issues. If they are debated by way of reference to the shari'a, it is because that is the very territory that the Saudi state, since its inception, has marked out as being bound up with its mission and reason of being. Challenges to the state from below tend to happen on the very ground defined and chosen by the rulers: Islam. In other words, the boundaries of contests are ostensibly religious whether such contests regard the economy, religious affairs or security matters.

To corroborate the above, one key benchmark in the Saudi political calendar – the Gulf War – of political opposition or challenge to the state is worth invoking. The use here of the terms 'opposition' and of 'challenge' is deliberate. The former is not part and parcel of the Saudi 'cake of custom'. There is nothing in the 'pattern of orientations' to politics that predispose Saudis towards opposition. If political culture is that set of tendencies shaped by tradition, norms, symbols or historical memories, then nothing in it suggests propensity towards political opposition.[12] This is not to say that there are no disagreements or contests. These abound even within the Saudi House itself, but the tendency has been to refer disputations to tribal adjudication, deliberation of the elders, inter-tribal marriages, and in the distant past feuds were not uncommon strategies for settling disputes. Opposition in the form of organised and licensed political activity for the advocacy of alternative policies or representation on behalf of partisan interests and preferences from society does not exist in Saudi Arabia. By this definition, political opposition has never been a cornerstone of Saudi politics. All expression and representation of conflicting ideas is proscribed and more often than not punished. In consequence, 'challenge' is a milder term that describes fairly accepted practices of advocating change loyally and from within the system, thus tending to persuade the powers that be to adopt the reforms as if they emanated from them. Saudi political history is littered with this brand of politics from within the establishment that may be seen to come under the remit of religious *irshad* (guidance), theoretically at least one duty of the ulema (learned scholars of Islam). In a country where political parties are banned, the ulema tended from time to time to function as an *ad hoc* interest group articulating, be it loyally and not in an opposition-type, agenda-setting way, *ad hoc* political preferences. From this perspective the challenges tended to be very sporadic and never continuous. However, it is not clear that the pattern of orientations that make up Almond and Verba's political culture are static. Challenges tend to be more common than opposition in Saudi Arabia, but the recent past points to emerging oppositional propensities.

This analysis now turns to the main political event that galvanised both establishment Wahhabi scholars and voices from within society into, respectively, forms of loyal challenge and more serious opposition. This event is none other than the Second Gulf War, following the 1990 Iraqi invasion of Kuwait and the subsequent US-led intervention on behalf of Saudi and other Gulf Co-operation Council states' interests, an intervention that was mandated by the UN. The rights or wrongs of the Saudi or US foreign policy options will not be addressed in detail here.[13] Suffice it to mention that, nearly ten years after the Grand Mosque takeover, the Saudi state's 'hosting' of foreign forces served as the rallying cry for both challengers and outright opponents. Since the parameters of contests were bound by religion, *islah* (reform) was the operative term not democracy, conceptually a minefield of conflicting understandings. None of the responses, challenges or outright opposition was couched in secular language or ideals. They were not about less religion in Saudi political and social life. Rather, they were concerned with reforming the political system by way of correcting the way official Islam is applied to polity, economy, society and even security. However, the type of reform advocated by those with a stronger oppositional bent and content, did not stop at questioning particular state policies. They questioned Saudi rule in its entirety. Challengers did not concern themselves with the question of whether the Saudi House deserve to rule or not. Unlike oppositional forces, challengers did not raise the spectre of an alternative political order replacing the Saudi House. Nonetheless, one point worth mentioning is that anti-systemic challenges did not end with the quashing of the Grand Mosque takeover. More importantly, the preoccupations of Juhayman al-Otaybi and his cohorts in the armed invasion of the mosque resurfaced in the 1990s. Had the Saudi House gone some way to addressing them, or at least debating them, it would have 'contained' many would-be challengers and opponents. Amongst al-Otaybi's preoccupations were corruption of the learned scholars and their subservience to the rulers, impiety of the power holders, close ties with the West (especially doing business with the US) and misuse of oil wealth:

> All Muslim rulers must be from the Quraish. Present Muslim rulers are co-operating with infidels and those who deny God ... The royal family is corrupt. It worships money and spends it on palaces not mosques. If you accept what they say, they will make you rich; otherwise they will persecute and even torture you. The *ulama* have warned the royal family about its corruption but Abd al-Aziz Ibn Baz is in the family's pay and has endorsed their actions.[14]

In reading the above quote one gets a strong sense of déjà vu. The quote suggests that perhaps events like the influx of hundreds of thousands of US troops into the Gulf region and Saudi Arabia may have only served to rekindle old issues and revive society's resolve to strike back. For the issues in more recent challenges and oppositional demands, as shall be shown below, tend to revolve around the same unresolved problems of corruption, impiety, misrule, and alliance with Western powers, principally the US.

If the 1990s is noted for increased politicisation of Sunni Islam, be it in its Wahhabi version, in Saudi Arabia the above problems have had some role in such politicisation. To an extent, though, this is also a reflection of sophistication at the state and society levels. The Saudi Arabia of the 1990s is more populous, more literate, more 'wired' to the global revolution of information, and is both more interdependent with the outside world as well as dependent on the international economy. Because it is more populous, it has more graduates from Islamic universities who continuously add to the soaring number of the unemployed. Pressing issues do not only concern indigenising the labour workforce, as one way of decreasing unemployment, but also how to limit the number and influence of expatriates (four to five million), through whom ideas ranging from liberal social patterns of behaviour to political dissension may disseminate. In the long term, replacing the millions of teachers and bureaucrats clogging the education sector and the public service may be achievable. But training enough Saudi technocrats and technicians to run the hydrocarbon sector, the mainstay of the national economy, will require more time as well as more serious strategic planning. The kingdom has more PhD holders per capita than any other Arab country. One has just to look at the composition of the ninety-member Majlis al-Shura (Consultative Council) and the Hay'at Kibar al-Ulema (Senior Scholars' Council) to realise that there is no shortage of intelligence in Saudi Arabia.

Petrodollars have opened up endless opportunities for Saudi investors, especially from the Saudi House, to concentrate media ownership within their hands. The Saudis are the rising media barons of the Arab world. Three of the most widely circulated Arabic dailies (*al-Hayat, al-Alam al-Yom* and *al-Sharq al-Awsat*) are Saudi-owned. But at last another forty-five magazines and other print media, circulating both in the Arab world as well as in Europe and North America, are Saudi owned. Saudis own three satellite TV networks, such as ART, Orbit and MBC, this latter being one of the most popular amongst Arab viewers.[15] Internet use is increasing and computers may not be as widely available as in other Gulf States, but they are becoming commonplace in education, business and the bureaucracy.

Saudi Arabia in the 1990s is also connected to the world not only through foreign labour, its thousands of graduates in Europe and North America, computers, bank accounts or petrodollars, but also through diplomacy and security arrangements. A country owning 25 per cent of the world's known oil reserves cannot be expected to be marginal to the major Western industrial powers whose prosperity depends on petroleum. The kingdom's own prosperity depends on continuous Western 'dependence' on its oil. Thus it is not surprising that Saudi Arabia is, besides Israel, the US's most important ally in the Middle East. Owing to their mutually reciprocated economic interests, they have in the 1990s become far more linked militarily than they were in any other period in the past. In fact, the most conspicuous paradox about the September 11 attacks was the fact that the Saudis were at once the US's and the Taliban's strongest Arab allies. With the US there has been a quasi Pax-Americana protective umbrella serving a form of 'dual containment' of their larger Gulf neighbours, Iran and Iraq. Economically, though, it has been 'business as usual', exporting petroleum in exchange for petrodollars. With the Taliban, until the cutting off of diplomatic relations in the aftermath of the September 11 events, the Saudis showed a quasi-missionary zeal for exporting another commodity: Wahhabism. In the Taliban they found a reliable 'customer'. Petrodollars exchanged hands. But this time it was from the Saudis to their Afghan clients.[16]

Society petitioning the state

Accordingly, at the core of the politicisation of Sunni Islam in Saudi Arabia lie the sophistication of Saudi society, in general, and its learned elites, businessmen and cadres. This sophistication can be seen in the composition of the challengers and opponents of the Saudi state as well as their political messages. Nothing captures this sophistication more than the mere fact that the ulema, supposedly the rulers' ideological last line of defence, do intermittently add their voices to those of challengers. Taking their loyalty for granted at all times is a big mistake despite their clientelistic ties to the apex of power. Theirs is a balancing act between the sovereignty of the shari'a and royal prerogative. As upholders of Islamic law, they are guided by one paramount value. That is, that the secular ways of modernisers and Westernisers around them in the Middle East region do not creep into their kingdom, with Islamic law, in its Wahhabi version, remaining the main source of legislation. As state clients, they are in the non-enviable position of being torn between the 'dictats' of men and of God. The dictats of men, in whose hands conflate financial and coercive power, are a constant reminder that the public goods that can most be achieved in a country like Saudi Arabia with its dynastic system is stability and order. These goods become the most important values that inform how the ulema function (i.e. with frustrating restraint, just as do judges, lawyers and the press living at the mercy of autocrats). The dictats of God, on the other hand, oblige the ulema to carry out their duty in the most disinterested fashion, unhindered by fear of any temporal authority or favour from rulers in general. That would have been more possible had the ulema owned their own petroleum companies, had the influence of the powerful Jiluwi or Sudayri clans, or commanded their own private paramilitary force as does the Crown Prince who has control over the National Guard.

So when the highest learned scholar in the land and another member of the Senior Scholars' Council joined the signatories of the 1991 *Khitab Shawwal* (Shawwal [name of a Muslim month] Statement), a two-page petition, they showed that the call for reform is not confined to non-establishment ulema. Both the late Shaykh Abd al-Aziz ibn Baz, for decades the kingdom's highest religious authority, or mufti, and Muhammad al-Salih ibn Uthaymin signed the petition along with another fifty Islamist reform-oriented Saudis, some of whom are qualified ulema. By signing the 1991 petition, the two scholars were helping stake out a new territory for a loyal challenge that stresses reform or guidance, be it incrementally. In so doing they were attempting to show that guiding from within the system could be serious and autonomous when it comes to the pursuit of public utility. Moreover, by signing the petition both widely respected scholars might have rendered their political masters an invaluable service. They could have intended their signature to do two things. First, to sensitise the power-holders to growing disaffection that needed to be addressed. Second, to nip in the bud the type of radical, violent or anti-Saudi rule opposition that might engage in a brand of political activism, which could be amenable to instability. Instability has traditionally been an anathema to all Muslim learned scholars, past and present. A petition signed by authoritative scholars and others, whose aim was not to oust the Saudi rulers, but rather to serve notice to the rulers to shape up, would always be less harmful than more radical tactics of an uncompromising opposition. Neither Ibn Baz nor Ibn Uthaymin had in mind delegitimising Saudi rule. But in signing *Khitab Shawwal* they must have considered their actions to be within the legitimate remit of the ulema to proffer guidance.

It is, therefore, not surprising that Ibn Baz did not support the 1992 *mudhakkirat al-nasiha* (Reform Memorandum).[17] Although the *mudhakkira* was more comprehensive, being long as well as more detailed in its assessment of the ills of the Saudi system, Ibn Baz criticised it as potentially destabilising. He definitely had qualms with its potential for causing *furqa* (division), *fitna* (conflict) and *tahazzub* (partyism). This was despite the fact that the *mudhakkira* reproduced similar demands contained in the *Khitab Shawwal*. What can be surmised from Ibn Baz's refusal to add his signature to the *mudhakkira* is that he primarily opposed its politically radical style and the disorder that could result from pitting a segment of society against the state. But there are other reasons. Ibn Baz knew the Saudi system more than the authors of the *mudhakkira*, especially the non-establishment young ulema, amongst its 109 signatories. Ibn Baz knew only too well that upping the ante would lead nowhere in Saudi Arabia. Saudi history is littered with examples of uprisings that were brutally quashed.[18] The example of the zealous Wahhabi protest against the introduction of TV in the kingdom in 1965, and which claimed the life of a prince who was amongst the leaders of the demonstration, illustrates the point. Ibn Baz must have also absorbed the historical lesson that change in Saudi Arabia was incremental and that multiplying petitions was not going to yield results since only one year passed since he and others signed *Khitab Shawwal*. Ibn Baz was not about to put his status on the line as a stabilising force over a forty-year career by giving his 'blessings' to the *mudhakkira*, especially given its style of discrediting the Saudi rulers does not square with his style of guiding. It is also quite possible that Ibn Baz read the *mudhakkira* as part and parcel of an emerging opposition, something he would not countenance. He might have appreciated the historical context of the *mudhakkira*, especially the devastating conclusion of the second Gulf War: financial ruin for the Saudi economy, unprecedented presence of foreign troops on Saudi soil, and uncompromising Saudi rulers who were concentrating efforts and synergies on foreign policy not domestic affairs.

More specifically, however, he criticizes the *mudhakkira* and its authors for a lack of objectivity. Ibn Baz's brief statement criticising the *mudhakkira* casts doubts on the 'Islamicity' of the *nasiha* or *munasaha* (counsel/advice) contained within it. For him Islamic *nasiha* must be objective and fair. Thus he charges the signatories of the *mudhakkira* to ignore *mahasin al-dawla* (the state's positive aspects), concentrating instead only on the rulers' failures.[19] The kingdom's senior religious scholar adds in his statement that 'although we [fellow ulema in the Senior Scholars' Council] condemn the Memorandum . . . we do not claim that *al-waqi'* [the current state of affairs] is perfect'.[20] Secondly, Ibn Baz and the senior scholars condemn the memorandum for its potential to divide, thus serving the interests of enemies of the Islamic community and the state. However, it must be mentioned that seven of the ulema sitting in the seventeen-member Senior Scholars Council conveniently missed the deliberations that led to the issuing of the *Bayan*, i.e. the 1991 petition.

By contrast to Ibn Baz, the young scholars attempted to seize on the context, hoping to force the Royal House to make concessions at a time when it was looking very vulnerable. The expensive and massive armament of the previous twenty years was in vain. The Saudi rulers had still to turn to foreign powers to seek protection. Defence expenses in the 1990s were twice as much as in the 1980s: recycling billions of petrodollars on the acquisition of state-of-the art weapon systems that, for all intents and purposes, were useless when it came to self-defence. On top of this, they, along with the Kuwaitis, had to bankroll the US-led war effort against Iraq. For the signatories of the *mudhakkira* none of this made political, economic or religious sense. The signatories of the *mudhakkira* allocate a whole section to foreign relations and another to the military, condemning ties with 'infidel' states or regimes, including Muslim states that combat Islam, and the stationing of troops and pre-positioning of military hardware on Saudi soil by 'untrustworthy' states. Politically, Saudi sovereignty almost ceased to exist during the 1991–92 period when the US pre-positioned a huge war arsenal and based troops on Saudi territory.[21]

Economically for the signatories of the *mudhakkira*, Saudi citizens were financially being squeezed between the demands of footing the huge defence bill and royal greed, with the princely caste keeping a big cut of all revenue from petroleum sales. Religiously, there is a consensus amongst the signatories that the rulers' authority was not sufficiently circumbsribed by the shari'a. Thus like *Khitab Shawwal* one year before, the *mudhakkira*, using harsher criticism and more political language, blamed the rulers for the deteriorating state of affairs and insisted upon reforms in the system of governance, the economy, the judiciary, religious affairs, and in the areas of foreign policy and national security. In particular, the *mudhakkira* made an issue of the country's oil wealth and its management, considering it to be a public asset that ought to be used for the good of the people as a whole. The question of more political accountability by the rules and adherence to the shari'a was made plain in the memorandum. Although the main frame of reference of the *mudhakkira*, which resonated with religious language, was the shari'a itself, the overall tone was far more political than that that of *Khitab Shawwal*, which neither mentioned the rulers by name nor sought to embarrass or discredit them. The section in the *mudhakkira* on 'Finance and the Economy' criticises the lack of financial accountability and the squandering of money on handouts given to secular Arab regimes. It singles out the Algerian 'military' regime for being brutal against its own people and the Jordanian regime, which was handed over billions of dollars in financial aid. It also criticises aid given to the former Soviet Union and the accruing of interest from investing in bonds issued by US banks.[22] Under the section on 'Social Amenities', the memorandum takes issue with the discrepancy of incomes and resources, noting the absence of schools in parts of the Kingdom and other services. It also contrasts the abject poverty of many Saudis with the vast wealth, manifest in the building of palaces, of a limited number of their compatriots.[23]

The memorandum was signed jointly by religious scholars, professionals and academics whose middle-class status and higher education, Western and Saudi, offered very little in terms of political participation.[24] Many were proactive in mosques and in the local press, carving out a small but nonetheless important margin of political existence. In particular, Safar al-Hawali and Salman al-Awdah, although not religious leaders in Ibn Baz's class, commanded followings in their tertiary institutions, respectively the Islamic University in Medina and the Imam Muhammad bin Saud University. The other two well-known religious scholars who supported the petition were Abdullah ibn Abdullah al-Jabrin and Abdullah al-Hamad al-Jalali. In the main, challenge or opposition remains within an Islamic framework.[25] Al-Hawali and al-Awdah were both unmistakably opposed to the US presence in the Kingdom and neither minced their words when criticising ruling corruption. When they were imprisoned for five years in 1994 it was because they were seen to have challenged the consensus of both the political and religious leaders about the key questions raised in the 1992 memorandum.

Specifically, from the Saudi rulers' point of view, the presence of US troops in the kingdom was rubberstamped by the 1990 fatwa (religious edict) of the Senior Scholars' Council. The fatwa, as far as they were concerned, closed the debate of foreign troops in Saudi Arabia. But there is more in that fatwa than meets the eye. The fatwa, which was principally authored by Ibn Baz, pandered to the Saudi rulers' pressing need at a time of a credible, not just perceived, threat from expansionist Ba'thist Saddam. Based on a reading of Taqy al-Din Ahmad ibn Taymiyya (1263–1328 AD), a leading scholar of the Hanbali school of jurisprudence, the fatwa averred the right of Muslim rulers threatened with invasion to seek non-Muslim protection. Two observations must be made in this regard. The fatwa was very general, using a credible scholarly authority that influenced the Wahhabi doctrine as its main frame of reference. Ibn Baz did not apply his counsel specifically to the Saudi context. Nor did he specify the US in his fatwa. In others words, he stayed out of the politics of the whole issue, leaving politics for the politicians even though theoretically demarcation between the temporal and the profane is not a professed Wahhabi philosophy. More importantly, in his fatwa Ibn Baz qualified his counsel with the condition that non-Muslim protection must cease once there was no longer a need for it. To an extent, al-Hawali, al-Awdah, and their co-signatories were motivated by the urgent need for US troops to depart once hostilities ceased with the 'liberation' of Kuwait. In fact, no other issue is more sensitive to Saudis, including members of the Royal House, than the presence of foreign troops in their country.

The emerging opposition

Likewise, individuals who might have shared concerns over the thorny question of US troops in the kingdom leaked the *mudhakkira*, which was sent to the office of the King. But if there was opposition to the *mudhakkira* it was not on the grounds of its disdain to the role of religion. Quite to the contrary, religiously it was sound. In fact, the memorandum's language, style and messages put its signatories in the category of Islamists, especially those influenced by the Muslim Brotherhood and its philosophy of *islah* (reform). It is wrong to conclude that the main motivation of the memorandum is political. There is an ostensibly religious motivation. Thus its signatories refer to *da'wa* (proselytisation) as an important mission for Muslims and

Muslim states. Throughout the memorandum the state is reminded of its role to uphold the shari'a and help the cause of *da'wa*. Opposition would have been on the basis that it was too critical of the rulers, which for many people in the elite and the religious establishment could potentially incite *fitna*. But by any standards, the *mudhakkira* enjoyed wide sympathy amongst the Saudi public. As rightly put by Dekmejian, the politicisation and radicalisation of Islam was on the rise, not only in Saudi Arabia, but also in the entire Arab world.[26] What is noticeable is the escalation of such politicisation and radicalisation, moving from loyal challenge obvious in *Khitab Shawwal* to the more serious criticism of the *mudhakkira*, which essentially questions the rulers' political legitimacy even if it did not openly articulate deposing them as one of its demands. A further escalation from the tactic of challenge is the quasi opposition of Lajnat al-Difa' an al-Huquq al-Shar'iyya (The Legitimate Rights Defence Committee). The Committee (which split up in the late 1990s) was headed by physicist Muhammad al-Mas'ari and lawyer Sa'd al-Faqih and was a more ambitious oppositional project. Its project differed markedly from previous challenges to Saudi rule. The split between the two and the widening of exiled opposition with the al-Faqih's founding of his Movement for Islamic Reform in Arabia, had resulted in opposition in the past few years becoming more systematic. It has obviously benefited from the cover of European immunity extended to many exiled Islamist movements, especially in the United Kingdom.

Political strategy has moved from simply deploying religion for lobbying, guiding or criticising to the purpose of opposing. Thus the strategy employed aims at wide recruitment, organisation and mobilisation.[27] However, organisation and mobilisation from exile have their limitations. Despite the environment of freedom of assembly, fund-raising, publishing, using the media and networking with sympathetic parliamentarians and politicians, the opposition does not have direct links with the street and public opinion in the homeland. Opposition from Riyadh is not the same as opposition from London. What is gained in enhanced physical security and impunity is lost in interaction with followers' sentiments and preoccupations in the homeland. Nonetheless, opposition from abroad should not be completely discounted, especially if it can mobilise international public opinion against the Saudi rulers to open up the system for greater accountability, contest, participation, and above all else more humane treatment of opponents. It must be noted that many Arab republics have a far worse human rights record than the Saudi Kingdom, the authors of the 1992 *mudhakkira* were not, for instance, harmed physically.

In general, what can be gleaned from the philosophy of the emerging Saudi opposition is that it questions the legitimacy of the rulers but not the legitimacy of Islam in the political process. Perhaps it contests the use of

Islam for personal ends by the Saudis, thus prolonging dynastic rule and privileges. Thus al-Mas'ari's main work, which articulates his politics, takes issue with *muhasbat al-hukkam*, also the title of the book – *Holding the Rulers Accountable*.[28] Despite al-Mas'ari's openness to Western proceduralism, he stresses accountability, which has roots in Islamic political thought, including that of Ibn Taymiyya, as intrinsic to his understanding of good government in a Muslim society. From this perspective, contest in modern Saudi Arabia may not be over the role of Islam in politics. Rather, contest is over how Islam, its symbols and institutions are used in value allocation, politically, economically, culturally, and socially. Value allocation, as can be gathered from al-Mas'ari's monograph, must be circumscribed by the paramount objectives of the shari'a and public utility. For the first condition to prevail just rule must be the basis of politics. For the second to be met, the good of the *umma* (Muslim community) must be paramount. Both are governed by the Islamic principle of *al-amr bi al-ma'ruf wa al-nahy 'ani al-munkar* (enjoining the good, and fending off the reprehensible).[29] Perhaps it is al-Mas'ari's training as a physicist and his scientific training in the West that makes him amenable to adopting forms of Western legalism and institutionalism, to which Saudi rulers have so far resisted as alien to, at least, their Wahhabi brand of Islam. Thus al-Mas'ari does not oppose political parties for embodying the *umma*'s sovereignty in organising and mobilising politically in the form of *jama'a* (group) or *jama'at* (groups).[28]

Al-Mas'ari adds that only when organised into *jama'at* can Muslims fulfil the Godly commandment of enjoining the good and forbidding the evil. That is, the Qur'anic call for Muslims to form *jama'at* is read by al-Mas'ari to apply to the forming of political parties, which would be in Wahhabi doctrine a *bid'a* (innovation). Al-Mas'ari goes even further by arguing for *ta'addud al-ahzab* (multi-partyism), almost an entirely new political discourse in Saudi Arabia.[31] He criticises the Saudi rulers' misinterpretation of Islam in order to disallow organised political life, going as far as describing their ways to be closer to unbelief than belief.[32] In so doing, he makes the mistake of other radical Islamic movements in the Arab world who engage in relegating rulers or selected Muslims to the realm of unbelief, a practice which has no basis in Islamic law. What is striking is the blending of liberal values of political openness with negative radicalism specific to extreme Islamist activists who take liberties with 'excommunicating' fellow Muslims – declaring them apostates. Nonetheless, al-Mas'ari strongly advocates many democratic reforms even if he does not mention democracy by name. Saudi rulers have continuously rejected democracy as non-Islamic. He shows appreciation of an independent judiciary to which the rulers must be accountable.[33] Generally, the crux of al-Mas'ari's monograph is an aspiration for a 'better' Islam in place of the self-serving Islam of the Saudi rulers. Accordingly, as far as the emerging but small exiled opposition is concerned, the Royal House has a crisis of legitimacy and the answer lies in replacing the entire political order.

Looking ahead

September 11 opened up a Pandora's box. Had the Saudi rulers taken notice of growing disaffection within society and paved the way for more equal and reciprocal state-society relations, would the attacks on New York have been avoided? This is an unanswerable question, but one can surmise that the issue that Saudi rulers have not been able to attend to has been the gap between socio-economic development and political reform. It is true that the Saudi population continues to increase and oil prices decrease, leading the per capita income to worsen, almost halving from the early 1980s to the 1990s. But it is equally true that the Saudis continue to spend massively on housing, education, health, agriculture and the country's modern infrastructure. However, performance legitimacy is no substitute for political legitimacy. In the long run Saudis will have to pay taxes and subsequently demand representation and a share of the 'political cake'. Writing nearly twenty years ago, Heller and Safran predicted that it would not be long before the disease of greater political representation gripping modernising societies would contaminate Saudi Arabia.[34] The emerging political challenges and opposition described above lends credence to the observation by Heller and Safran that 'As the new middle class continues to grow and more junior princes with modern education come of age, co-optation will become a progressively less satisfactory response to the aspirations of individual Saudis or the political norms of the class as a whole'.[35] Had Bin Laden been given the opportunity to represent his political position, that the US presence be opened up for debate as a way of either terminating it or prolonging it, would the world have witnessed those 'two hours that shook the world', as Fred Halliday put it.[36] It is an academic question with no precise answer, but the point being stressed here in support of Heller and Safran is that the Saudi state has to reinvent its inventory of mechanisms for dealing with challenge and opposition. Stripping critics of their citizenship, exiling them, or jailing them are all short of sophisticated politics that demands dialogue. Closing all avenues of legalised dialogue, political expression, organisation and representation radicalises many activists. If Bin Laden can be implicated in the 1996 Khobar Towers bombing that left nineteen US soldiers dead, the 1998 bombings of the US embassies in Kenya and Tanzania, and the hideous attacks of September 11, so can those who did not seek political answers to religious radicalism and opposition in general. His Saudi interlocutors, who eventually closed all communication and banished him, dismissed Bin Laden:

By 1990 Bin Laden ... returned to Saudi Arabia to work in the family business ... After Iraq's invasion of Kuwait he lobbied the Royal Family to organize a popular defence of the Kingdom and raise a force from the Afghan war veterans to fight Iraq. Instead King Fahd invited in the Americans. This came as an enormous shock to Bin Laden. As the 540,000 US troops began to arrive, Bin Laden openly criticized the Royal Family, lobbying the Saudi *ulema* to issue *fatwas* ... against non-Muslims being based in the country.

Bin Laden's criticism escalated after some 20,000 US troops continued to be based in Saudi Arabia after Kuwait's liberation. In 1992 he had a fiery meeting with Interior Minister Prince Naif whom he called a traitor to Islam. Naif complained to King Fahd and Bin Laden was declared persona non grata. Nevertheless he still had allies in the Royal family ...

In 1992 Bin Laden left for Sudan ... Bin Laden's continued criticism of the Saudi Royal family eventually annoyed them so much that they took the unprecedented step of revoking his citizenship in 1994.[37]

The above quote strengthens still further the view that the absence of institutions and democratic, or at least consultative, channels of representation and the facility to collate political interests and preferences, is partly to blame for the inadequacy of the archaic Saudi political system. By weakening society, the Saudi state has unwittingly weakened itself. Saudi rulers have historically responded by fragmenting society – divide and rule – rather than build a strong popular power base.[38] Princes are part of the economy, owning billions of shares, holdings and hundreds of companies. They can equally become politically involved in politics from below, forming parties or contributing to parties and NGOs, thus fostering the growth of a Saudi civil society that can sustain pluralist politics, one that is informed by Islam. They can partake in transforming the political landscape in their country either as leaders, cadres or ordinary citizens. Just as there are dividends from business activities there are political dividends to be gained from civic participation. Personal arrangements, as Islami and Kavoussi argue, have become substitutes for institutional ones. In continuing to rely on personalist politics, Saudi rulers have ignored the fact that the 'integration of [Saudi Arabia] into the world market has had a revolutionary effect on the structure of ... society'.[39] As oil wealth unites society through increased contacts, and the level of conflict over distribution of wealth or political organisation soars, the state becomes faced with difficult political choices that personalist politics can no longer resolve. There has been slight political change since 1984 when Islami and Kavoussi wrote on Saudi Arabia. There is still no representative and autonomous organisation 'to channel' increasingly complex political demands 'in an orderly institutionalized manner'.[40]

Three distinct responses stand out: regulative, coercive and distributive. There is a definite need to increase regulative responses. Any initiatives that strengthen legal and institutional frameworks enhance regulation, at the expense of coercion, in the long term. Positive responses include the decision by King Fahd to restore the female academics who participated in the 1990 protest to be given the right to drive, to their lecturing positions in various universities. He was instrumental in the decision to compensate them financially for time and income lost out of work.[41] But so far the creation of *Majlis al-Shura* in 1993 is by far one of the most important innovations in the Saudi political system. As Abir rightly notes, its creation was in response to the petitions of the early 1990s.[42] While the *Majlis* is still lacking in representation, since it is appointed by the King and not elected by the people, it is a positive step in the right direction. Saudi history and political culture seem to favour gradual change. The *Majlis* was expanded to ninety members in 1997 and to one hundred and twenty in 2001. It is not impossible that, in ten years hence, a new political class of Saudi rulers will opt for a partly elected council. This would be one way of defusing the question of political legitimacy as well as equalising state–society relations, in the long term. The demands for better rule are not new. The so-called 'liberal princes' in the 1960s, led by Prince Talal, expressed demands for a constitutional monarchy, limiting royal prerogative, and a partially elected parliament.[43] Preserving tradition should not be taken to be antithetical to good government or democratic government. The tendency to treat *shura* and democracy as mutually exclusive has to be questioned. Writing on the *shura* system in Saudi Arabia, Amin Sa'ati sees *shura* to be superior to democracy. He justifies this by noting that *shura* is a godly system applicable to all times and places. Furthermore, he finds democracy's advocacy of political parties to lead to divisiveness and malice, observing that Muslims are commanded to close ranks. Basically, he does not champion democracy because it divides Muslims.[44] This kind of scholarship oversimplifies the question of democracy in a Muslim society, reducing *shura* to a system that is inimical to modernity and incapable of cohabitation with other notions of good government. That is one reason why Sa'ati rejects democracy's suitability for his country, observing that *shura* and appointed *shura* councils must not be underestimated in realising good government in Saudi Arabia.[45]

Coercion remains but, as mentioned above, the Saudi and generally Gulf States' record of brutality is less shameful than that of Iraq, for instance. However, coercion becomes more important as the state's function to regulate and distribute. The obverse is also true. The challenge therefore is to improve distribution, politically and economically. Politically, as the petitions of the early 1990s have shown, there is a pressing need for overhauling the political system and opening it to society. The days when governments can rely solely on the power of bread to pacify society or buy political allegiance are quickly passing. Distribution through political inclusion or participation is the route to shared political values, stability, legitimacy and citizenship. That does not lessen the importance of equity in the distribution of wealth or other economic goods, to Sunnis and the Shi'a, allies and opponents. Here again the memorandum accentuates the importance of equitable distribution, a question inextricably linked with corruption. But Saudi rulers have at the same time distributed a fraction of the oil wealth internationally, showing unique generosity and Islamic philanthropy, giving to Muslim countries strapped for cash as well as to Western universities, where they endowed many chairs in the fields of Arab and Islamic studies. In so doing, they were acting in the name of Islam. Those challenging them are today doing so in the name of Islam too. The scene in Saudi Arabia is set for more contests between state and society, further implicating Islam in the political process. The outcomes of these contests are very difficult to predict, although the capacity of the Royal House for adjustment is increasing, especially as young, savvy, tolerant and worldly Princes become more integrated in the machinery of government. Similarly, their interlocutors from society are likely to share with them preference for dialogue and consensus building as well as political values of power sharing. There is no reason why al-Hawali or *al-Awdah* would not in the future find a common ground with like-minded reform-minded princes amongst the upcoming generation of Saudi decision-makers. There are already signs supporting this trend. In January 2003 the royal family allowed Human Rights Watch to undertake its first fact-finding mission in the Kingdom. A month earlier, Crown Prince Abdullah called for more inclusive politics in the Arab world, a message with no precedent in Saudi political rhetoric. What can be gathered from all of this is that only through regulation can Saudis, rulers and ruled, hope to make politics the art of the possible. In Islam they all share a common platform. The challenge is for them to learn together where to look for values of dialogue, mutual tolerance and co-existence in that common platform.

I would like to thank my friend Mansour Chams (Abu Ammar) for his brief but helpful comments on a draft of this chapter.

Notes

1 Edward W. Said, *Orientalism* (London: Routledge & Kegan Paul, 1985).
2 The adjective from Wahhabism, which is the Hanbali creed of Sunni Islam that Muhammad Ibn Abd al-Wahhab elaborated in the early eighteenth Century. At the core of this puritanical brand of jurisprudence is to return all matters of life to a literalist reading of the Qur'an, the Holy Book of Islam, and to a pristine Islam that is unpolluted by heretical additions (ban of music, worship of Saints etc.) and innovations (opposition to *qiyas*). Thus *tawhid* (Unity of God) forms

part of the crux of the Wahhabi School, whose adherents and scholars were known by the name of *muwahhidun* (preachers of Unity of God).
3. Abd al-Rahman Ibn Khaldun, *Muqaddimat Ibn Khaldun* (Beirut: al-Matba'ah al-Adabiyya, 1900).
4. It is considered the first capital of Saudi Arabia, as state-formation was launched from it. Geographically, it is not far from the capital Riyadh, also in Najd.
5. The alliance was not only about the conversion of Ibn Saud to the Orthodox teachings of Abd al-Wahhab. Ibn Saud protected Abd al-Wahhab from various enemies of the founder of the Wahhabi doctrine.
6. The *Ikhwan*, as a fighting force, dates back to the early 1900s. From 1913 they grew into a formidable force, becoming effectively the 'praetorian guards' of the newly emerging Saudi state. Until then, *Ikhwan* referred to adherents of the Wahhabi doctrine of *tawhid*. In the modern state, the *Ikhwan* make up the National Guard, which comes under the remit of the Crown Prince.
7. Generally, there is agreement that the capture of Riyadh in 1902 by Abd al-Aziz ibn Saud was a major turning point in the history of Saudi state formation. In 1926 he took control of the Hijaz, becoming the following year King of the Najd and of the Hijaz. But the year 1932, which is important in the Saudi political calendar, marks the naming of the state: The Kingdom of Saudi Arabia. On the question of the *Ikhwan*, Kostiner shows how they were instrumental in state formation, helping Ibn Saud prevail over his enemies militarily. But in the phase of consolidation after the establishment of the new state, the *Ikhwan* had to be restrained. See David Howarth, *The Desert King: A Life of Ibn Saud* (London: Collins, 1964), and Joseph Kostiner, 'On Instruments and their Designers: The Ikhwan of Najd and the formation of the Saudi State', *Middle Eastern Studies*, 21 (3) 1985, 298–323.
8. Christine M. Helms, *The Cohesion of Saudi Arabia: Evolution of Political Identity* (London: Croom Helm, 1981), pp. 76–126.
9. James A. Caporaso (ed.), *The Elusive State: International and Comparative Perspectives* (New York: Sage, 1989); John A. Hall and G. John Ikenberry, *The State* (Buckingham: Open University Press, 1989); Andrew Vincent, *Theories of the State* (Oxford: Blackwell, 1987).
10. Article 1 of the Government's General Principles adopted by Royal decree in March 1993 reads as follows. 'The Kingdom of Saudi Arabia is a sovereign Arab Islamic state with Islam as its religion; God's Book and the *Sunna* (deeds and Sayings) of His Prophet, God's prayers and peace be upon him, are its constitution, Arabic is its language and Riyadh is its capital.' See http://www.uni-wuerzburg.de/law/sa00000_.html#A001_19/02/02.
11. Said Aburish, *The Rise, Corruption and Coming Fall of the House of Saud* (London: Bloomsbury, 1994), pp. 241–72.
12. Gabriel Almond and Sydney Verba (eds), *The Civic Culture: Political Attitudes and Democracy in Five Nations* (Princeton, NJ: Princeton University Press, 1963).
13. Frederick Hartman and Robert Wendzel, *America's Foreign Policy in a Changing World* (New York: HarperCollins, 1994), pp. 10–19.
14. Al-Otaybi quoted in James Buchan, 'Secular and Religious Opposition in Saudi Arabia', in Tim Niblock (ed.), *State, Society and Economy in Saudi Arabia* (London: Croom Helm, 1982), pp. 106–24.
15. Safran al-Maktay *et al.* 'A-Q-Study of Reactions to Direct Broadcast Satellite Television Programming in Saudi Arabia', *Journal of South Asian and Middle Eastern Studies*, 20, 4 (1997).

Saudi Arabia in the wake of September 11   49

16 Ahmed Rashid, *Taliban: The Story of the Afghan Warlords* (London: Pan Books, 2001).
17 See *Mudhakkirat al-Nasiha* (Saudi Arabia: n/p, July 1992).
18 Buchan, 'Secular and Religious Opposition in Saudi Arabia'.
19 See text of Ibn Baz's *Bayan* or Statement in the appendices of the *Mudhakkirat al-Nasiha*, pp. 122–5.
20 *Mudhakkirat al-Nasiha*, p. 123.
21 See *Mudhakkirat al-Nasiha*, pp. 94–8 and 114–19.
22 See the *Mudhakkirat al-Nasiha*, pp. 78–9.
23 See the *Mudhakkirat al-Nasiha*, pp. 85–92.
24 R. Hrair Dekmejian, 'The Rise of Political Islamism in Saudi Arabia', *Middle East Journal*, 48 (4) 1994, pp. 635–43.
25 Joshua Tietelbaum, *Holier than Thou: Saudi Arabia's Islamic Opposition* (Washington, DC: Washington Institute for Near East Policy, 2000).
26 R. Hrair Dekmejian, *Islam in Revolution: Fundamentalism in the Arab World* (Syracuse: Syracuse University Press, 1995).
27 Mamoun Fandy, *Saudi Arabia and the Politics of Dissent* (London: Palgrave, 2001).
28 Muhammad Al-Mas'ari, *Muhasabat al-Hukkam* (London: Mu'assat al-Rafd Lial-nashr wa al-Tawzi, 1997).
29 Al-Mas'ari, *Muhasabat al-Hukkam*, pp. 10–64.
30 Al-Mas'ari, *Muhasabat al-Hukkam*, pp. 65–73.
31 Al-Mas'ari, *Muhasabat al-Hukkam*, pp. 73–7.
32 Al-Mas'ari, *Muhasabat al-Hukkam*, pp. 76–7.
33 Al-Mas'ari, *Muhasabat al-Hukkam*, pp. 78–80.
34 Mark Heller and Nadav Safran, *The New Middle Class and Regime Stability in Saudi Arabia* (Cambridge, Massachusetts: Harvard Centre for Middle Eastern Studies, 1985), p. 13.
35 Heller and Safran, *The New Middle Class and Regime Stability in Saudi Arabia*, p. 22.
36 Fred Halliday, *Two Hours that shook the World* (London: Saqi, 2002).
37 Ahmed Rashid, *Taliban: The Story of the Afghan Warlords* (London: Pan Books, 2001), p. 133.
38 A. Reza S. Islami and Rostam M. Kavoussi, *The Political Economy of Saudi Arabia* (Seattle: University of Washington Press, 1984), p. 35.
39 Islami and Kavoussi, *The Political Economy of Saudi Arabia*, p. 35.
40 Islami and Kavoussi, *The Political Economy of Saudi Arabia*, p. 35.
41 Mordechai Abir, *Saudi Arabia: Government, Society and the Gulf Crisis* (London: Routledge, 1993), p. 193.
42 Abir, *Saudi Arabia*, p. 189.
43 Buchan, 'Secular and Religious Opposition in Saudi Arabia', pp. 113–15.
44 Amin Sa'ati, *Al-Shura fi al-Mamlaka al-Arabiyya al-Saudiyya* (Cairo: al-Markaz al-Sa'udi li al-Dirasat al-Istiratijiyya [The Saudi Strategic Studies Centre], 1992), pp. 30–5.
45 Sa'ati, *Al-Shura fi al-Mamlaka al-Arabiyya al-Saudiyya*, pp. 152–5.

4 The politics of reform in the Islamic Republic of Iran

Farideh Farhi

Introduction

'Persevere, as your son has been imprisoned for his faith and religion,' said Ayatollah Hossain Ali Montazeri in his telephone call of support to Hojjatoleslam Abdollah Nouri's father in late 1999.[1] Abdollah Nouri, a midranking cleric with impeccable revolutionary credentials, had just been briskly sent to prison for five years on a variety of made-up charges regarding the violation of press laws, a few days after his valiant defence of free expression and religious tolerance and rejection of arbitrary rule in front of a special clergy court. If one didn't know better, one would think that the Ayatollah was talking about opposition to a regime oblivious to religious sensitivity and righteousness. But Ayatollah Montazeri, an eminent Shi'a source of emulation (*marja-e taqlid*) once destined to become the most powerful religious leader of Iran but now under house arrest for his opposition to what he calls a 'club-wielding' clerical rule, was speaking about persevering against an Islamist regime he helped put in power. Indeed the irony and power of his words were lost to no one inside Iran. It was only a generation ago that clerics, along with many others, were put in prison for their faith and opposition to what they considered to be an illegitimate secular regime. The capture of state power by Islamists was reputedly their innovative solution for creating a popularly based legitimate regime. Twenty years later it is the Islamist regime that has to face open challenges to its legitimacy.

This open competition and confrontation between different versions of Islam – one that emphasises clerical prerogative and duty to interpret religious commands for the faithful and guide their daily activities through various religious and political injunctions and the other that insists on the importance of endowing the religious community itself with the right to make political choices on the basis of a democratic process – is clearly suggestive of a vibrancy in Iranian political thought about the nature of Islamic political rule; a vibrancy perhaps not as present in other countries populated by Muslims. At the same time this rather open-ended and at times seemingly endless conflict threatens to undermine the Islamist project of revamping the Iranian state, questioning its legitimacy, as a population tired of turmoil and political impasse becomes increasingly sceptical of the possibility of the conflict being resolved gradually through a process of negotiation.

Notwithstanding popular scepticism, open competition and conflict remain the hallmark of Iranian politics today, justifying the attempt in this chapter to understand their roots. Oddly enough, the sources of this confrontation between different versions of Islam may be found in the republican as well as the Islamist dimensions of the revolution that occurred more than twenty years ago. The 1979 Iranian revolution was made possible by the disintegration of a personalist state in face of a broad, multi-class coalition of forces that, at least in public and certainly in the beginning, agreed on some form of republicanism.[2] Being republican was to be against a rule that was personal, lifelong, hereditary, and arbitrarily defined. Indeed, the complex negotiations that led to popular support for the establishment of the provisional revolutionary government boiled down to two concrete rejections: neither monarchy nor dictatorship. To be sure, in Iran's prerevolutionary history those two rejections amounted to more or less the same thing, since there was hardly any example of an enduring personal power that had not become royal *and* dictatorial. The Shah had to be refused because of Iran's experience of the past century, in the course of which all monarchs, including the ones that had a constitution imposed on them, turned out badly. Even Muhammad Reza Pahlavi, the last shah, who began as a weak monarch both politically and temperamentally, ended up thinking he was God's gift to earth before his intricate system of personal rule crumbled in a hurry.

It was only after the revolution that monarchy and dictatorship were decoupled and the latter reinstated, this time in the name of an odd creation called Islamic republicanism. It was republicanism, Iranian-style, in so far as personal, hereditary and lifelong rule was rejected, and popularly elected republican institutions, such as the office of the presidency and the parliament (*majles*), as well as a complex set of negotiating rules among key players, and soon to be publicly revealed political factions, replaced a monarch-dominated system. It was 'Islamic,' as will be discussed below, in so far as powerful and non-elective politico-religious institutions, such as the office of *Rahbar* (*vali-ye faqih* or supreme leader) and Guardian Council (*shura-ye negahban*), were created on the side of republican institutions, constitutionally empowered with a variety of oversight tasks to ensure that the democratic processes enshrined in the constitution would not result in 'un-Islamic' ends. In addition, the created system was also dictatorial because it was exclusive to a tight circle of revolutionary elite and demanded a very strict code of public conduct on the part of believers or those pretending to be believers in the newly created Islamist state.

With Nouri's trial and his unadulterated defence of the real or imagined republican ideals of twenty years ago,[3] the Iranian revolution has come full circle. Once again the revolutionary demand for a republican form of government, a law-based state without a hereditary monarch, has been coupled with the rejection of dictatorship, this time in any form or shape. More significantly, as reflected in the support he received from Ayotallah Montazeri, Nouri's demand was not an isolated call of a dissident. It was the voice of a religious insider; the voice of a man who had served in a number of executive and legislative positions before he was chosen to be the Minister of Interior by a new reformist government headed by Hojjatoleslam Muhammad Khatami, also an insider; himself overwhelmingly and unexpectedly voted into office in May 1997 by an electorate responding affirmatively to his political call for the creation of law-based society and government.

Future historians will have to render a more distant and perhaps sober judgement about whether what is going on in Iran currently is the culmination of the revolutionary processes that began more than twenty years ago or a detour. Meanwhile, however, Nouri's trial has made at least one point crystal clear. Some clerics and many other supporters of the early turn towards a dictatorial Islamist state have every intention of being part of Iran's future and probably still highly contested political system, as players as well as diehard republicans! To be sure, as will be explained below, the commitment is to the democratic participation of religion in politics, instead of the separation of religion from politics. Nevertheless the republican aspects of this political game and challenge from within cannot be ignored.

In what follows I will attempt to shed light on the complex interplay of Islamist forces and their various versions of Islam, offering explanations for the current 'democratic challenge' in Iran and within the Iranian religious establishment. I will argue that although this democratic challenge was generated from the top as a strategy for survival on the part of an embattled political faction, it has managed to slip the hands of its initial formulators and turn into something with much wider democratic implications and possibilities. Possibilities are of course just that: mere possibilities. Yet the existence of an open-ended competitive political game among forces, all self-identified as loyal to Islamic principles, cannot be overlooked. This chapter will attempt to glean and chart the particularities of the post-revolutionary experience in Iran that have yet again led to challenges of legitimacy, this time for the Islamist state.

A consolidated Islamist state, an ensemble of fiefdoms or both?

Oddly enough, the place to begin the search for the roots of the current turn towards pluralistic politics in Iran is the Islamist post-revolutionary state itself and the success the state builders had in consolidating power in terms of state control of the society. I say oddly because the understanding of the Iranian post-revolutionary state has generally been in terms of its ability to coerce the population into submission and certainly not in terms of its embedded institutional pluralism. To be sure, success in consolidation was a very important part of the post-revolutionary experience. But this success had its unintended consequences as well. It was also not necessarily accompanied with co-ordinated and centralised institutionalisation.

Political consolidation came swiftly and mercilessly.[4] With the rapid collapse of the *ancien régime*, the existing institutions as well as abundant resources of the Iranian state were taken over and decapitated through a series of purges. Parallel security and military institutions were erected to defend against possible deviations within the remnants of *ancien régime* institutions, and the legal system was brought under religious jurisdiction. The resultant institutional arrangement that came out of the fluid revolutionary context was codified in the Constitution of the Islamic Republic of Iran, which, as Asghar Schirazi points out, was replete with contradictions, reflecting the extraordinary range of political forces involved in the revolution.[5]

Schirazi identifies two fundamental contradictions that have had decisive impacts on the development of the Iranian post-revolutionary state: contradiction between the constitution's Islamic legalist and non-Islamic secular elements and the contradiction between its democratic and non-democratic elements arising essentially from two notions of sovereignty, one of the people and one of the Islamic jurists. The democratic and secular elements can be found, for instance, in the idea of adopting a constitution, the partial recognition of the will of the people to be expressed in elections for the president, members of the parliament and local councils as well as Assembly of Leadership Experts (a clerical body in charge of choosing and dismissing the leader). It can also be found in the powers vested in the parliament despite restrictions imposed through oversight by other bodies and partial recognition of fundamental rights (such as the equality of all Iranians as well as a number of freedoms including of opinion, press, and to form political parties).

The Islamic legalist elements of the constitution, on the other hand, are laid out in the establishment of a state explicitly identified as Islamic, with an Islamic character, its legislative process bound by shari'a, and ruled by Islamic jurists. In addition, the constitution imposes Islamically defined restrictions on the democratic rights of individuals as well as ethnic groups. Finally it sets up institutions such as the office of the *Rahbar* (*vali-ye faqih*) and the Guardian Council whose task is to ensure the Islamic character of the state.

More specifically, Article 2 of the constitution defines 'continual *ijtehad* (jurisprudential reasoning) by qualified jurists' as a principle of the Islamic system of government. Article 5 stipulates that a *faqih*, a supreme individual jurist (or a supreme council of jurists), endowed with uprightness, purity, and expertise, has the right to exercise leadership in the Islamic Republic as long [as] the Twelfth Imam of the Shi'a remains in occultation. Identified as Rahbar (supreme leaders), the powers of this *faqih*, which are specified in the constitution, far exceeds a mere supervisory role but is not absolute. They include, to name a few, the appointment of the jurists to the Guardian Council as well as the appointment of the highest judicial authority in the country. Rahbar also holds supreme command over the armed forces and can dismiss the president if the Supreme Court declares that the president has violated his legal duties or parliament judges that he is politically incompetent. At the same time, Rahbar's powers do not include either legislative authority or the exercise of direct judicial powers. There are, however, other non-elective institutions run by Islamic jurists that exercise control over the legislative and judicial processes. For instance, six of the twelve-member Guardian Council, a body which has the right of veto over parliamentary resolutions, must be jurists and these six alone have the right to vote on whether acts of parliament are in conformity with the shari'a. The Guardian Council is also vested with the task of interpreting the constitution and supervising presidential and parliamentary elections and referendums.

This heavy Islamist tint of the constitution was further buttressed in the immediate post-revolutionary period by a process, pursued in full force, to 'Islamicise' society and social institutions, perhaps out of ideological commitment, but with the effective result of confirming the supremacy of a loose coalition of Islamic revolutionaries that had come to accept the absolute leadership of Ayatollah Khomeini, and initially the institutional medium of the Islamic Republican Party (IRP), as a means to resolve internal conflicts as well as maintain control. Moves such as forced veiling of women and suspension of some of their previously gained rights were complemented by a highly charged takeover of the American Embassy in Tehran, which facilitated the downfall of the moderate Provisional government of Mehdi Bazargan, and later a successful mobilisation to defend the country against an 'imposed' war initiated by the Iraqi incursion into Iran in 1980. Led by a parallel military institution, the Islamic Republic Guards Corp (IRGC), countless sacrifices were made in the duration of the war between 1980 and 1988 in the name of 'Sacred Defence,' and a vast repository of heroic deeds was created to use in crushing dissent but also for reference in later political struggles. In fact, the Iran–Iraq War became the basis of a new political milieu that remained even after the war, despite the rise of other ways of thinking about and conceiving politics.

Muhammad Javad Gholamreza Kashi identifies emphasis on Shi'a values, Shia-generated epic aspects of the war, mourning, opposition to existing values in the city, martyrdom, action as opposed to words, purity and devotion, and spiritual rewards in the afterlife as the most important elements of the culture of war propagated by the war machine in Iran.[6] To be sure, the propagated ideal type of behaviour was not completely distinct from the images generated for an ideal Islamic revolutionary during the revolution.[7] However, while the revolution brought out a multiplicity of voices, at times emphasising contradictory aspirations (submission to Islam and the spiritual leader as well as democracy and freedom), the war offered a univocal venue for both crushing domestic opposition to the newly emerging political order as well as 'sacred defence' against international aggression. According to Kashi, 'this discourse has specific practical implications, the most important of which are emphasis on war and courage, worship, control of passions, avoidance of fame and material interests, unconditional adherence to the leadership and avoidance of any questioning in this regard'.[8]

Moreover, what was developed during the war engulfed the society far beyond the war front. In the cities, the locale from which volunteers were sent to war and stations for the mobilisation of *basij* (militia) forces became important centres of social gathering. In addition, the constant broadcast of war chants from radio, television and loudspeakers, television programs celebrating sacrifices made in the war front, ceremonies held for the funerals of war martyrs, and re-written school textbooks imbued with values emphasised during the war reflected the encroachment of the values of the war front into the daily life of all Iranians.

In retrospect, speed and efficiency were the two characteristics that can be identified as the distinguishing features of the post-revolutionary consolidation period. The opposition was methodically and systematically eliminated or exiled, step-by-step. Never having to deal with a significant or serious counter-revolutionary force, the regime found it relatively easy to dispense with its early revolutionary partners, of liberal, socialist or Stalinist varieties, and move on. More importantly, this elimination was accompanied with ideological emasculation. In short, a variety of opposition forces simply lost credibility. The royalist opposition could not be a factor so soon after an anti-royalist revolution. The secular opposition lost credibility for being in exile and constantly bickering. They also suffered through calculated assassinations of their key leaders by the Iranian state operatives. The left, in its secular, Islamist and Stalinist varieties, lost credibility by becoming identified with the early excesses of the revolution. The most important organised opposition of left Islamists, the Mujahedin, also lost credibility through its own fateful decision to come out on the side of the opponent in the war with Iraq and its own undemocratic, or cult-like as some would have it, internal structure.[9]

With a rather quick and effective handling of the counter-revolutionary or opposition movements, there was really no overwhelming threat to keep the diverging fundamental differences of interest and ideology within the ruling coalition in check. The divergence of interests was further intensified by the fact that the ruling coalition itself was the result of the intersection of a variety of social forces (bazaari merchants, clerics, intermediate classes, poorer sectors of the society) that in real life were competitors in their pursuit of the state's economic – read oil – resources. To be sure, the Iran–Iraq War and Ayatollah Khomeini's forceful presence kept the loose coalition together for a while. Yet the differences were so overwhelming that they ultimately led to the abandonment of the idea of one revolutionary party keeping the differences under hierarchical or co-ordinated control. Democratic centralism, Iranian style, was only made possible temporarily and haphazardly not through ideological justification but through the forceful personality of Ayatollah Khomeini who acted as the central commander once he spoke. Not even the principle of *velayat-e faqih* (guardianship of the jurist/supreme religious leader) could fully serve to unify all political forces ideologically due to the conflicts that existed from the beginning over the way the office was interpreted. As mentioned above, the principle was affirmed in the constitution but debates surrounding it regarding the distinction between *velayat-e faqih* and an 'absolute' *velayat-e faqih* hinted at the tensions that were going to come out more fully later, after Ayatollah Khomeini's death.[10] Even when alive, on many occasions, Ayatollah Khomeini chose to stay above the fray, either due to temperament, religious/ideological beliefs, or political exigency. At the end, even he could not keep things firmly in hand and factions formerly operating under the rubric of the IRP were set loose after the party was declared defunct in 1986.

With Ayatollah Khomeini's death, the stage was set for full-fledged competitive politics, and here comes the second caveat about the post-revolutionary state. Although, as described, the Islamist revolutionaries were quite capable of consolidating their hold over society, this consolidation did not translate into a centralised system of control over state institutions and structures. To be sure, they were able state builders, but of the extreme opportunistic type.[11] They looked at the state, whose bureaucratic structure had essentially remained intact and continued to be the most important source of economic resources and rent because of its control over the means of oil production and distribution, both as a lever of power and a source of income. As such, rather than joining forces to build a centralised state structure, various competing factions simply began to disassemble the state and turn it into a series of multi-layered, parallel and often competing fiefdoms. New parallel institutions were also built in some cases as a means to check institutions with similar objectives, when direct control was deemed impossible. Added to this process, was a layer of institutions such as the Foundation for the Oppressed (*Bonyad-e Mostaz'afan*) consisting of what has become known as parastatal economic foundations that found their origins in the property confiscated from the extended royal family as well as many others.[12]

Ultimately, out of necessity, the political system in the Islamic Republic did not merely embody institutions that were worked out within a broader constitutional framework in the early stages of the revolution, such as the parliament or the Guardian Council. It also included institutions, such as the Expediency Council, that were created at particular historical junctures to avert or reduce systemic crises or political tensions and then became permanent features of the system.[13] Perhaps no political system in the world is characterised by so many interconnected and parallel political institutions. Added to this situation is the lack of any transparent organisational chart that identifies the relative importance of one institution over another constitutionally or a revolutionary party that can establish the superiority of one institution over another in practice and through tacit agreements. Amidst all this, it is a wonder how post-revolutionary authority was even maintained.

Post-revolutionary authority and sources of legitimacy

In fact, post-revolutionary state authority has been maintained through a divided state structure that entrenches political and economic competition among social groups that ranges from traditional trade-centered interests located in the bazaars, to modern professional middle classes, to more service-oriented interests of the new Iranian political economy.[14] The so-called Islamic state of Iran, rather than becoming the medium through which competition among these classes became regulated and hence controlled, has itself developed into an institutional repository of these varied interests and an arena in which multiple claims over various parts of the state were constantly negotiated rather than resolved. Meanwhile, as mentioned above, the heavy hand of the state's ideological and repressive apparatus is used to make legitimate the clerical claim to state power.

The term 'clerics' should of course be used delicately here. The idea of clerical guardianship from the beginning was not intended to mean that all clerics should be politically involved or that it is through their unanimity that clerical rule is made possible. Rather, it simply suggested that first there was a will to rule, no matter at what cost, and, second, that there existed certain interpersonal and non-transparent dynamics among the revolutionary clerics that would allow them to negotiate their way out of political conflict and crisis.

In short the notion of clerical guardianship portrayed the revolutionary clerics as deliberate, determined, and flexible in their claim to power and this ended up being an important source of political legitimacy in a society in search of stability in the aftermath of a period of tumultuous revolution and war.

Ayatollah Khomeini was undoubtedly the most important figure in the construction of the idea of clerical guardianship. He not only resurrected the idea as a purely political formulation in the notion of *velayat-e faqih*, but also epitomised the idea in flesh. He was himself deliberate, determined, and flexible. He was a political man who could rise above it all and be the final arbiter. Yet, Ayatollah Khomeini's dominant presence should not overshadow the ideological dimension of clerical rule. Even without Ayatollah Khomeini, the Iranian revolutionary leadership always strove to derive legitimacy by relying on the existence of seemingly invincible authority, be it vested in individuals, institutions, or behind-the-scene negotiation processes, that could rise above the everyday scenes of partisan politics and define the parameters of accepted public speech and actions. The idea was that a non-transparent, non-tangible tacit agreement among the clerics would always prevent policy disagreements and, more importantly, power struggles from getting out of control.

From internal bickering to open competition and conflict

The first public display of flows in this source of clerical authority came during the fifth parliamentary elections of 1995.[15] During these elections, disagreement over the list of candidates led to the creation of a new political faction (*Kargozaran-e Sazandegi*, or Servants/Executives of Construction), which had previously operated under the political umbrella of *Jame'eye Rohaniyat-e Mobarez* (Society of Combatant Clergy). This emboldened another faction, *Majma'eh Rohaniyoon-e Mobarez* (Association of Militant Clerics), which had previously splintered and become politically marginalised, to enter the election process as well. The first round of elections suggested important gains for the new faction in particular. However, intervention on the part of Rahbar, Ayatollah Seyyed Ali Khamenei, and warnings against the 'creeping influence of the 'liberal' or 'secular' forces closed the competitive window that was opened and led to the reversal of some of the gains in the first round. But the reversal in the election results could not hide the damage done to the idea of clerical guardianship as the final arbiter among competing factions.

The damage done in the fifth parliamentary elections became clearly manifest in the 1997 presidential election. By the time it became possible to think of Muhammad Khatami's presidential challenge as real, it was clear that the idea of clerical guardianship was being taken prisoner of partisan politics rather than acting as a mechanism to rise above it. This became apparent when attempts were made to appropriate the notion of clerical guardianship as a tool to manipulate the outcome of the election. Making a move to take control of the political system and put an end to factional disputes and competition, political forces representing a coalition of bazaari merchants and conservative clerics made an argument that reputable clerics (and by implication, Rahbar) could and should render judgment on who is the most religiously rightful (*aslah*) candidate.

This rather unwise political move undermined the legitimacy of the notion of clerical guardianship in two ways. On the one hand, by openly coming out in favour of one candidate and then justifying it in religious terms, the conservative clerics opened themselves to the charge of using religion in an instrumental fashion, a charge that has dogged them since. On the other hand, by not controlling the outcome of the election, they publicly revealed their inability to manipulate at least some events in Iran. This latter point is particularly important in the light of the fact that the Iranian electorate fully expected the election results to be tampered with.

The election platforms of the two candidates also reflected a turning point in Iranian politics. The establishment candidate, Ali Akbar Nateq Nouri, came into the fray with confidence and not much else. Security, prosperity, 'melting' in *velayat-e faqih*, and 'just Islamic government' were slogans loudly hooted without much concern for popular resentments. On the other hand, forces fearful of total elimination, represented by Mohammad Khatami, had a ready made slogan handed to them: they were simply against forces of monopoly (*enhessar*). In this process they were aided by the fact that they had managed to tap an appealing presidential candidate who turned the anti-monopoly slogan into something broader and more appealing to the whole population: the need to overhaul the rules of the political game, making them and the way Islamic ideas are practised more inclusive, tolerant, and democratic. How else could have an embattled political faction staged a comeback? The only option left was to ask for help outside the elite circles.

Whether improvised or clearly thought through, the new slogan struck a chord with a variety of social forces that one way or another had come face to face with an increasingly exclusionary elite in the political as well as economic arenas. However, the call for a tolerant and inclusive polity also echoed well within, as well as was fed by, sectors of the Iranian religious community that had already been going through what some people have called a process of religious reformation. Influenced by the works of such lay religious thinkers such as Abdolkarim Soroush[16] but also reform-oriented clerics such as Muhammad Mojtahed Shabestari and Mohsen Kadivar, they charged that a legalistic version of Islam had replaced the spirit of the faith in Iran. In fact, they argued, by imposing and practising a harsh and unforgiving Islam, the ruling clerics were in the process of secularising society, ultimately putting themselves (as an establishment) in a position of being eventually rejected by the society in the same way secular Marxist parties were in the former communist states. Contending that Islam as a faith was larger than Islamic jurisprudence (*fiqh*), they rejected the Islamic Republic's interpretation of Islam as a series of immutable religious laws. Political Islam, by definition, had secularised Islam in so far as making it concerned with the organisation of the present temporal world. As such, and in order to be relevant, its practices must be critically and perpetually examined, questioned, critiqued, and reinterpreted. For this to work, Islam must recognise individual rights and not merely confer obligations on people. Such critical work cannot be dependent upon a class of people (i.e. clerics) who are dependent on maintaining a particular interpretation in order to sustain themselves economically and politically. It must be the work of people endowed with assured individual rights, infused with religion enthusiasm, and engaged in the protection and enrichment of the spirit of Islam in their daily lives. Interpreted this way, religious or Islamic democracy is not merely a right but a necessity for the health and vibrancy of a pious community.

While Khatami did not explicitly draw upon these arguments to criticise clerical rule, his call for a 'religious democracy' echoed elements of these arguments. As mentioned above, the idea of creating a more democratic understanding of religious governance based on the rule of law was in many ways a natural slogan for an elite faction facing the possibility of political elimination. But it is also important to note that even Khatami and his embattled faction had thoroughly underestimated the extent to which the general public was ready for this. This diverse general public, weary of years of abuse and intrusions in their daily lives, began to watch the very fluid and delicate political game while consistently siding with the forces that were, granted perhaps only for the moment, on the side of political and cultural opening. Through an incredibly vibrant and continuously expanding print media as well as a number of parliamentary, presidential and local and town council elections, this 'public' repeatedly stated its desire for the state to pull back and let the society live. But it also did something more basic. It established itself as a player, or more accurately a set of players, that competitors for power could no longer take for granted as either mute or made mute.

But this is, perhaps rather predictably, a difficult disposition for the conservative forces to accept. After its stunning defeat in the 1997 presidential election, the efforts of these forces became more defensive. Not being able to count on their tenuous relationship to the electorate, the traditional bazaari forces and their allies in various parts of the state, including some sectors of the Revolutionary Guards and security forces, began to use institutions that could undermine increased popular participation in democratic institutions. The judicial system, the Guardian Council, and the institution of *velayat-e faqih* were the ready made institution for them to rely upon.[17] They also still had control of the fifth parliament. But the reformers, many of whom had been in the government before, also began to play the political game, this time with much more adeptness about the key institutions that they felt would enhance their power. The massive participation of the people in the 1997 presidential election was a learning experience for them, creating an understanding that society had changed and their strength lay in parts of state structures that could further ease popular participation.

This understanding came to play an important role in the complex negotiations and bargaining that took place over the selection of Khatami's cabinet members. Khatami was willing to relent in areas considered to be important for the traditional right, such as the economy. He also made compromises in other ministries but in two areas of direct impact on popular participation – Ministry of Culture and Islamic Guidance (simply known as Ershad in Iran) and the Interior Ministry – he refused to buckle under. The results ended up being decisive. Ershad began and steadfastly continued a policy of giving licenses to pro-democracy newspapers as the Judiciary kept closing them and the Interior Ministry, which is in charge of internal security as well as the appointment of provincial governors, simply began putting reformists in charge at the provincial and local levels.

Another important state institution that the reformists earmarked as important, but could only make inroads in after a fight, was the dreaded Information Ministry. This ministry, which had been the most important arm of the state in crushing dissent, was exposed as the source of a series of murders that occurred after Khatami's election and was at least partially neutralised as a body to be used for factional politics.

The result of all this was that by the time the sixth parliamentary elections came around in February 2000, the reformists had far more resources in their arsenal than the previous elections. First of all they had the institution of election itself. No matter how manipulated, this institution had always been considered a signpost for the legitimacy of the system. Furthermore, the decision in the 1997 presidential election to keep it relatively free of manipulation on election day had created a precedent that was difficult to subvert. Most importantly, elections provided an easy avenue for forces that were not keen on using violence to make their choices public. Indeed, the shift of the competitive venue from back rooms and rough and tough street politics to the ballot boxes was already the most important strategic victory of the reformists. Second, the control of the Interior Ministry proved extremely useful as that institution became an important, although by no means fully effective, counter to reckless disqualification of candidates by the

Guardian Council and also an effective counter to possible voting violations at the provincial and local level. Third, the policies followed by Ershad bore fruit as the independent and reformist press effectively became the most important sounding board for the reformist candidates. Finally, tapping on the popular energy that had responded so favourably to their more limited objective of 'ending monopoly' in the previous elections, the reformist were now bold enough to be pushed further in the realm of ideology as well. Indeed a simple campaign slogan of 'Iran for all Iranians,' presumably religious or secular, clarified the stakes as well as aspirations in terms of the need for political equality for all as well as fairer rules of the political game. Ultimately, the combination of a competitive election and a vibrant public discourse about the stakes involved kept the larger public involved.

The role of democratic Islamist forces also proved decisive. Self-identified as 'religious intellectuals', and using the pens and newspapers they now controlled, they replaced religious preachers as the most important shapers of public opinion. They became the voice as well as conscience of a 'nation is search of inclusion and respect'. Theirs was a struggle to end 'humiliation' and also 'instrumental' or ideological use of Islam as a means to maintain state power. Once again everyone was surprised at how well the message was received.

For democratic Islamist forces, the May 1997 election proved to be a turning point. In that election something fundamental became evident: that a body of resources, secular as well as religious, is available in the society to be tapped. Suddenly the real possibility that these democratic forces could mobilise their followers independently and through alliance with other forces close to them (some of whom may be secular) became evident. This was an important revelation because while the democratic Islamist forces had been around from well before the 1979 revolution, dwelling on the fundamental question of how to modernise Islam, their historical experience suggested failure when they chose coalition with secular forces over alliance with traditional clerics and their bazaari backers. As succinctly pointed out by Morad Saghafi, historically, collaboration with secular forces had made them targets of extremist opponents, who had connections to conservative clerics who, in turn, mounted 'the pulpit denouncing them as apostates'. The question for democratic Islamists was always and continues to be 'whether they can withstand the pressure, denunciations and the mobilisations against them. Their predecessors either did not or were defeated.'[18]

Political deadlock or paralysis

That the democratic Islamist forces have made a choice to offer a different path to the participation of religion in politics can no longer be doubted.

Whether they will be successful is of course an entirely different matter. The overwhelming victory the reformists registered in the 2000 parliamentary election in no way signalled the end of factional power politics in Iran. If anything, it intensified it. Of course, most people expected that the reformists, having won control of both executive and legislative branches, could now pursue their objectives with greater ease. But as it turned out, popular rejection did not weaken the will of anti-reform forces but in fact spurred them to step up their efforts. Before the newly elected parliament took over, for instance, they used their clout in the outgoing parliament to pass a draconian law that allowed courts to force news reporters to reveal their sources and barred anyone involved in 'anti-establishment' activities from holding a position in the press. Most important, they continued to use the non-elected institutions they controlled to relentlessly block proposals that would facilitate political competition and open discourse. They undermined reformist legislation, shut down newspapers, forced Khatami's key ministers out of office, sent militia forces to disrupt student rallies and meetings, and arrested reformist journalists and government and elected officials, as well as active members of civil society. And they have done all this with the open, albeit itinerant, support of both Ayatollah Khamenei and former president Ali Akbar Hashemi Rafsanjani.

This strategy – an 'attack from below' coupled with 'consent from above' – has placed Khatami in a difficult and delicate position. Every time a newspaper has been closed, a political rally or meeting disrupted, or an ally arrested on fabricated charges, Khatami's inability to condemn or counter the act (beyond expressing his regret) has exposed his limited powers (as well as the limited powers of all democratic institutions) within the political system. Unwilling to engage in direct confrontation, Khatami has called for patience and slow reform – an approach that has placed him at odds even with some of his own supporters. These so-called radical reformists have pleaded for a more unequivocal stance and greater reliance on the 'people power' that put Khatami in office. But concerned that such an approach might lead to violent, uncontrollable street riots (similar to those that occurred in the summer of 1998 after security and militia forces attacked students at the University of Tehran), Khatami has been mostly reticent and non-resolute under pressure.

These circumstances underlie what can be considered a political deadlock in Iranian politics. Openly embarrassed about his inability to counter the onslaught of anti-reform tactics, Khatami even remained hesitant to stand in a second presidential election in May 2001 unless he was assured of a less hindered presidency. With that assurance not forthcoming, Khatami's no-win predicament developed into a no-win quandary for the entire nation. Even the anti-reform forces could not count on outright success. Incapable of coming up with a popular candidate or platform, yet unable to forcibly rule through non-elected institutions, these forces have remained wedded to their obstructionist strategy. Although effective in impeding reform, their strategy continues to lack a realistic vision of how to govern a multi-voiced country ready for non-violent, coherent reform.

Such gridlock has created the potential for the Iranian electorate to trade its patience for indifference, robbing the Islamic republic of all its legitimacy. Of course this situation did not happen in the 2001 presidential election as 63 per cent of the electorate voted,[19] overwhelmingly (79 per cent) for Khatami. But the continuing obstructionist stance of anti-reform forces after the 2001 election suggests that Iran's political problems are far from over.

To be sure, some observers maintain that democratic legitimacy has never been a concern for the anti-reform forces, as long as their political power can be assured through their opaque economic dealings with and through various governmental and semi-governmental institutions. Some even argue that as a 'power Mafia' (a term openly used in Iran), the anti-reform forces actually thrive in chaos and confusion. Although this observation may be partially correct, the intense political competition that has pervaded Iran over the past several years has now reached a point where no single political force can administer and control the country without some sort of truce or agreement among all the key political players. Various forces each have enough political muscle to obstruct the progress of their opponents, even if they are not strong enough to defend themselves against similar attacks. But none of these forces is individually capable of thwarting a popular rejection of the Islamist regime. This is a real concern, given that Iran's electorate (65 per cent of which is under 25 years old) increasingly sees the state as paralysed by internal conflicts and unresponsive to popular demands and needs.

Conclusion

The Iranian democratic discussion has not yet been able to generate answers to some fundamental questions about the basic contradictions that exist in the Iranian Islamic constitution between its democratic and undemocratic as well as secular and religious elements. Furthermore, at the practical level it has not been able to politically emasculate the anti-democratic impulses of forces that are operating within the institutions established by the post-revolutionary constitution. Whether it will be able to do so can only be determined by time. With the continuation of open conflict, the impasse itself has been an important source of discontent and erosion of legitimacy for the Islamist regime.

At the same time, the messiness of current political dynamics should not overshadow some important moves toward clarity and transparency. The most important trend is towards the acceptance of relatively free and open elections as the means to decide the balance of power, making the idea of electoral democracy as the 'only game in town' a real possibility, no matter how particular that possibility is to the Iranian political context. The conservative clerics, through their control of the Guardian Council, still have the power of vetting the candidates prior to the elections and all signs suggest that in the next parliamentary and presidential elections they will do their best to prevent the candidacy of candidates deemed dangerous to their interests. But even then they will be faced with a dilemma since they are confronted with an electorate that will register its vote by non-voting, hence making the election a vote not for a particular candidate but against the Islamic Republic itself. As such, elections now serve as important transparent mechanisms to gauge public mood and disposition.

A second and related trend involves the partial move away from shadowy politics to transparent politics. The making public of positions, powerful personalities, and their relationships has been a very important part of the Iranian political process. Indeed the conversation that has been generated in Iran about the way politics is conducted and the changes that are needed to end back room politics has itself been one of the most important reasons for maintaining the interest of the population in electoral politics. This interest in public conversation in turn has been an important boost for the push for more transparency. Extensive discussions in the print media, despite all the restrictions imposed on it, about the role of religion in politics, different interpretations of Islam, Islamic justice, respect for individual rights, limits on the power of the state, and freedom of expression have been a significant part of the democratic turn in Iran.[20] Conversations about basic freedoms and rights presumably guaranteed in the constitution have also gone a long way in educating the public, which in turn has become more demanding in terms of the implementation of these rights and guarantees.

With Khatami's election Islamic Iran seems to have begun a process of moving away from politics shaped by the unbridgeable rift between the state and society and towards a situation in which the 'democratic temptation' is replacing the 'authoritarian temptation'.[21] A consensus seems to have developed among many, although by no means all, elite and non-elite actors and forces, religious and secular, that a democratic process is the best foundation upon which to redraw the relationship between the state and society as well as resolve conflicts among the contending interests within the political system. The idea, in the words of one well-known Iranian theorist of reform, Saeed Hajjarian, is to push gradually for reform through a process of 'pressure from below and bargaining from the top'.[22]

However, even this proposition is perhaps a mischaracterisation since the elements of actual democratisation that are established with the involvement of popular forces are by definition unpredictable and cannot be kept within any predefined limits. Within the Iranian context, it is important to remember that the idea of limited elite competition was hampered from the beginning by the fact that one section of the elite, because it did not have sufficient resources within the elite circles, was forced to look for support outside the closed ruling cliques. In this process it was aided by a democratic Islamic strain of thought that had always had a standing in Iranian society but was unable to make an autonomous stance of its own because of the organisational weakness of its proponents vis-à-vis the popular appeal of the clergy. With popular backing, that strain of thought has gained support not only as a possible vehicle for ending dictatorship but also as a means to resolve societal and political deadlocks. The result has been the movement of a limited and presumably managed political game into a territory in which very little seems predetermined. The concern at this point is not about the 'realness' of the struggle to democratise the Islamic state but, given the almost blind internal opposition to it by a minority, the possible chaotic implications of this very fierce struggle. Obviously there is much more to tell about this story as events of incredible speed unfold in Iran. The only certain thing is that judgment about the nature of Iran's 'Islamic' revolution of more than twenty years ago will very much depend on the trajectory that unfolds.

Research for this chapter was made possible by a grant from the United States Institute of Peace. I would like to thank Shahram Akbarzadeh for the very helpful comments in the re-writing of this chapter.

Notes

1. As reported by Ali Raiss-Tousi, 'Iranian Cleric Nouri Defied Appeal Calls.' Reuters (December 1, 1999).
2. For an analysis of the nature of personalist rule and its particular vulnerability to revolutions see Farideh Farhi, *States and Urban-Based Revolutions: Iran and Nicaragua* (Urbana, IL: University of Illinois Press, 1990).
3. Abdollah Nouri's defence was later published in a book called *Showkaran-e eslah* (Hemlock of Reform) (Tehran: Tarh-e No, 1378/1999) that immediately became the best-selling book in Iran. In this defence, Nouri relied solely on guarantees and protections laid out in the Iranian Constitution as passed immediately after the revolution and amended in 1989. He even relied on the same document to question the constitutionality of the Special Clergy Court that had brought charges against him. He argued that the court was unconstitutional, having never been specified in the constitution. He also argued that its act of bringing charges against him for press violations as the publisher of daily *Khordad* was outside the purview of the Special Clergy Court since Iran also has a press court.
4. See my own *States and Urban-based Revolutions in Iran and Nicaragua* as well as John Foran and Jeff Goodwin, 'Revolutionary Outcomes in Iran and Nicaragua: Coalition Fragmentation, War, and the Limits of Social

Transformation.' *Theory and Society* 22, 2 (April 1993). For detailed discussion of the immediate political and ideological struggles see Shaul Bakhash, *The Reign of the Ayatollahs: Iran and the Islamic Revolution* (New York: Basic Books, 1984).
5 Asghar Schirazi, translated by John O'Kane, *The Constitution of Iran: Politics and the State in the Islamic Republic* (London: I. B. Tauris, 1997). On the debates surrounding the writing of the constitution, particularly as they related to the question of the relationship between dominant Shi'a and religious minorities, also see Eliz Sanasarian, *Religious Minorities in Iran* (Cambridge: Cambridge University Press, 2000), ch. 2.
6 Muhammad Javad Gholamreza Kashi, *Jadouye Goftar: Zehniat-e Farhangi va Nezam-e Ma'ani dar Entekhabat-e Dovom-e Khordad* (The Magic of Discourse: Cultural Consciousness and the System of Meanings in the 2 Khordad Election). (Tehran: Ayandeh Pouyan, 1379/2000), pp. 326–34.
7 For a comprehensive analysis of revolutionary images see Peter J. Chelkowski and Hamid Dabashi, *Staging a Revolution: The Art of Persuasion in the Islamic Republic of Iran* (New York: New York University Press, 1999).
8 Kashi, *Jadouye goftar*, p. 336.
9 On the origins, history, and internal structure of Mojahedin see Ervand Abrahamian, *The Iranian Mojahedin* (New Haven: Yale University Press, 1992).
10 The institution continues to rest in an uneasy tension with the republican aspects of the constitution. In general, most people agree that the institution was a 'garment only fitting of Khomeini'. In his trial, Abdollah Nouri made a distinction between the 'leader' of the revolution who as the originator of the system is endowed with extra-systemic rights and prerogatives and the 'position of leadership' which derives its legitimacy from the already established laws and hence cannot rely on the same prerogatives accorded to the original leader/founder.
11 By able I mean the ability to increase the size of the state. Quoting the now-banned opposition journal, *Iran-e Farda*, Anoushiravan Ehteshami writes that government payroll grew from 800,000 in 1977/8 to 2 million in 1992/3 (*After Khomeini: The Iranian Second Republic*, London: Routledge, 1995, p. 119). Abdolali Rezai uses figures for the number of salaried and waged workers in the broader public sector category to suggest a 254 per cent increase in the twenty-year period from 1,673,092 to 4,257,967 in 1996. ('Nimeyeh por-e livan' [The Full Half of the Glass]. In *Entekhab- e No* [New Choice], edited by Abdolali Rezai and Abbas Abdi, Tehran: Tarh-e No, 1998). No matter the variation in numbers, the jump seems to hover around a 2.5-fold increase. Rezai suggests that the jump can be explained by the more inclusive employment practices of the new state managers who recruited from the more marginalised strata.
12 Susan Maloney has done the most extensive study of these parastatal organisations. See for instance her 'Parastatal Foundations and the Political Economy of Postrevolutionary Iran'. Delivered at the 1999 annual meeting of the Middle East Studies Association, November 19–22, 1999.
13 The Expediency Council, which was created at the time of the Iran–Iraq War, was intended to resolve conflicts between the Parliament and the Guardian Council. The permanence of this body as well its rejuvenation under the leadership of the former president Ali Akbar Hashemi Rafsanjani since 1997, created all sorts of questions regarding the power of this body and its status in

relation to other bodies such as the Guardian Council and the Assembly of Leadership Experts, particularly since many of the members are the same. Another question relates to the origins of this body. Born out of a crisis situation as a mechanism to reduce tension among other political bodies, some argue that this institution thrives on crisis for maintaining and enhancing its power. This view has been most clearly laid out in an essay on the 1977 presidential election by Tschanguiz Pahlavan in *Rah-e No* 1, 5 (May 23, 1998).

14 Some numbers here are worth mentioning and of course worth further study. According to Rezai, 'Nimeyeh por-e livan,' while the total number of people employed in the private sector has only witnessed a small jump (6.5 per cent) between 1976 and 1996, the number of self-employed, including managers, has increased dramatically. In fact the number of independent managers has tripled and the number of independent economic actors has increased by 189 per cent. All this means that a lot of people in the private sector are their own bosses. My guess is that, if anything, there is quite a bit of under-reporting here as many people, particularly women who run thriving or semi-thriving businesses from their homes, are not recorded in this data. Another important point about this category of people is that they are probably more secular than religious, many of them forced into their own businesses because of the lack of opportunities afforded to them after the revolution in the state bureaucracy. Many were pushed out of their jobs, others resigned because of lack of potential for upward mobility. Stripped of their political voice and defensive about their more secular lifestyle, this group of people is making a political comeback through the ballot box.

15 For detailed discussion of the dynamics that led to the disagreements and splits within the ruling coalition during Ali Akbar Hashemi Rafsanjani's presidency and events that followed see Ali M. Ansari, *Iran, Islam and Democracy; The Politics of Managing Change* (London: Royal Institute of International Affairs, 2000).

16 For a concise selection of the ideas of Abdolkarim Soroush in English see his *Reason, Freedom & Democracy in Islam: Essential Writings of Abdolkarim Soroush*, translated, edited, and with a critical introduction by Mahmoud Sadri and Ahmad Sadri (Oxford: Oxford University Press, 2000).

17 Here it is important to reiterate the use of the office of *velayat-e faqih* as part and parcel of the opposition to republicanism. In other words, it is important to see the use of the institution by the conservative forces not as a sign of personal allegiance to Ayatollah Seyyed Ali Khamenei, the current spiritual leader, but rather as serving the anti-republican cause. This is an important point because it underscores the movement away from personal politics and personal political control even among forces with authoritarian tendencies.

18 Interview with Morad Saghafi in *Middle East Report* 212 (Fall 1999).

19 The turnout was lower than the 77 per cent turnout in Khatami's first run at the office but still much higher than expected for a second run at the presidency.

20 For a more detailed analysis of the expanding public sphere in Iran see Farideh Farhi, 'On the Reconfiguration of the Public Sphere and the Changing Political Landscape of Postrevolutionary Iran', in John L. Esposito and R. K. Ramazani (eds), *Iran at the Crossroads* (New York: Palgrave, 2001).

21 Adam Przeworski writes most aptly about the authoritarian temptation being generated out of the messiness of democracy. I am suggesting the generation of democratic temptation from the failure of an authoritarian regime unable to resolve internal conflicts and faced with an educated population able to seize on

the internal conflicts. Adam Przeworski, *Democracy and the Market: Political and Economic Reforms in Eastern Europe and Latin America* (Cambridge and New York: Cambridge University Press, 1991), pp. 93–4. On the 'temptation of democracy' see Morad Saghafi's interview with *Middle East Report*.
22 Interview with Saeed Hajjarian in *Rah-e No*, no. 5 (Khordad 1377/May 1998).

5 Pakistan and the struggle for 'real' Islam

Samina Yasmeen

Since the terrorist attacks on the United States on 11 September, Pakistan has experienced an open struggle between liberal and orthodox Islam. While President Musharraf has promoted a moderate interpretation of Islam and its place in Pakistan's domestic and foreign policy, the orthodox groups have insisted on realising the country's 'true' identity as an Islamic state. This struggle, which also has implications for the US 'War on Terrorism', raises a number of questions about the place of Islam in Pakistan. Is the struggle between liberal and orthodox Islam a new phenomenon in Pakistan, or does it represent the continuation of trends apparent in the past? What factors account for the origin and continuation of this struggle? Is the struggle drawn along the lines of the state and the civil society, or is the picture a mixed one? What is the future of Islam as an instrument of political legitimacy in Pakistan?

While attempting to address these questions, this chapter makes a distinction between state-sponsored and societal Islam. It argues that for three decades, liberal Islam dominated the scene in Pakistan. While Islamic institutions were established, they remained largely powerless in affecting the course of events in Pakistan. But General Zia-ul-Haq changed the situation after taking power in July 1977. His search for legitimacy caused him to initiate a state-sponsored orthodox version of Islam that gradually influenced and altered the nature of societal Islam. Combined with the lack of political institutionalisation, the process set the scene for the proliferation of orthodox Islamic groups in Pakistan that established both co-operative and conflictual relationships with those in the decision-making circles. The process reduced the space available to liberal Muslims in the country as the elected leaders continued to give in to the symbolic strength of the orthodox groups. The military regime also remained hostage to this pressure until the terrorist attacks of 11 September. Since then, the military has reverted to the policy of promoting Pakistan as a modern state for Muslims. The orthodox groups, however, question such re-configuration of Pakistan's identity. Taking place against the background of the US 'War on Terrorism', the struggle between liberal and orthodox Islam is unlikely to be resolved in favour of one or the other. Both sides are likely to use their version of Islam to seek legitimacy for them and deny it to their opponents. The continuing struggle will contribute to the already existing instability in the country.

Pakistan and Islam: the historical context

The debates on the place of Islam in any state or society can be understood in terms of two ends of a spectrum. At one end, Muslims argue that the divine will is paramount as the primary determinant of how social and political relationships are to be organised.[1] For them, the Holy Qur'an and Sunna, (as interpreted by religious scholars and imams across the centuries) are the only source of guidance and law for a state containing Muslims. While for some on this end of the spectrum, absolutist and orthodox interpretations of Islam are not only justified but also mandatory, others admit the relevance of human will in providing time-relevant interpretation of the Qur'an and Prophetic practices. On the other end of the spectrum, some Muslims argue that the Qur'an did not provide any specific injunctions on the nature of political order in a society of Muslims. Hence, while the social life of Muslims could be shaped by their religious beliefs, the political structures in these societies can and need to be secular in nature. Essentially, for the subscribers to the idea of the paramountcy of the human will, Islam remains in the private domain of the individual. While the sum total of the interactions growing out of these individual wills could manifest itself in an Islamic culture, the state remains secular in nature. In a mirror image of those insisting on the primacy of divine will, some on the human will end of the spectrum also accept the role played by religion in societies. While remaining committed to the idea of human will as significant, they accept the notion that in Muslim societies Islam provides the main operational context and hence, by extension, needs to be taken into account in determining the nature of political order and structures. They stand for what could be identified as liberal Islam.

A multiplicity of views on what is 'real' Islam often coexist in Islamic societies. The relative balance of power between those subscribing to different versions of the paramountcy of the divine or human will determines the manner in which political and social lives of Muslims in a particular society are organised. A shift in the balance, therefore, can cause a society to move from the absolutist to the secular end, or vice versa. Similarly, societies and states can experience shifts in the balance of power that are concentrated either on the human or divine will end of the spectrum. For instance, they may move from absolutist to more moderate interpretations of Islam and its role in society. Also the balance may tip against those supporting the notion of a secular state in favour of those admitting the role of religion in a Muslim society.

These shifts in balance of power and attendant ideas can be caused by a combination of domestic and/or external factors in which the role of agency becomes important. In some cases, state structures appropriate the role of guiding society along the spectrum of ideas. This process can be identified as state-sponsored Islam. In other cases, non-state actors and societal groups react to domestic and/or international contexts and become agents of change in what could be described as societal Islam. This change can ultimately transform the political and social structures of a Muslim society. The relationship between the state and societal Islams is a symbiotic one in which state-sponsored Islam can lead to societal Islam and vice versa. The symbiosis, however, does not exclude the possibility of adversarial or conflictual relationships between and among those acting as agents of change. Often groups differ on the real meaning of Islam, and how it can be manifested in the social, political and cultural spheres of Muslim societies. The difference of opinion can take the form of theological debates but can also find expression in violent clashes between variants of liberal and orthodox Islam.

Pakistan is a classic example of a state which has experienced shifts along the spectrum of liberal and orthodox Islamic views. It also stands out for the role played by the state in sponsoring Islamic orthodoxy and then finding itself a hostage to the societal forces thus unleashed. At the same time, co-operative and conflictual relationships have developed between those supporting various understandings of Islam. To some extent the origin of this conflict resides in the independence struggle for Pakistan. The leaders of the Muslim League used Islam to mobilise support among the masses for carving out an independent state for Muslims from British India. The idea, while originating in central India, was used to garner support for such a state comprising East Bengal, North West Frontier Province (NWFP), the Punjab, Sindh and Baluchistan.

Despite the use of Islam as a unifying force, however, the founders of Pakistan did not envision a theocratic Islamic state. On the contrary, they either did not address the issue of the nature of the state that was to be created for Muslims of British India, or favoured a liberal Islamic state. This was evident in the approach adopted by Mohammad Ali Jinnah, the founder of Pakistan, around the time of the partition of India in August 1947. He avoided identifying the place of Islam in the proposed state for Muslims. When religion was mentioned, he clearly expressed his opposition to turning Pakistan into a 'theocratic state ruled by priests with a divine mission'. Equally significantly, in his inaugural address to Pakistan's Constituent Assembly on 11 August 1947, he presented a vision of state for Muslims which was liberal and moderate enough to accommodate cultural and religious differences. 'You will find', he said, 'that in the course of time Hindus would cease to be Hindus and Muslims would cease to be Muslims, not in the religious sense, because that is the personal faith of each individual, but in the political sense as citizens of the State'.[2] The separation of the state and societal religious values suggested that he favoured the notion of a state that admitted divine will but not to the exclusion of the rights of citizens who followed other religions.

The liberal Islamic ideas were clearly reflective of the socio-economic and educational background of the leadership in central India that had been educated overseas and fought for independence to avoid political and economic persecution. That the new leadership was determined to move beyond the realm of ideas to actual practices was evident in the fact that the first meeting of the National Assembly of the nascent state was chaired by a non-Muslim, Mandal. Soon, Mandal, a Hindu, was inducted into the country's first cabinet as the Law Minister. At the same time, Pakistan's first Foreign Minister was chosen from the Ahmadiyya community – a sect identified as heretic and non-Muslim by a number of Islamic scholars in Pakistan.[3]

Religious groups in Pakistan, however, opposed the liberal Islamic notions of a state. Interestingly, they had initially opposed the creation of Pakistan on religious grounds. They argued that nationalism and state sovereignty were Western ideas that ran counter to the notion of the *umma* in Islam. Muslims were seen as part of a global community of believers who could not be bound by or restricted to artificially created state boundaries. So opposed were they to the creation of Pakistan that some of them declared Jinnah to be a *kafir* (non-believer).[4] Once Pakistan was created, some of these religious scholars, notably Mawlana Abul Kalam Azad, adhered to their opposition and chose India as their home. Others, including Mawlana Mawdudi of Jamaat-i Islami opted for Pakistan. The choice was accompanied by a shift in the views on Pakistan. Instead of adhering to the idea of a global *umma*, Mawdudi and other scholars including Mawlana Shabbir Ahmed Othmani of Jamiat Ulama-i Islam, came to emphasise that Pakistan was created as an Islamic state and not merely a state for Muslims. The emphasis on the theocratic nature of the state prompted them to demand that the primacy of divine will be acknowledged in the construction of the new political order. The orthodox interpretations of the Qur'an and prophetic traditions were to be the source of law in the new state and not some liberal notions of humans determining the constitution of Pakistan.

In this struggle for opposing notions of the Pakistani state, liberals/ modernists held sway for a major part of the country's formative years. They acknowledged the ideas presented by the ulema and even incorporated into the constitution but stopped short of changing the liberal Islamic nature of the state. The ulema assisted them in this process by generally not agreeing among themselves. The First Constituent Assembly, for instance, adopted the 'Objectives Resolution' on 12 March 1948 which affirmed that Pakistan would be an Islamic state, and that its laws would be drafted on the basis of Qur'ān and sunna. To facilitate this process it also established the Basic Principles Committee (BPC) which was supported by a board of Talimat-i Islamia (Islamic Teachings) under the chairmanship of Mawlana Nadvi. But the first BPC report ignored the advice given by the board while drafting its suggestions on how to ensure that Islam formed the basis of the polity. The attitude caused an uproar among ulema who tried to jointly enunciate the principles of an Islamic state. In response to this reaction, the second BPC report issued in December 1952 accorded a special status to ulema in ensuring that no proposed legislation ran counter to Islamic principles. However, when Pakistan's first constitution was adopted in 1956, no mechanism was provided for that purpose. Instead, the constitution restricted itself to declaring Pakistan an Islamic Republic, emphasising the role of Islam, and requiring the President to set up an organisation of Islamic research. Specifically, no legal procedure was established to ensure that laws repugnant to Islam could not be enacted.[5]

This process of acknowledging but not allowing the orthodox ulema to determine the place of Islam in Pakistan continued as the military gained strength and ultimately took over power in 1958. As a successor to the British Indian army, and by virtue of being trained and equipped by the United States during the early days of the Cold War, the military stood for liberal/modernist ideas. Instead of subscribing to orthodox Islamic ideas, it favoured the idea of realising Pakistan's true potential as an Asian state. The process was spearheaded by the Chief Martial Law Administrator and later the President of Pakistan, Ayub Khan. The 1962 Constitution, drafted under his leadership, for instance, originally dropped the term 'Islamic' from the title of the country, only to be reinstated at the first meeting of the National Assembly. The 1962 Constitution also provided for two institutions that could provide the ulema an avenue to voice their opinions: an Advisory Council of Islamic Ideology (ACII) and an Islamic Research Institute (IRI). Their powers, however, were limited to conducting research and advising *when asked* if certain laws were repugnant to Islamic teachings.[6] Meanwhile, the regime engaged in reinterpreting Islamic laws in the light of changed circumstances. One of the most vivid examples of this modernist interpretation was the introduction of the Muslim Family Law Ordinance, 1961. The ordinance provided for limiting men's right to marry more than one woman, registration of the marriages, and avenues for preventing divorces. As such it attempted to change the established cultural practices that derived authenticity from religious injunctions. While opposed by a number of ulema, the military regime remained committed to the implementation of the ordinance and hence empowerment of Pakistani women.

The reluctance to let the orthodox ulema determine the place of Islam in Pakistan, however, did not mean that those subscribing to liberal Islamic ideas shied away from using Islam for their own political ends. On the contrary, they carefully and creatively incorporated ideas presented by the orthodox ulema into their modern vocabulary and used it to attract support, seek legitimacy or question the position of their adversaries. During the mid-1960s, for example, Zulfiqar Ali Bhutto introduced the idea of Islamic socialism as a basis for his newly constituted Pakistan People's Party (PPP). By claiming to bring alive the real socialist spirit of Islam through the PPP, he not only questioned the policies of Ayub Khan's regime but also laid claim to his leadership in a post-Ayub set up. The strategy paid off in 1970 elections when the PPP secured the largest number of seats in West Pakistan. It also paved the way for Ali Bhutto's rise to power in Pakistan after the secession of East Pakistan in December 1971.

The Ali Bhutto regime (1971–7) was marked by a continuation of the previously established patterns. The state persisted with supporting liberal interpretations of Islam and ensuring that the political structures reflected this preference. The 1973 Constitution, which was supported by a large majority of those elected in the 1970 elections, acknowledged the role of Islam in Pakistan by declaring it to be the state religion. It also committed itself to not enacting un-Islamic laws in the country. To this end, it established the Council for Islamic Ideology (CII). The council was to include not less than four of its fifteen members with at least fifteen years of experience in Islamic research or instruction, and was to draw its membership from various schools of Islamic thought. Its advisory role was replaced with the idea that the President or two-fifths of the legislature could seek advice on the suitability of laws enacted or proposed. The CII was also to prepare interim reports and a final report after seven years on a host of proposed or promulgated laws and bring them into line with Islamic injunctions.[7] The council recommended the creation of a Ministry of Religious Affairs (MORA) and prepared thirty-one recommendations for making the society 'Islamic' during the 1974–7 period.[8] Bhutto accepted the idea of the ministry but ignored the other suggestions of the council. This happened while the regime focused on establishing a close link with Muslim states in the Middle East, hosting the Islamic Summit (1974) and using Islam to attract support for its nuclear programme.

The state policies, however, coexisted with an imperceptible shift in societal attitudes towards Islam. The shift was caused by a number of factors. Paramount was the traumatic experience of the Indo-Pakistan War of 1971 which resulted in the secession of East Pakistan as Bangladesh and the imprisonment of more than 90,000 Pakistani prisoners of war by India. As in the case of Egypt following the Arab–Israeli war of 1967, the war with India caused a reassessment in Pakistan of the place accorded to Islam in the country. People wondered if the defeat had been caused by them veering away from the 'true' path of Islam. The process was paralleled by the rise of an educated middle class after the developmental policies of the 1960s. At the same time mass migration of an unskilled labour force to the Middle East enabled a new group of Pakistanis to experience fast, up-ward social mobility. As in other Muslim states, these new entrants into the middle class felt unsure and insecure in a system where the elite predominantly subscribed to Western and liberal Islamic ideas. The situation provided a fertile ground for Islamic parties, including the Jamaat-i Islami and the Jamiat Ulama-i Islam which presented themselves as the interpreters of 'real' Islam. They also targeted educational institutions, including colleges and universities, where student wings of the Islamic parties emerged as major contenders for power. The tide slowly began to shift away from the emphasis on the pre-eminence of the human will and towards accepting the significance of divine will. By 1977, enough change had taken place for the opposition parties to join together and campaign for the elections on the grounds of introducing *Nizami-e-Mustafa* (a system of government based on the traditions of the Prophet Muhammad) in Pakistan.

The Bhutto government remained impervious to these changes until after the 1977 elections which were heavily rigged. Faced with the backlash from the opposition, the Pakistan National Alliance (PNA), he resorted to the selective use of Islam for retaining power. In the interest of regime maintenance, he responded favourably to the suggestions by the CII to ban gambling and horse-racing, alcohol, and night clubs. He also declared Friday to be a weekly holiday. The PNA refused to accept these changes and demanded his removal. The resulting tension and civil unrest finally created the justification for the military regime to intervene in July 1977 and take over power.

The military regime and state-sponsored Islam

The military's intervention ushered Pakistan into an era of state-sponsored Islam. General Zia had initially expressed the intention of holding fresh elections within ninety days. Soon he shelved these plans and chose to rule Pakistan indefinitely. To legitimise this shift and ensure the process of regime maintenance, he resorted to a revised interpretation of Islam's place in Pakistani society and politics. In marked contrast to the previous regimes, Zia shifted to the divine will end of the spectrum. Repeating the arguments presented by orthodox ulema over the last three decades, he argued that 'as a soldier of Islam' he was determined to realise Pakistan's true identity as an Islamic state. This was to be done by implementing Islamic teachings enshrined in the Qur'an and sunna under the guidance of religious leaders. Such an approach led to a de facto alliance between the military and Islamic parties, particularly the Jamaat-i Islami under Mawlana Mawdudi's leadership.

Building upon the ideas of Mawdudi, General Zia took a number of steps aimed at truly Islamising Pakistan. A number of institutions were set up for the purpose and the process was gudied by the CII. Although the 1973 Constitution had been held in abeyance, the council was allowed to function, and its area of operation widened. It was entrusted with the task of making recommendations and advising the government on the Islamic nature of proposed or already promulgated laws. It was also to engage in the process of 'Islamising' the constitution. To facilitate the process, the membership of the council was increased from fifteen to twenty. Together, these ulema recommended the creation of additional Islamic institutions. The military regime accepted a number of these suggestions and established the Federal Shari'a Court (FSC) and the Islamic University in 1980. The FSC was initially to consist of four judges from the High Court chaired by a retired judge from the Supreme Court. The number was increased in 1981 with the appointment of three ulema as judges. A Shari'a Appellate Bench was also established in the Supreme Court. The FSC was to respond to petitions filed by any citizen on the Islamic character of promulgated and proposed laws. Later, it was also authorised to examine the laws *suo moto*.[9] The Islamic University, the first of its kind in Pakistan, was to conduct research on Islamic issues, as well as impart knowledge in the fields of shari'a and law, *usul al Din* and social sciences. Apart from its educational programme, the Islamic University was also to take on the task of increasing the awareness of Islam among the general public.

The process of institutionalisation also extended downwards into society. Religious schools (dini madaris), became the main beneficiaries of this process. Madaris (sing. madrasa) had traditionally coexisted with formal educational institutions in Pakistan. Zulfiqar Ali Bhutto had attempted to streamline them and also formally recognise their qualifications. But the number of these madaris, with their focus on religious education, had remained limited. The Zia regime changed the pattern by providing support to those enrolled in the madaris and, hence, encouraging the proliferation of such institutions. The support, it is imprtant to mention, was not extended evenly to all schools of religious thought in Pakistan. The orthodox Deobandis received more patronage from the government than the madaris established by Ahl-i Hadith, Brelwis and the Shi'a. The number of students enrolling in these schools, therefore, increased, as did the number of graduates from the madaris. During a short period of five years (1981-5), for instance, on average 853 Deobandi candidates appeared annually for examinations called Shahadat al-Alamiyya. This was in marked contrast to the average of 279 candidates appearing for the same qualifications during the 1960-80 period.[10]

A process of Islamic legislation paralleled the creation or strengthening of already established institutions by the military regime. A number of new laws were introduced which were to transform the character of Pakistani society. It is, however, instructive that these laws generally targeted the weaker sections of the society, such as women and religious minorities, who were least likely to react or attract support from the dominant religious clergy in the country. Of the laws affecting women, the Hudood Ordinance stood out as having the most serious ramifications.[11] Promulgated in February 1979, the Ordinance dealt with crimes of 'theft, drunkenness, adultery, rape and bearing false witness'. The clauses dealing with adultery (*zina*) and rape (*zina bil jabr*) were apparently introduced to tackle the problem of moral decay. The manner in which they were introduced, however, contained the possibility for the exploitation and abuse, not protection, of women. Zina, according to the Ordinance, was classified as a crime against the state and not the husband as was the case in the penal code inherited from the British system. Specifically, in line with the Islamic principles, it required four witnesses who could testify that *zina* had taken place. Based on the testimony of these witnesses, the ordinance provided for the maximum punishment under *hadd* of stoning to death for married people and 100 lashes for unmarried individuals. In cases where four witnesses were not available, the ordinance provided for the lesser punishment under *ta'zir* consisting of 'imprisonment for up to ten years, and flogging of up to thirty strips and/or a fine'. The Ordinance, however, did not distinguish between *zina* (adultery) and *zina bil jabr* (rape) and hence created a situation in which a woman who got pregnant through rape could be punished under the Hudood Ordinance without much recourse. It also did not provide for a distinction between adultery and failure to report a second marriage, thus opening the possibility of women being accused of *zina* even though they had been religiously married.

The law dealing with *qisas*, or retribution for harm done, and *diyat* (blood money in lieu of a murder or bodily harm) was drafted by the CII in 1980 and passed in August 1984. It provided for blood money equivalent to the value of 30.63 kg of silver for a man and half that amount for a woman murdered. The provision was defended on the grounds that while men are the breadwinners, women remain dependent on men. The clauses related to *qisas* also discriminated against women. They required two male witnesses for a murder to be proven. By excluding women, they provided for situations where the testimony of women could go unnoticed. The Law of Evidence proposed by the CII in 1982 aimed at literally halving the value of testimony by women. It argued that two women witnesses equalled one man! Faced with opposition from women's organisations, the draft law was modified and made applicable to financial cases only. For other cases, determining the value of a single woman's testimony was left to the discretion of individual judges.

Religious minorities became the other major target of the symbolic Islamisation in Pakistan. As 3.3 per cent of the country's total population, Christians, Hindus, Ahmadis, Sikhs and other religious groups were given rights as equal citizens in the 1973 Constitution. Soon after coming to power, General Zia-ul-Haq ended this equality. In September 1978 he introduced an amendment to the electoral system which was later embodied in the 1973 Constitution (Articles 51 and 106). By virtue of this amendment, separate electorates were created for non-Muslims in National and provincial assemblies which became operational in 1985. Not only could non-Muslims not vote for Muslim candidates, but they also had to elect their own representatives from across the country and/or the provinces.[12] The psychological space available to non-Muslims was also reduced by an amendment to the Pakistan Penal Code (295–C) which made blasphemy punishable by death. While blasphemy had always been a criminal act, by making even insinuation a criminal act, the law opened the doors to those who did not want non-Muslims to practise their religion freely. At the same time, Ahmadis, who were declared non-Muslim by the Parliament in 1974, were barred from calling their places of worship 'mosques', reciting *Azaan*, and directly or indirectly passing themselves as Muslims or referring to their religion as Islam.

These discriminatory acts would have normally drawn criticism from western liberal societies. But regional developments created conditions in which General Zia's agenda for introducing orthodox interpretations of Islam was supported by western liberal democracies. The Soviet invasion of Afghanistan in December 1979 caused the United States to identify Pakistan as the front-line state that could help roll the Soviets back. In return for economic and military assistance, General Zia accepted this role and opened up Pakistani territory for training camps where people could be prepared for Jihad. Dini madaris played a major role in this process. They emerged as the centres where the language of jihad was communicated to those enrolled with the ultimate aim of using them in the war against the Soviet Union. The process necessitated a working relationship between the US Central Intelligence Agency (CIA) and Pakistan's Inter-Services Intelligence agency (ISI). The ISI became the main conduit for weapons and funds to those engaged in jihad in Afghanistan. It also developed an interest in retaining and further promoting the cause of jihad as a means of strengthening its own position within Pakistani governmental structures.

The logic of jihad in Afghanistan also provided an avenue for regional actors to play a role in the pre-eminence of orthodoxy in Pakistan. A number of Arab Muslims came to Pakistan to support and participate in the fight against the 'god-less communism'. The Saudi Arabian government supported the process by providing assistance to dini madaris. Unlike the military regime, the Saudi aid was targeted towards the madaris run by Ahl-i Hadith/ salafi groups. These moves were countered by the recently established Islamic regime in neighbouring Iran. They provided support to Shi'a schools in Pakistan. The net result was a confluence in the domestic and external trends that facilitated the spread of varieties of 'Pakistani Islams'. The groups had different opinions as to who was following the 'real Islam'. The process indirectly and directly contributed to the application of these different interpretations in the cultural sphere. Religious opinions were expressed on the role of women in an Islamic society, appropriate methods for purifying Pakistan and helping it attain its true goal as an Islamic state. Such discourse and the insistence by the military regime and the ulema on its application reduced the space available to those who continued to subscribe to liberal Islamic ideas.

The democratic experience (1988–99)

The return to democracy after General Zia's sudden death in August 1988 did not mark the end of the primacy of orthodox Islam in Pakistan. To a great extent this stemmed from the political structure General Zia had established during his eleven years of rule. As a quid pro quo for return to nominal democracy in 1985, he had secured an amendment to the 1973 constitution and altered the balance of power between the president and the prime minister. Upon his death, therefore, a troika emerged in which the military remained the balancer. It became apparent that any elected prime minister would remain in power for the term of the pleasure of the president and/or the Chief of the Army Staff (COAS). This, in turn, added a strong element of uncertainty among the two dominant political parties: the Pakistan Muslim League (PML) led by Nawaz Sharif and the PPP led by Benazir Bhutto. Unsure of how long they would remain in power, both the parties and their respective leaders focused on retaining the goodwill of other parliamentarians and the military. They also engaged in rampant corruption with the view to recouping the amount they had already spent in the elections. Cumulatively, these practices created a situation in which the democratically elected governments could not last, on average, for more than two and a half years.

The apparent weakness of the state provided the context in which the statesponsored Islam of Zia's days gave way to multiple versions of societal Islam. The process was marked by alliances between non-state actors and Islamists in the decision-making circles. The eleven years of state-sponsored Islam had created groups within government circles with a vested interest in perpetuating orthodoxy. The military, for instance, had metamorphosed from being a secular and professional organisation to one which included elements that believed in and supported the policies initiated by General Zia. His death did not weaken their views. On the contrary, they built upon the orthodoxy introduced during the military regime and introduced the notion of religiously based strategic depth. Believing that they had succeeded in pushing the Soviets out of Afghanistan, they opted for pursuing a similar policy vis-à-vis the Indian part of Kashmir. The unfinished agenda of the partition, they maintained, could also be finished in Kashmir by waging a jihad. By installing a pro-Islamabad Islamic regime in Afghanistan, the argument evolved, Pakistan could also acquire a strategic depth that would deny the Indians any significant gains in a war. The logic necessitated the continuation of an active role by the ISI as the promoter of the concept of jihad, as well as the supplier of weapons to those willing to operate in the Indian part of Kashmir. This, in turn, contributed to a proliferation in the number and variety of Islamic groups in Pakistan. They were able, and allowed, to raise funds from private sources while receiving money from the sympathetic elements within the government. Effectively, therefore, Islamic groups in society became the instruments of regional policy for the Islamists in the Pakistani government. Like their patrons, these groups also developed an interest in promoting the language of jihad to protect their position in society. Their ability to insist on the validity of their messages also increased as they acquired more weapons to wage a war in Indian Kashmir.

The links between elements in the state and non-state Islamists were further strengthened after the rise of the Taliban in Afghanistan. That the Taliban were educated in the language of jihad in madrasa was evidence for others that 'real Islam' could prevail. As the Taliban proceeded to implement an extremely rigid version of Islam in Afghanistan, the Islamists in Pakistan came to develop their own history of regional struggles. The criticism in international circles was seen as evidence for the validity of true Islamic ideas and was placed in a historical context: like the first Islamic state in Medina, a number of those subscribing to orthodox Islamic ideas argued, the Taliban were also facing opposition and oppression from non-believers. But the oppression was to be short-lived with a pre-destined victory for Taliban. The 'success' of the Taliban was seen as proof that similar ideas could prosper in Pakistan as well.

The creeping Talibanisation in Pakistan was paralleled by a rise in sectarianism. The inability of the state to streamline the activities of dini madaris, coupled with the continued involvement of Iran and Saudi Arabia, created a situation where the trends already apparent during the Zia regime became stronger. The competition over 'real Islam' reached a level where Sunnis identified the Shi'a as *kafir* (non-believers), and the Shi'a criticised Sunnis for not following real Islamic injunctions. Accompanied by the proliferation of small arms in a gradually failing state, this opened the way for sectarian violence. Mosques lost their place as sanctuaries and became targets of sectarian attacks.

The democratically elected governments did not attempt to control these negative manifestations of societal Islam. This was not because orthodox Islamist groups had gained leverage in the parliament. On the contrary, Islamist groups had failed to secure any significant support in the elections held in 1988, 1990, 1993 and 1997. Nonetheless, the elected governments were reluctant to take any decision that could cost them support from their own party colleagues or attract the wrath of Islamists in the civil society. They feared the ability of the Islamist parties to mobilise support among the masses in the name of protecting Islam. Consequently, while occasionally criticising orthodoxy and sectarianism, both Benazir Bhutto and Nawaz Sharif chose to remain silent on the question of Islam's place in Pakistani state and society. Benazir Bhutto did not repeal the Hudood Ordinance despite the growing evidence that the law was frequently abused, and that a number of women were languishing in jails on trumped up charges of *zina*. The blasphemy law also remained in force despite the fact that it was abused for vindictive purposes.

The silence of liberal elements in state structures was compounded by their willingness to use orthodoxy to maintain their respective regimes. Benazir Bhutto, for instance, opted for covering her hair in public to appease those who had come to expect Muslim women to follow a strict dress code. Nawaz Sharif went a step further in his second term as prime minister. Interested in neutralising any possible opposition after removing the chief justice of the Supreme Court, the president and the COAS, he chose to introduce the 15th Amendment to the constitution which was to allow him to 'introduce Islam' in Pakistan.

To say that orthodox interpretations of Islam persisted during the democratic era is not to suggest that those subscribing to liberal Islamic ideas did not voice any concern. A number of groups in civil society expressed their apprehensions about the possible 'Talibanisation' of Pakistan. They also questioned the weakness of the democratic regime in opposing such trends and highlighted that Pakistan was created as a state for Muslims and not as a theocratic Islamic state. The weakness of the state and the elected leaders' willingness to occasionally use orthodoxy to seek legitimacy, however, severely limited the available space for liberal Islam in Pakistan. Any articulation of the importance of human will was branded as 'un-Islamic' and as representing Western alien values. The balance of power had tilted towards the orthodox end with a combination of co-operative and conflictual relationships between the Islamists in the state and civil society.

Return to military rule and liberal Islam

On 12 October 1999, the military once again seized power in Pakistan. General Pervez Musharraf presented a vision of a united, prosperous and secure Pakistan as the agenda for the regime which was 'forced to intervene' in politics. By emphasising the comprehensive, and not fractional, nature of security, he clearly established his liberal outlook. Combined with his identification of Kamal Atatürk of Turkey as his role model, this articulation of a security concept favoured a liberal-Islamic outlook. Interestingly, however, initially General Musharraf avoided openly steering the country away from the orthodox interpretations of Islam. In fact, two parallel approaches were apparent in his position on Islam's place in Pakistan. While willing to support liberal Islamic ideas, he was reluctant to alienate the ulema. This tendency resulted in the silence that soon descended on the question of his preference for the 'Turkish model' after criticism from the ulema.

The tendency not to alienate the ulema also led to his volte-face on the issue of revisiting the blasphemy law. The law had been misused by a number of people as a means of harassing their enemies. Both Muslims and non-Muslims had suffered from the fact that any insinuation of blaspheming could be treated as an offence and result in incarceration of the accused. Human rights organisations in Pakistan had raised the issue on a number of occasions. In response to this voice from the liberal elements of civil society, General Musharraf promised 'procedural changes in the registration of blasphemy cases' to make the registration of such charges more difficult.[13] The announcement met with widespread criticism from the ulema. The Milli Yakjehti Council – a coalition of Islamic groups – not only demanded that the announcement be retracted but also demanded that Islamic provisions be included in the Provisional Constitution Order (PCO) under which the military regime was ruling. The list of demands also extended to reverting to Friday as a weekly holiday, allowing the dini madaris to operate freely and banning non-governmental organisations (NGOs) that had come to be identified as projecting a 'Western agenda'.[14] On 16 May 2000, three days before a planned strike by religious groups, General Musharraf retracted the planned revisions of the blasphemy law.

By mid-2001, however, the military regime was once again tried to address societal Islam. Interested in improving relations with India and resolving the Kashmir issue, General Musharraf wanted to curb the activities of Islamic militant groups. Within a month of returning from the Agra Summit, in August 2001 he banned a number of sectarian religious groups including Lashkar-i Jhangvi (LJ). Given that the LJ had been involved not only in sectarian killings but was also closely aligned to the Taliban regime, the decision indicated a move away from orthodoxy and state patronage of militancy as an instrument of domestic and foreign policy. It was, however, not until the terrorist attacks on the United States on 11 September 2001 that the General gained an opportunity to openly address the issue of rampant orthodoxy and Islamic militancy.

The terrorist attacks placed Pakistan in an unenviable position of being the only state that had not only sponsored the Taliban but had also maintained close contacts on the ground with the ultra-orthodox regime. Paradoxically, these links and the geographical realities turned Pakistan into the front-line state against the Taliban regime and the al-Qaeda based in Afghanistan. Faced with a possible choice between joining the US 'War on Terrorism' or being 'sent back to the stone age', General Musharraf opted for the former option. He agreed to provide logistical facilities and access to airspace to the US forces on the condition that Indian and Israeli troops would not be involved in any planned strikes against Afghanistan. The decision inflamed the Islamic orthodox groups in Pakistan.

A number of groups that had established close links with the Taliban argued that the attacks had been perpetrated by 'anti-Islamic forces' who wanted to use it as a pretext for establishing a foothold in the Central Asian region. Echoing neo-Marxist analysis, they argued that General Musharraf had become a pawn in the hands of the US government and was being used to target the only truly Islamic state established by the Taliban. General Musharraf was engaged in an un-Islamic act of colluding with non-Muslims against the Taliban. Such a portrayal of the general's plans prompted Islamic groups to support the idea of jihad against the US and the Pakistan government in support of the Taliban.

The recourse to Islamic language as a way of analysing a regional development opened the way for the military regime to respond in kind. General Musharraf explained and defended his decision to join the alliance in terms of Islamic history and practice. Drawing examples from the policies adopted by Prophet Muhammad, he argued that Islam calls upon its followers to abhor killing innocent civilians, and make strategic decisions based on existing circumstances. He also introduced the idea of protecting Pakistan on the grounds that God would protect Islam. The duty of Pakistanis was to protect their country. The use of liberal Islamic language was supplemented by General Musharraf's decision to sideline Islamists within the military hierarchy. The head of the ISI, a known Islamist, was removed along with two other generals who had helped bring Musharraf to power in October 1999. The ISI as an organisation was also targeted with a view to cleansing it of Islamist influence.

The presence of two alternative conceptions of a regional development and the role of Pakistan in this scenario brought the struggle between orthodox and liberal Islam out in the open. While Islamic groups threatened jihad, joined Taliban in Afghanistan, and organised demonstrations, the military regime became the harbinger of liberal Islamic values. The rapid demise of the Taliban regime after the US attacks further paved way for the liberal Islamic agenda. Against the background of the rising tensions with India after the attack on the Indian parliament on 13 December 2001, General Musharraf adopted a more aggressive strategy targeting Islamic orthodoxy and militancy in Pakistan. He banned the Islamic militant groups in Pakistan on 12 January 2002. This decision directly targeted groups like Lashkar-i Taiba, Jaish Muhammad and Harkatul Mujahedeen which had been operating from within Pakistan with assistance from groups within the army. But realising that the militant groups had found a fertile ground in the dini madaris, the General also targeted the religious schools. Instead of closing them down, he argued for madaris that took into account the requirements of the modern era and educated their students accordingly.[15] The demand for a revision of the curriculum was accompanied by the requirements of making these institutions more transparent. The suggestion that Muslims need to take into account changed circumstances, however, was not restricted to the dini madaris alone. General Musharraf has argued that the Muslim *umma* needs to revert back to the liberal, enlightened past in which Muslims played a major role in various fields. The language being used for this, however, is conciliatory: instead of drawing a distinction between liberal and orthodox approaches, General Musharraf has been arguing for the 'middle way' where Muslims shun extreme modernism as well as militancy.[16] The military regime in Pakistan, after a lapse of more than two decades, has emerged as an agent for liberal Islamic values in Pakistan.

The future of the struggle for 'real' Islam

The military regime's careful shift away from orthodox to liberal Islam has not marked the end of the struggle between religion, state and culture in Pakistan. Having been bolstered by state structures, Islamic groups have developed a vested interest in retaining their position of pre-eminence in the country. With access to small weapons over the last decades with help of domestic and external patrons, the militant wings of these groups retain the capability of coaxing the state and citizens into accepting their version of the place of Islam in the society. This trend can be seen in the initial silence among Islamic groups after the overthrow of the Taliban regime and the crackdown of militant groups within Pakistan. The caution was soon followed by a strategy of engaging opinion-makers in the country in favour of dini madaris and against the idea of 'liberal Islam'. These groups have argued that there is only one 'real' Islam and that references to change the nature of Islam in Pakistan are based on western notions.

While such a portrayal of the military regime's approach to Islam does not automatically lead to militancy, some of the banned groups have used it to justify their co-ordination as a re-emerging threat to the regime. General Pervez Musharraf's government is projected by these groups as 'un-Islamic', and one which has colluded with the enemies of Islam. Such a portrayal has gained prominence since the government has tightened the controls over the groups operating from within Pakistan for 'Kashmir's independence'. Claiming that, after Afghanistan, they could not accept selling out another 'Muslim cause', these groups have engaged in a series of attempts to isolate and weaken the regime. The spate of terrorist attacks, which have carefully targeted western groups and organisations, are designed to achieve such an aim.

The ability of orthodox Islam (both militant and non-militant versions) to assert itself in Pakistan depends on a combination of factors. The extent to which Western states, especially the United States, side with the Pakistani government, will determine the future course of events. If Washington reduces the level of its support for Islamabad, the militant groups may feel emboldened. Paradoxically, increased level of interaction between Washington and Islamabad also carries the possibility of strengthening the resolve among militants to threaten the regime. This threat could be controlled if Pakistan's economy is managed and supported by external donors so that the temptation to join Islamic militant groups for economic reasons is brought under control. The future of the struggle between liberal and orthodox Islam, however, equally depends upon the process of democratisation. The manner in which the military regime transfers power to elected leaders may open up the space for Islamists to assert themselves. A failure to work for broad-based democracy may create the conditions in which Islamists could use orthodoxy to demand and fight for a different Pakistan. A military regime, with its preference for liberal Islamic ideas, may still end up contributing to more Islamic orthodoxy than it intends to or what Pakistan can cope with. The end result could cause instability not just in Pakistan but also in the adjoining regions.

Notes

1 The discussion on the ends of the spectrum draws heavily upon the seminal work by Ishtiaq Ahmed, *The Concept of An Islamic State* (Frances Pinter, 1987)
2 *Quaid-e-Azam Mohammed Ali Jinnah: Speeches as Governor General, 1947–1948* (Karachi: Pakistan Publications, no date), pp. 8–9.
3 Samina Yasmeen, 'Islamisation and Democratisation in Pakistan: Implications for Women and Religious Minorities', *South Asia*, vol. 22, Special Issue (1999), p. 185.
4 Andrew Wilder, 'Islam and Political Legitimacy in Pakistan', in Muhammad

Aslam Syed (ed.), *Islam and Democracy in Pakistan* (Islamabad: National Institute of Historical and Cultural Research, 1995), p. 34.
5   Mohammad Amin, *Islamization of Laws in Pakistan* (Lahore: Sang-e-Meel Publication, 1989), pp. 33–42.
6   Mohammad Amin, *Islamization of Laws in Pakistan*, pp. 42–6.
7   Mohammad Amin, *Islamization of Laws in Pakistan*, pp. 46–9 and *The Constitution of the Islamic Republic of Pakistan* (Islamabad: Government of Pakistan, Federal Judicial Academy, 1989), pp. 157–60.
8   Mohammad Amin, *Islamization of Laws in Pakistan*, pp. 48–9.
9   Interview with Justice Fida Mohammad Khan, Federal Shariat Court, Islamabad, January 2002.
10 Information based on data provided by Jamal Malik, *Colonialization of Islam: Dissolution of Traditional Institutions in Pakistan* (Lahore: Vanguard Books, 1996), p. 227.
11 The following discussion of the legal changes draws heavily upon: Khawar Mumtaz and Farida Shaheed, *Women of Pakistan: Two Steps Forward, One Step Back?* (Lahore, Vanguard Books, 1987), chapter 7; and Anita M. Weiss, 'The Consequences of State Policies for Women in Pakistan', in Myron Weiner and Ali Banuazizi (eds), *The Politics of Social Transformation in Afghanistan, Iran and Pakistan* (New York: Syracuse University Press, 1994), pp. 412–44.
12 For this purpose Christians and Hindus were given four seats each in the National Assembly, while Sikhs, Buddhists and Parsi communities and other non-Muslims were given one seat. Ahmadis were given one seat as well. At provincial level, the minorities were allocated twenty-three seats with Sindh and Punjab accounting for seventeen of the seats.
13 Amber Rahim Shamsi, 'The General's Labyrinth', *Herald*, July 2002, p. 101.
14 Amber Rahim Shamsi, 'The General's Labyrinth', p. 102; and interviews with Pakistani journalists.
15 'Selected Madaris may be given University Status', *Dawn*, 3 April 2002.
16 See, for example, President General Pervez Musharraf's Address to the ulema and Mushaikh Conference, Pakistan Government's Website, *http://www.pak.gov.pk*, downloaded on 1 August 2002.

6 The Islamic dilemma in Uzbekistan

Shahram Akbarzadeh

The leaders of post-Soviet Uzbekistan have had a paradoxical relationship with Islam. On the one hand they have fostered Islam and presented themselves as true believers. On the other, they have rejected any suggestion that Islam should play a role in the political life of that state and have systematically suppressed unsanctioned Islamic groups. This is, of course, not a uniquely Uzbek dilemma. Other societies in the Muslim world have experienced similar conflicting imperatives, but the Uzbek case is made special because it was controlled, until recently, by a regime that attempted to eliminate Islam, at least in the public sphere, and is now led by the same leaders.

The transition to independence did not mean a change in the leadership. Instead the Communist Party (CP) leaders, with President Islam Karimov at the helm, have managed to remake their public image and transform themselves to champions of independent Uzbekistan. President Karimov has taken a lead here. An upwardly mobile member of the *nomenklatura*, Karimov chaired the republican State Planning Committee (Gosplan) before he was appointed Uzbekistan's minister of finance in 1983. By late 1986 he was deputy chairman of the Council of Ministers and chairman of *Gosplan* as well as the CP first secretary in the Kashkadar'ya region. In June 1989, with Moscow's backing, Islam Karimov became the first secretary of the CP of Uzbekistan, and was subsequently appointed president by the republican parliament in 1990.[1] His presidency was confirmed in the December 1991 elections, and in subsequent polls (in March 1995 his term was extended for five years and in January 2000 he was overwhelmingly re-elected).[2] This successful evolution from being appointed by Moscow, to a leader elected by popular vote (however questionable), was the result of a public image revamp, with significant implications for Islam.

Although Karimov and most of the current leaders in Uzbekistan received their training under Soviet rule and were suspicious of the political force of Islam, they were also aware of Islam's inherent potential for social stability and legitimising the government of the day. They were mindful of the Soviet failure to eliminate Islam and the growth of Islamic manifestations, as attested by mosque attendance, and the availability of religious literature in public in the final years of the Soviet Union. They rightly interpreted Islam's resilience under Soviet rule and its 'revival' on the eve of the Soviet collapse as a sign of its integration with the cultural identity of Uzbeks, and other Muslim minorities in Uzbekistan.[3] This realisation, and the Soviet experience of top-down control over civil society, have come together to inform the state policy on Islam. These two seemingly contradictory considerations have led the political leadership to make a sharp distinction between two types of Islam: a sanctioned version that is closely supervised by the state and a renegade version that is persecuted by state agencies.

The renegade version of Islam is presented as violent and fanatical with links to outside sources and labelled Wahabbi. State security agencies and judiciary have pursued an uncompromising policy on political manifestations of Islam in Uzbekistan, now represented by the Islamic Movement of Uzbekistan (IMU) and Hizb ut-Tahrir (Liberation Party). This policy received US endorsement in the aftermath of the terrorist attacks on the United States and the military operation in Afghanistan against Osama bin Laden and the Taliban. The most conspicuous evidence of this endorsement was the US administration's inclusion of the IMU on its list of terrorist organisations and a pledge of $400 million aid to Uzbekistan following that country's participation in the US-led anti-terrorist campaign.[4] As will be discussed below, the increasingly close relations between Uzbekistan and the United States have significant ramifications for Islam in this Central Asian state and the political legitimacy of the ruling political elite.

However, before turning to the role of political Islam in undermining the legitimacy of the leadership it is important to set the stage by exploring the nature of Islam in Uzbekistan and how it has been treated by the post-Soviet regime. This chapter opens with an examination of the relationship between Islam and cultural identity and the Soviet administrative response to Islam. It then proceeds to ascertain post-Soviet state policy on Islam. The subsequent section will look at the effectiveness (political implications) of state supervision over the authorised form of Islam, followed by an examination of the unofficial or renegade version of Islam and the challenges it poses to state authority.

Cultural Islam

Islam is entwined with cultural identity and is, therefore, inseparable from the self-definition of Uzbeks as a community. This is a truism. But for Soviet planners there was nothing true about this statement. Moscow made every effort to separate Islam from Uzbek and other Central Asian cultures. Islam was treated as a 'vestige of the past', a brew of superstition and reactionary practices that were incompatible with the socialist project.[5] Soviet planners resolved to replace Islam with 'progressive', 'optimistic' and secular national identities that were demarcated on the basis of language. The Uzbek nation was supposed to be one such project. This Soviet initiative seemed to enjoy particular success, at least in part. A sense of loyalty in the Uzbek nation grew rapidly, especially among the cultural, administrative and political elite. But to the surprise of Soviet planners, this new object of loyalty did not replace Islam. Instead it appeared as though the parameters of the Uzbek nation were being reformulated to incorporate Islamic traditions, with Islamic practices being reinterpreted as part of the national heritage.

The merger of Islamic traditions and modern Uzbek nationality (especially one that was designed to be secular) presented a serious challenge to Moscow. The line between Islamic and national traditions was blurred even for those responsible for implementing Soviet policy. It was not uncommon to see members of the Communist Party attend Islamic feasts, follow the Islamic burial ritual and ensure that their newborn boys were circumcised.[6] In the mind of ordinary Uzbeks and many in the leadership, an Uzbek could not be anything but Muslim.

This popular perception may be held responsible for the continued adherence to Islamic practices and the use of social gatherings to reaffirm collective observance of Islamic rituals. A common practice was the illicit conversion of many Central Asian teahouses (*chai khona*) to places of prayer. In other instances, imams, or an elder (*aqsaqal*) with knowledge of the Qur'an, would be discreetly invited to wedding parties to perform the Islamic *nikah* to complement the secular, Soviet-controlled marriage ceremony. Without this the newly-weds would not be recognised as legitimately married by the joining families.

Moscow's response to this challenge was predictable. If Islam could not be eliminated it had to be controlled. Two institutions were set up to achieve that goal. The first was the office of Mufiyat, officially known as the Muslim Spiritual Board for Central Asia and Kazakhstan, formally established in 1943. The board was headed by a Mufti in Tashkent and was responsible for registering and directing all imams in Central Asia. It trained imams in the only operating madrasa in the Soviet Union and had the authority to appoint them to one of the few officially registered mosques or remove them. In other words the board was responsible for bringing the Islamic clergy under a unified umbrella organisation. Concentrating the imams in a hierarchical organisation was designed to facilitate greater Soviet supervision and control.

The second institution was the Council for Religious Affairs. First established in 1944, the council was attached to the Council of Ministers of the

Soviet Union, based in Moscow, but had corresponding branches at the republican level which dealt with local religious matters.[7] The council worked as a tier between all religious establishments (including the Muftiyat) and the Soviet government. It was responsible for regulating the conduct of religious activities, it negotiated with the clergy over the opening of new prayer houses and checked relations between Soviet denominations and members of those confessions beyond the borders.

The collapse of the Soviet Union affected both institutions, but did not remove them. The Muftiyat, with authority over Central Asia, was divided along national borders in 1992–3 and the Mufti's jurisdiction was physically limited to the territory of Uzbekistan. At the same time the Council for Religious Affairs in Tashkent was freed of Moscow control and became fully responsible to the Cabinet of Ministers in Uzbekistan. Notwithstanding this organisational rearrangement, the nature of the relationship between Islam and the state continued to be defined by political expediency and the struggle for control.

Islam in independent Uzbekistan

In December 1991, the Soviet Union ceased to exist and Tashkent set upon finding an independent course for Uzbekistan. The post-Soviet relationship between the political leadership in Tashkent and Islam has been fraught with contradictions. On the one hand the leadership has been conscientious of the importance of Islam in lending it public legitimacy; while on the other hand it does not welcome Islamic actors' involvement in the political arena, lest the leadership's authority be challenged. These contradictory considerations have informed the response of the Uzbek state to Islam in the post-Soviet era.

President Islam Karimov has exhibited an acute awareness of the importance of Islam to Uzbek national identity. Eager to present himself as an unblemished Uzbek nationalist, President Karimov has paid special attention to symbols of Islam. On the eve of the first direct presidential elections in December 1991, President Karimov spoke reverently about Islam and its place in the Uzbek way of life. He has emphasised the centrality of Islam in regulating Uzbeks' familial and social life. For example in an interview with the Uzbek daily *Khalq Sozi* he referred to Islam as the 'conscience, the essence of life, the very life of many of our countrymen'.[8] Following this lead, the Uzbek government has actively sponsored religious celebrations. *Kurban bairam* (*'id al-qurban*) and *Uruza bairam* (*'id al-fitr*), the two main Islamic festivals, are enshrined in Article 77 of the Uzbek labour code as national holidays.[9] President Karimov ritually calls on local administrators (*hakims*) and local government apparatus to work closely with the registered Islamic authorities to celebrate these Islamic feasts.

In a parliamentary speech, President Karimov personally identified such great Islamic thinkers as Imam Bukhari, al-Tirmizi and Khoja Bahoutdin Naqshband as the great ancestors of Uzbeks.[10] In 1994 Tashkent was the venue for a seminar on Imam Bukhari's theological writings.[11] In the following year, President Karimov decreed the establishment of a Centre for International Islamic Studies in Tashkent. This centre is attached to the Uzbek Academy of Sciences and works closely with Islamic teachers in the Muftiyat office. According to the presidential decree the centre will study the teachings and philosophy of Islam and 'explore the religious, historic, and cultural heritage of the people of Uzbekistan'.[12]

In line with this policy, the Uzbek government has banned missionary work by Christian sects for 'offending the Uzbek soul and spirituality'. In May 2002 Uzbek officials called for the cessation of Uzbek-language sermons in Christian churches and detained eighteen Christians suspected of publishing Christian literature in Uzbek.[13] Uzbeks have traditionally assumed synonymity between Uzbekness and Muslimness, and the leadership appears to be keen to reinforce that assumption. A recent government-run survey found that more than 80 per cent of Uzbeks are Muslim.[14] By reinforcing this link, the leadership is sending a clear message: it is safeguarding Uzbek traditions and values. This position has of course been criticised by European and North American NGOs and governments as contravening the freedom of religious beliefs. But as far as Tashkent is concerned, being at the receiving end of mild international scorn is a small price to pay for shoring up domestic approval.

Concurrent with this paternalistic approach to Islam, the leadership has embarked upon a policy of eliminating independent Islamic groups in order to eradicate their ability to launch Islamically inspired political initiatives. As far as the Uzbek leadership is concerned there is no room for such autonomy in a 'secular' Uzbekistan. The Uzbek Constitution, adopted in December 1992, enshrines the separation of the state and religion and promises non-interference by the state in 'the activity of religious associations' (Article 61). This clause is complemented by banning religious organisations' interference in state affairs, namely prohibiting the formation of political organisations based on 'religious principles' (Article 57). This is a peculiar interpretation of the separation of the state and religion, as it moves to exclude Islamic organisations from public life.

Secularism in Uzbekistan seems to have a unique meaning. Far from separating religion and politics, it is understood as curbing the scope of Islamic actors' autonomy in the public sphere, while allowing for the state to stage-mange and direct publicly sanctioned Islamic activities. This paradoxical approach is likely to have unforseen consequences for the state, as discussed in the assessment of policy implications below.

The principle of state non-interference in religious affairs is routinely violated by the leadership's desire to emasculate existing Islamic bodies, namely the Muftiyat, by administrative means. The State Committee for Religious Affairs, and various arms of the state continue to exercise control over the Muftiyat. In 1993, Uzbekistan adopted the law 'On Freedom of Conscience and Religious Organisations' which severely restricted religious activities by granting regional governors (*hakims*) and their local agencies supervisory control over the activities of Islamic institutions, even over the content of sermons at Friday prayers.[15] In the same year the leadership managed to remove the increasingly vocal Mufti of Tashkent.[16] The replacement of Mufti Muhammad Yusuf with Imam Mukhtarjon Abdullah was a serious blow to the growing self-confidence of the official Islamic establishment. Mukhtarjon Abdullah has been described by many imams in Uzbekistan as unassertive, a quality that no doubt appealed to the Uzbek government. Mukhtarjon Abdullah himself was soon replaced with Abdurashid qori Bahromov whose political orientation may be gleaned from his endorsement of the American campaign in Afghanistan and Tashkent's policy of allowing US forces into Uzbekistan.[17]

The Uzbek government's move against Muhammad Yusuf signalled a growing anxiety in the leadership regarding Islam's potential to erode its legitimacy. In line with the policy of promoting Uzbek nationalism, Tashkent had enlisted the Muftiyat on the eve of the Soviet collapse to deal with social and political unrest, and Mufti Muhammad Yusuf seemed ready to play his part. In May 1990, he was sent on a tour of the Ferghana Valley, which had been the scene of ethnic violence, to preach tolerance and good will. He then visited Jizak and Nukus to restate this message and warn against the dangers of fanaticism.[18] Mufti Muhammad Yusuf later gave an interview to the Soviet newspaper *Komsomol'skaya Pravda* on the theme of Islam and politics. Commenting on the formation of the Islamic Renaissance Party of Uzbekistan,[19] he asserted that Muslims already had a party: Islam, and that it would be wrong to form a party under the pretext of Islam because that would inevitably lead to divisions among Muslims. Islam, he claimed, transcended earthly categories of clubs and parties.[20] This argument was adopted by the state-run Uzbek daily *Pravda Vostoka* which repeated the thrust of the Mufti's point and rejected the formation of Islamic political parties as illogical and contradictory.[21] The article warned of the devious intentions that lay behind this transgression against the border separating Islam and politics.

Mufti Muhammad Yusuf's preaching for social harmony, however, did not stop him from seeking involvement in politics. It was perhaps a sign of the times that for the first time in Soviet history a member of the Muslim clergy ran for the parliament. Mufti Muhammad Yusuf was elected to Uzbekistan's parliament (Supreme Soviet) in 1989. He was increasingly embroiled in political issues, least of which was the future of Uzbekistan as an independent entity. Although he never openly challenged the justification for Uzbek statehood, Mufti Muhammad Yusuf was highly critical of the separation of the Muslims of Central Asia along linguistic lines which had led to the break-up of the Central Asian Muslim Board into separate nationally based Muftiyats. Language 'egoism', it was argued, had undermined Muslims' commitment to the path of Allah and clouded their judgments. The Muftiyat's *Muslims of Mowarounnahr* magazine became the mouthpiece of this position. This was a subtle, but unmistakable, challenge to national sovereignty for the five separate states in Central Asia, and put the Mufti on a collision course with the nationalist government of President Karimov.

Another measure of Mufti Muhammad Yusuf's assertive leadership was his ability to attract hitherto unregistered mullahs to the Muftiyat. At the time, the government encouraged this process as it promised to make all mullahs subject to state supervision, but as will be discussed below, this initiative offered a boost to the Tashkent Muftiyat both numerically and psychologically. The office of the Mufti, by late 1992, could speak as the authoritive representative of Islam in Uzbekistan. This was widely understood by the government and Islamic dissidents alike. Even the IRP, despite earlier tensions with the Muftiyat, was eager to gain approval from the Mufti for their political objectives which involved the Islamisation of Uzbekistan through improved education in Islam and political reforms.[22]

The increasing assertiveness of the Muftiyat under Mufti Muhammad Yusuf and the growth of the Islamic Renaissance Party of Uzbekistan and a host of smaller Islamic organisations in the Ferghana Valley were cause for concern in Tashkent. But one episode seemed to convince the leadership of the need to curtail independent Islamic activity and bring Islam firmly under state control. This episode was the escalation of political tension in neighbouring Tajikistan, where the Islamic Renaissance Party of Tajikistan spearheaded a campaign for an 'Islamic' state. The Uzbek leadership came to view, and officially present, the Tajik civil war (1992–7) as a stark reminder of the devastating potential of autonomous Islamic actors.

Assessing policy implications

Tashkent's heavy-handed approach to Islamic autonomy seemed quite effective in silencing Islamic dissent. By 1997, the Muftiyat was no more than a shadow of its vibrant self in 1991–2. The Islamic Renaissance Party was practically removed as a player in Uzbek politics with its members in prison, in exile or in hiding. Other opposition parties (ie. Erk and Birlik), which were not religious in their outlook but accepted the grievance of the Islamically minded dissidents and were prepared to work with the IRP, were also eliminated. It looked as though the government was finally eradicating the much-feared 'Islamic threat', and making way for the state-sanctioned clergy under the umbrella of the Muftiyat and the watchful eye of various state agencies as the only spokespeople for Islam. The message of Islam in Uzbekistan appeared to be carefully manufactured to conform to guidelines set by the government.

However, this apparent success may be transient and short-lived. Two separate developments suggest that the government's self-congratulations may have been premature. The first involves the growth of clandestine Islamic networks that espouse radical political views and are much harder to track than the IRP and unregistered mullahs. In 1997, a new Islamic player appeared on the scene: Hizb ut-Tahrir. Although Hizb ut-Tahrir was originally linked to the Muslim Brothers in Jordan, with specific attention to Palestinian national liberation, the party shifted its objective towards a more universal goal, namely the establishment of an 'Islamic caliphate'.[23] The message of Islamic unity and social justice, espoused by Hizb ut-Tahrir appears to have found resonance among Uzbek youth who are being alienated by the absence of employment prospects and a comprehensive social security network to protect them against the adverse effects of the market economy. Estimating the degree of support for Hizb ut-Tahrir is difficult as it is organised clandestinely in small cells in a pyramidal network where members of one cell are not known by those of the other cells. But the growing appearance of leaflets by Hizb ut-Tahrir, especially in Andijan and Kokand suggests that the party is gathering support. Some analysts credit the non-violent doctrine of Hizb ut-Tahrir for its apparent success, as the party has not been involved in terrorist activities and is not cited on the United States list of terrorist organisations.[24]

Another clandestine organisation that has championed political Islam is the Islamic Movement of Uzbekistan (IMU). The IMU does not concern itself so much with the transnational objectives of Hizb ut-Tahrir, and is focused on deposing the government of President Karimov and the establishment of an Islamic state in Uzbekistan.[25] With its narrower national focus, the IMU has proven to be a serious challenger to President Karimov's rule which it rejects as illegitimate. The IMU has no qualms about political violence in pursuit of its goals. A series of co-ordinated bombings in Tashkent in February 1999, thought to be carried out by the IMU, marked the entry of this organisation on the scene. The IMU's audacity was demonstrated again later in the year when it moved its fighters from bases in northern Afghanistan via Tajikistan to infiltrate Kyrgyz territory close to the borders of Uzbekistan.[26] Similar operations were carried out in the following year, throwing Kyrgyzstan's state security into mayhem and highlighting the ease with which Central Asian borders could be crossed. The American led 'war on terrorism' which toppled the Taliban, delivered a below to the IMU, as there have been reports that its leader Juma Namangani was killed in the fighting near Mazar-e Sharif. Notwithstanding the veracity of this information, Russian intelligence reports claim the IMU still has substantial forces in Afghanistan and Tajikistan. There are also reports of a 3000-strong IMU contingency living under cover in the Ferghana Valley which is shared by Uzbekistan, Tajikistan and Kyrgyzstan.[27]

Despite tactical differences in the use of violence, these two Islamic organisations, and other smaller groups operating in Uzbekistan, pursue a radical overhaul of Uzbek politics. They reject President Karimov's rule as *kafir*,[28] and champion the establishment of a shari'a-based polity. The government has responded to these organisations and the challenge of political Islam by dismissing them as common criminals and drug-traffickers who use Islam as a smokescreen.[29] Another tactic has been to emphasise the external connections of the IMU and Hizb ut-Tahrir and portray them as pawns in the hands of foreign players, be it Pakistan, Saudi Arabia, Iran or Tajikistan. In essence, the government response seeks to undermine the public support that these groups might have enjoyed by virtue of their Islamic message and to justify suppressive measures against them. Denying the Islamic nature of these organisations and pointing to their external links tends to confirm a monopolist perception of Islam whereby only the state-sanctioned Islamic authorities can speak in the name of Islam – only the Islam of the Muftiyat can be authentic. Accordingly, other Islamic contenders are dismissed as false-pretenders, which leads us to another potential minefield.

The second issue that could prove to be even more challenging for the political leadership is the potential for loss of control over the official Islamic hierarchy. The promotion of a centralised Islamic establishment in the shape of the Muftiyat and a unitary interpretation of Islam to help legitimise the post-Soviet order steers Islam away from a way of life toward a structured social institution. The concentration of disparate local prayer-readers and mullahs under the umbrella of the Muftiyat has been intended to facilitate state control. But at the same time, this practice tends to transform Islam into a de facto political player, even if in the limited role of sanctioning and approving government policies and presidential decrees. By elevating Islam onto the political level and incorporating it in the official ideology of the state, Islam is bestowed an unprecedented authority in the public domain. The symbiosis of Islam and cultural identity which informed believers on daily rites, and was limited to immediate local community affairs is being infused with a prescriptive, albeit highly controlled, quality that is political in nature.

Islam in its centralised form is concerned with national affairs. The centralisation and institutionalisation of Islam help expand its scope of competence, not just geographically but also politically. The uniform interpretation of Islam by theologically trained clergy, helps transform it from a representation of ritual practices among Muslims to a guide for appropriate social behaviour and ultimately government. This new Islam draws its strength and inspiration from the Qur'an and hadith, not daily practices of Muslims. For that reason it is less influenced by cultural traditions which are held by Islamic puritans, such as the Wahabbi, to corrupt the teaching of Islam. Islam in this form is pure, original and inspirational.

By the same token, the scripture-based form of Islam represented by the Muftiyat, as opposed to the tradition-based variations in different localities, has the potential to sit in judgment on national politics. This is a very significant shift with far-reaching potential. The fact that the Muftiyat can now comment on a variety of political issues is fully appreciated by state officials. This is evident in solicited endorsements of state policies from the ulema. Extracting political legitimacy from the ulema affirms, and contributes to, the politicisation of Islam. But if Islam is politicised, it can, by the same token, refrain from providing celestial support (or tacit resignation) to the temporal state. That the Muftiyat has not already taken a more assertive stand in relation to government policies relates to the passive personality of the ulema and the weakness of pure scripturalism among Uzbeks. It is likely that more resolute clerical leaders would conclude from Islam's newly established pervasiveness the need for their independence from the state. The precedents of Mufti Muhammad Yusuf, and Qazi-kalon Akbar Turajonzoda in Tajikistan, offer examples of such assertion of independence.[30] The logic of scripturalism and politicisation facilitates the emergence of Islam, not simply as a legitimising force, but as an independent political actor with the potential to be critical of temporal leaders.

In this context it may be revealing to note that the present Mufti, despite his explicit endorsement of government policies, has politely refrained from using government-prescribed terminology in relation to radical Islamic groups. In a televised meeting between the Mufti, chairman of the Cabinet Office for Religious Affairs and the Minister of Internal Affairs (in January 2000), religious leaders were criticised as 'cowards' for not waging 'jihad' against Islamic radicalism. The response of Mufti Bahromov was intriguing as he diplomatically deflected this criticism by stating that there is an urgent need to fight illiteracy and ignorance as the source of such misinterpretation of Islam.[31]

The second factor hampering the development of the Muftiyat into an independent agency, implied in the Mufti's response above, is the very limited public knowledge of the tenets of Islam. Over seventy years of forced insulation from the Muslim world and constraints on Islamic education in Central Asia have seriously undermined public familiarity with Islamic teachings, save for basic (often incomplete) prayers used in traditional rituals. This superficial familiarity with Islam, has favoured the non-scriptural traditional (folkoric) quality of Islam, which now acts as a barrier to the growth of Islam as a political ideology. It is revealing to note that a 1993 public opinion survey documented very low levels of familiarity with the basic principles of Islam in Central Asia. The survey discovered that the principal Muslim precept of *shahada* (declaration of faith: There is no God but Allah and Muhammad is his prophet), when proclaimed in Arabic, was not understood accurately by many respondents.[32]

The third, and perhaps the most obvious, reason for the absence of independent Islam in Uzbekistan is the state persecution of the more outspoken members of the clergy. Local human rights groups estimate that at least 7,000 independent Muslims were in prison in May 2002.[33] Hizb ut-Tahrir puts the number of prisoners much higher at 50,000, detained in concentration camps in western Uzbekistan.[34] Among some of the more notable detainees, now missing, are the imam of the Andijan Jami Mosque, Sheykh Abdul Vali and his assistant.[35] On a more general level, devout Muslims are held under suspicion in Uzbekistan. Recent reports indicate that bearded men were closely watched by the security forces for fear of connections with the IMU or Hizb ut-Tahrir. Others have complained of restrictions on wearing *hijab* at high school or government offices. It may sound ironic that a government so concerned with ensuring that it has Islam on its side, harbours such salient apprehension of that religion. The irony is not lost to Uzbeks who see state control over religious sermons and the state's watchful eye on mosque attendance, which to many mirrors Soviet techniques, as a Machiavellian effort to retain the reins of power.

Conclusion

The fact that Islam was going to play an important role in the post-Soviet politics of Uzbekistan was not disputed by anyone. Neither the emerging Islamic activists in the Muftiyat and the multitude of Islamic groups, who gravitated toward some form of political Islam, nor the political leadership that inherited power was in any doubt that the future of the independent republic of Uzbekistan was inseparable from this essential component of Uzbek identity. Islam had survived Soviet repression and had helped Uzbeks maintain a sense of who they were. Consequently, it seemed only natural that it should become a more prominent feature in the aftermath of the Soviet collapse. But here is where the common ground between Islamic activists and the political leadership ends. While Islamic activists tended to favour a greater role for Islam in setting the political agenda and transform Uzbekistan into an Islamic polity, no matter how diversely and vaguely understood, the political leadership adopted a utilitarian approach and sought to extract legitimacy from a subservient Muftiyat. The divergence of views on the role of Islam in the politics of Uzbekistan reflected a more profound division on the concept and practice of political legitimacy. The point in dispute has been the source of legitimacy.

The Islamic Renaissance Party and its successors in the shape of the IMU and Hizb ut-Tahrir, as well as the Muftiyat under the leadership of Mufti Muhammad Yusuf, to greater and lesser degrees subscribed to the principle of the shari'a as the source and inspiration of public life and political rule. The call for the establishment of an Islamic state, explicitly espoused now by the IMU and Hizb ut-Tahrir, flows from the starting point that only God can make law and that government is only just if it is based on, and implements, divine judgments as articulated in the shari'a. The Muftiyat in 1991–3 had an awkward position on this proposition. Although Mufti Muhammad Yusuf may have personally favoured it and worked through his office to promote a greater public appreciation of Islamic teachings and their implications for social organisation, he could not openly espouse that view for fear of antagonising the Uzbek government.

The above perspective is deplored as 'fundamentalist' and 'Wahabbi' by the political leadership. It advances an alternative vision: a non-religious state which 'protects' the authentic Islamic values and traditions of the Uzbek people. Its source of legitimacy, therefore, is not Islam per se, but the national Muslim community. This nationalist orientation has caused some international embarrassment for Tashkent, but the domestic benefits of this strategy in terms of perpetuating the myth of President Karimov's devotion to Islam outweigh other concerns. At any rate, the new realignment between Uzbekistan and the United States against a common enemy has eased international pressure on Tashkent for its lack of democratic reform and the frequent flouting of the 'rule of law'. In the emerging international setting, the Uzbek leadership would find it easier to monopolise Islam through state agencies and the official hierarchy of the ulema while persecuting alternative/radical interpretations. All indications point to the success of this strategy in the short term. But this approach is fraught with contradictions and likely to re-enforce the political role of Islam in the long term. An irony that is lost to Tashkent.

Notes

1 Biography extracted from *Pravda Vostoka* (30 November 1991).
2 Abdumannob Polat, 'Karimov will stay in office, but recent elections send mixed messages', *RFE/RL End Note* (7 January 2000). The 2000 election results were questioned by the Organisation of Security and Co-operation in Europe as unreliable due to the absence of a genuine democratic contest. Reported on *Uzbekistan Daily Digest*, www. EuasiaNet.org (14 January 2000).

3 Uzbekistan had a mixed population on the eve of independence in 1991. In recent years, however, many Russian residents have left that country due to social discrimination and fear of persecution. The Russian population declined from 8.3 per cent in 1991 to 5.5 per cent in 2000, while the Uzbek population grew from 71.3 per cent to 80 per cent.
4 'Uzbek president visits Washington', *Transitions Online*, Week in Review 12–18 March 2002 <www.tol.cz>.
5 Geoffrey Wheeler, 'The Muslims of Central Asia', *Problems of Communism*, 16, 5 (1977) p. 77.
6 Chantal Lemercier-Quelquejay, 'From Tribe to *Umma*', *Central Asia Survey*, 3, 3 (1984), p. 22. 1989 Soviet research discovered that adherence to Islam was 'alarmingly' high among the educated strata; see RFE/RL, *Report on the USSR*, 17 March 1989, p. 27.
7 Jim Forest, *Religion in the New Russia* (New York: Crossroad, 1990, p. 188).
8 Reproduced in the Russian language daily, 'U nas est' svoi put', *Pravda Vostoka* (20 December 1991), p. 2.
9 Islam Karimov, 'Zakon o prazdnichnykh dnyakh v respubliki Uzbekistan', *Pravda Vostoka* (16 July 1992), p. 1.
10 Islam Karimov, 'Dovesti do kontsa blagorodnoe delo', *Pravda Vostoka* (24 September 1994), p. 1.
11 'Shkola: vremya peremen', *Pravda Vostoka* (20 September 1994), p. 2. Imam Muhammad al-Bukhari lived between 810 and 870 AD. His collection of hadith, known as *al-Sahih*, remains the most respected source after the Qur'an among Hanafi Sunni Muslims.
12 *OMRI Daily Digest* (22 May 1995).
13 *Uzbekistan Daily Digest* (28 May 2002) www.eurasianet.org/resource/uzbekistan/hypermail/200205/0019.shtml.
14 *Uzbekistan Daily Digest* (28 May 2002), www.eurasianet.org/resource/uzbekistan/hypermail/200205/0020.shtml.
15 Lerman Usmanov, 'Opredelit li "Islamskii faktor" budushchee strany?', *Nezavisimaya Gazeta* (6 January 1994), p. 3.
16 'Muftiya smeshchayut v pyatnadtsatyi raz', *Nezavisimaya Gazeta* (28 April 1993), p. 2.
17 In an interview with the Russian media, qori Bahromov rejected the Taliban's behaviour as un-Islamic and declared that the American operation in Afghanistan was not aimed at Islam. He went on to cite the number of pilgrims to Mecca (7,000 each year) and the operation of Islamic schools as significant achievements under the leadership of President Islam Karimov. *Rossiskaya Gazeta* (16 November 2001).
18 *Muslim of the Soviet East*, No. 3 (1990).
19 The founding congress of the Islamic Renaissance Party of Uzbekistan (January 1991) was dispersed by police as illegal (*Pravda Vostoka*, 1 February 1991). The Uzbek government drafted and passed a new law on public organisations to ban political parties inspired by religion. The law was signed on 15 February 1991 by Islam Karimov, head of the Council of Ministers: 'Ob obshchestvennykh ob'edineniyakh v Uzbekskoi SSR', *Pravda Vostoka* (26 February 1991), p. 2. This law was subsequently incorporated in the 1992 Uzbek Constitution.
20 'My-partiya Allakha', *Komsomol'skaya Pravda* (8 December 1990), p. 1.
21 'Komu i zachen ponadobilos' sozdanie "islamskoi partii"?', *Pravda Vostoka* (1 February 1991), p. 3.

22 Shahram Akbarzadeh, 'Islamic Clerical Establishment in Central Asia', *South Asia: Journal of South Asian Studies*, 20, 2 (December 1997), pp. 73–102.
23 Olivier Roy, '*Qibla* and the Government House: The Islamic Networks', *SAIS Review*, 21, 2 (Summer–Fall 2001), p. 61 (see also web-page www.)
24 See for example Olivier Roy, '*Qibla* and the Government House'.
25 Mikhail Gerasimov, 'Religioznyi narkotrafik', *Nezavisimaya Gazeta* (3 November 1999).
26 Viktoria Panfilova, 'Grazhdane yaponii obreli svobodu', *Nezavisimaya Gazeta* (26 October 1999).
27 Armen Hanbaian and Mikhail Hodarenok, 'Pered geostrategicheskoi razvilkoi. Tashkent vinuzhden lavirovat' mezhdu Rossiei i zapodom', *Nezavisimaya Gazeta* (15 April 2002).
28 Vitalii Ponomaev, 'Griazet li islamskaia revoliutsiia v Uzbekistane?', *Kontinent*, no. 8, 2000 accessed on <www.continent.kz/2000/09/16.html>.
29 According to the International Crisis Group this accusation is widely used in Uzbekistan and was tacitly endorsed by an international conference on security and stability (held in Tashkent, 19–20 October 2000), organised by the UN Office for Drug Control and Crime Prevention and the Organisation of Security and Co-operation in Europe. See International Crisis Group. *Central Asia: Islamist Mobalisation and Regional Security* (Osh/Brussels: ICG Asia Report No.14, 1 March 2001).
30 Akbar Turajonzoda was appointed Qazi-kalon (Supreme Judge) of Tajikistan in 1988. In the aftermath of the Soviet collapse, both men welcomed the opportunity to consolidate the Islamic clergy (both official and unofficial) and took a critical view of their respective governments. Both were forced to flee their republics in 1993. See Shahram Akbarzadeh, 'Islamic Clerical Establishment in Central Asia'.
31 Uzbek Television channel 1 (27 January 2000), reproduced in *Uzbekistan Daily Digest*, www. EuasiaNet.org (28 January 2000).
32 See Dobson, Richard B., 'Islam in Central Asia: Findings from National Surveys', *Central Asia Monitor*, 2 (1994), p. 19.
33 See report: http://www.eurasianet.org/resource/uzbekistan/hypermail/200205/0025.shtml (accessed 1 June 2002).
34 *Central Asia: Islamist Mobalisation and Regional Security* (Osh/Brussels, ICG Asia Report No. 14, 1 March 2001), p. 7.
35 Bureau of Democracy, Human Rights, and Labour, US Department of State, *1999 Country Reports on Human Rights Practices: Uzbekistan*, 25 February 2000.

7 Failure of the 'welfare state'

Islamic resurgence and political legitimacy in Bangladesh

Taj I. Hashmi

The emergence of Bangladesh in 1971 in the name of Bengali nationalism signalled a break with the Islam-based state ideology of the Pakistani period (1947–71). To some scholars, the creation of Bangladesh delegitimised the 'two-nation theory', which in 1947 justified the communal partition of the Indian subcontinent into India and Pakistan. Soon after its emergence, Bangladesh adopted the four-pronged state ideology of nationalism, democracy, socialism and secularism. However, not long after the emergence of that state, Islam re-emerged as an important factor in the country, both socially and politically. The not-so-democratic regime of Sheikh Mujib ur-Rahman (1972–5) retained 'secularism', along with 'democracy', 'socialism' and 'nationalism', as state principles, but his assassination and the overthrow of his government by a military coup d'état in August 1975 brought Islam-oriented state ideology at the expense of 'secularism' and 'socialism'. Not long after his ascendancy as the new ruler in November 1975, General Zia ur-Rahman replaced the outwardly secular 'Bengali nationalism' with 'Bangladeshi nationalism'. One may argue that 'Bangladeshi' is inclusive of the different non-Bengali minorities; nevertheless the term also highlights the Muslim identity of the country, differentiating its Muslim majority Bengalis from their Hindu majority counterparts in West Bengal in India.

It is noteworthy that most Bangladeshi Muslims suffer from a tremendous identity crisis. They are not sure which comes first – their loyalty towards Islam or towards Bangladesh. After the failure of the 'socialist-secular-Bengali nationalist' Mujib government in 1975, his successors realised the importance of Islam to legitimise their rule – hence the rapid Islamisation of the polity. This type of state-sponsored Islam reflects the hegemonic culture of the civil and military oligarchies seeking political legitimacy. The successors to Mujib adopted Islam after the failure of the 'welfare state' or the promised socialist utopia.

Bangladeshi Muslims have adopted various types of Islam – escapist, fatalist, puritan and militant, for example – as alternatives to their failed 'welfare state'. An understanding of these variables in the context of Bangladesh requires an intimate knowledge of what the people need and what the leaders have been promising since the inception of the separatist movement for Bangladesh in the 1960s. The gap between what the people have attained since independence and what the liberal-democrat, socialist-secular and nationalist leaders (both 'Bengali' and 'Bangladeshi') have been promising to deliver is the key to our understanding of the problem.

This chapter is an inquiry into the re-emergence of Islam in Bangladesh as a socially and politically significant force by exploring the local and external factors in this regard. It presents an historical appraisal of the state–Islam–ulema nexus and its gradual transformation. This study shows that both the state and large sections of the population have been using Islam for political purposes. While secularism, democracy and independence of the country are burning issues in the political arena, nobody can ignore the cultural and political aspects of Islam in Bangladesh. Various groups of nationalists, sections of the ulema representing both the political and non-political organisations and even members of the armed forces from time to time champion the cause of Islam – some of them by openly demanding the transformation of the country into a shari'a-based 'Islamic state' and some by opposing liberal democratic and secular institutions.

Since Bangladesh is the third largest Muslim country in the world (after Indonesia and Pakistan), it is only natural to assume that Islam will play an important role in moulding its politics and culture while around 90 per cent of the population are Muslims – most importantly, representing one of the poorest, least literate and most backward sections of the world population. If mass poverty, illiteracy and unequal distribution of wealth have any positive correlation with Islamic resurgence and militancy, then Bangladesh has to be a fertile breeding ground for what is wrongly defined as 'Islamic fundamentalism'. The Awami League (the party under Sheikh Mujib which championed the cause of greater autonomy for East Pakistan, ultimately leading to the independence of Bangladesh) has been projecting its main political opponents – the Bangladesh Nationalist Party (BNP) and the Jamaat-i Islami (partners in the BNP-led coalition government since October 2001) – as 'fundamentalist' with a view to gaining political leverage after its abysmal performance in the parliamentary elections held in October 2001.[1] However, despite its poverty, backwardness and the preponderance of Islamic ethos in the main streams of its politics and culture, Bangladesh is not just another Afghanistan, Iran, Saudi Arabia or even Pakistan. Despite having many striking similarities with the Islamic movements elsewhere, their Bangladeshi counterparts have striking dissimilarities with them as well.

The nature of Islamic movements in Bangladesh

Here, Islamic movements have another dimension – they are primarily rural-based, agrarian and reflect peasant culture and behaviour. The country is predominantly agrarian, more than 80 per cent of the population being rural, mostly impoverished peasants primarily depending on primitive modes of cultivation, having incomplete access to the means of production, lacking power, security of tenure and viable means of sustenance and employment. Bengali peasants, being traditional, fatalist and religious if not pious by nature, often resort to religion as a means of identity. The peasant political behaviour and culture are not devoid of religion. Their mundane activities, including the political ones (in power perspectives) are inspired by their 'moral economy',[2] which again, is subject to their religious belief system. Consequently peasants' violent acts and proclivity to anarchy in the name of religion, often classified as 'pre-political' activities of the 'pre-modern',[3] are generally labelled 'Islamic' militancy, fanaticism, and 'fundamentalism' if they happen to be Muslims. Hence the significance of the 'peasant factor' towards understanding Islam in Bangladesh society and politics.

Although the 'peasants' Islam', or what we may call the 'little traditions', to paraphrase Redfield, represents the main stream of Islam in Bangladesh, urban Muslim elites and their rural counterparts, representing the 'great traditions' of Islam, have been the main custodians and guardians of Islam in the country. It is, however, interesting that not only the 'little traditions' of Bangladesh are very different from their counterparts elsewhere, but the 'great traditions' of Islam as believed and practised here are also unique. The synthesis of the two traditions, leading to syncretism, is what prevails as 'Islam' in Bangladesh. Despite their concerted efforts, the Islamic puritan reformers, the 'Wahhabis', Faraizis, Tayyunis and others since the early nineteenth century, have been unable to make significant changes in this regard. While sections of ultra-orthodox Muslims claim to be adherents of the Islamic 'great traditions', they have also inherited syncretistic beliefs and rituals as their forebears were not immune to the 'little traditions' of Arabia, Central Asia, Iran and north-western India and Bengal.[4]

Who are the Islamists?

Two parties have been championing the cause of Islam – one, on behalf of the government since 1975 and the other, various Islamic groups, parties and individuals with both pro- and anti-government inclinations. These groups and individuals may be classified as (a) the fatalist/escapist, (b) the Sufis/*pirs*, (c) the militant reformist ('fundamentalist') and (d) the 'Anglo-Mohammedan' ('opportunist'/'pragmatist'). The fatalist/escapist groups represent the bulk

Islamic resurgence and politics in Bangladesh 105

of the poor, unemployed/underemployed people having a next-worldly outlook and philosophy. They often belong to the Tabligh Jamaat, a grassroots-based puritan movement originating in northern India in the 1920s, which has millions of adherents in Bangladesh. Unlike the militant reformists belonging to the Jamaat-i Islami and other groups, including the clandestine ones, the Tablighis represent a pacifist, puritan and missionary movement. Every winter they organise a mammoth rally at Tungi, near Dhaka, attended by more than a million devout Muslims from Bangladesh and elsewhere. The Sufis and *pirs* represent mystic Islam. They belong to several mystic orders or *tariqas*, having *muridan* or disciples among all sections of the population, especially among peasants. They exert tremendous influence on their *muridan*. They may be politically motivated having renowned politicians, including General Ershad, as their *muridan*. The Sufis are generally opposed to the Jamaat-i Islami and Tabligh movements, but there are instances of Jamaatis and Tablighis paying respect to certain *pirs*. While the militant reformists, including the Jamaat-i Islami, are in favour of an Islamic state as an alternative to the existing system of government in Bangladesh, the 'Anglo Mohammedans' are the anglicised or Westernised Muslims aiming at synthesising Islamic and Western values for temporal benefits. They can be believers, agnostics and even atheists, but for the sake of expediency, political legitimacy, and social acceptance and above all, power, are often vacillating. They popularise a version of Islam which could be avowedly anti-Indian and tacitly anti-Hindu. They are very similar to the Pakistani ruling class who, since the inception of the country, has been promoting the communal, anti-India/anti-Hindu Islam for the sake of legitimacy. It is noteworthy that the followers of the above groups can easily shift allegiance. A Tablighi might join the Jamaat-i Islami (as Jamaat leader Ghulam Azam did) and an 'Anglo-Mohammedan' might turn Tablighi one day.[5]

However, despite their mutual differences and enmity, especially between the orthodox ulema/pirs and the Jamaat-i Islami, these groups have certain commonalities. All except the 'Anglo-Mohammedans' oppose women's liberation, Western codes of conduct, law and ethics (even dress and culture) and are in favour of establishing shari'a or Islamic law. The most important aspect, which is common to all the four categories, is their stand vis-à-vis India and Pakistan. They are invariably anti-India and pro-Pakistan. It may be mentioned that the ulema belonging to the 'Wahhabi' school of thought, who run thousands of madrasa or Islamic seminaries with an ultra-orthodox and conservative curricula throughout Bangladesh, are inimical to the Jamaat-i Islami and its founder, Mawlana Mawdudi (1903–79).[6] The counterparts of these seminaries in Pakistan and Afgahnistan, known as *qaumi* (national) madrasa, produced the Taliban. The 'pro-Taliban' groups in Bangladesh, for ideological reasons, are opposed to the Jamaat-i Islami.

However, as happened in Pakistan, they might unite against common enemies at the height of polarisation between Islam and some other forces, especially in the wake of September 11, the war in Afghanistan (2001–2) and the Israeli invasion of the Palestinian territory in March and April 2002.

An historical overview

Muslim peasants and the economically disadvantaged joined the Pakistan movement with a view to circumscribing the power of the Hindu landlords, middle classes and traders. Their eventual overthrow and replacement by the weaker/budding Muslim middle classes and upper peasantry were parts of the Bengali Muslim 'peasant utopia'.[7] The emergence of Bangladesh after the overthrow of the dominant non-Bengali Muslim elites by the subjugated Bengali Muslims did not signal the disappearance of the age-old fault line between the Muslims and Hindus of the subcontinent. The creation of Bangladesh did not destroy the 'two-nation-theory' of the founding fathers of Pakistan. Renowned Indian journalist, Basant Chatterjee, has the irrevocable arguments in this regard:

> Somebody should ask these hypocrites if they could give one good reason for the separate existence of Bangladesh after the destruction of the two-nation-theory. If the theory has been demolished, as they claim, then the only logical consequence should be the reunion of Bangladesh with India, as seems to be the positive stand of the Bangladeshi Hindus ... for the people know that had Pakistan not been created then, Bangladesh too would not have come into existence now.[8]

Chatterjee further contends that with the gradual shifting of Hindus to India due to the prevalent anti-Hindu feelings in the country, 'Bangladesh would by itself become 'Muslim Bengal'.[9] Consequently, one may argue, that with the creation of Bangladesh, the 'Hindu phobia' of Bengali Muslims, a legacy since the British colonial days, transforming into 'Indophobia' during the Pakistani period (1947–71), is still around in the psyche of the average Bangladeshi Muslim. As the 'peasant factor' is important for understanding the Islamisation process in the country, so is the 'India factor'. An understanding of the predominant petty bourgeois and lumpen culture is also essential in this regard. They are equally, if not more, violent, anarchical and vacillating as the peasantry.

Bengali peasant support for various Islamic movements since the early nineteenth century not only project the violent, 'pre-political' and non-committal aspects of the peasant community, they also suggest how vulnerable Muslim peasants have been to the manipulative leaders who mobilise mass support in the name of Islam or any other ideology. It is noteworthy that before their political mobilisation took place in the early nineteenth century by Islamic reformists-cum-militants, the 'Wahhabi' and Faraizi leaders – East Bengali peasants and aboriginal tribesmen had come under the influence of 'warrior-Sufis' in the late medieval period. The 'warrior-Sufis' were mainly responsible for the rapid Islamisation and peasantisation of the region in the sixteenth and seventeenth centuries converting the bulk of the indigenous population who had not yet fully integrated into the Hindu and peasant communities. Sufis played a leading role in reclaiming land by clearing forests in the deltaic south-eastern 'frontier land'. They introduced a new religion, Islam, and new agrarian implements and technology, such as the plough and other methods to contain the turbulent rivers, which were shifting eastward.[10]

The 'Wahhabi' and Faraizi leaders, and especially the most influential Mawlana Karamat Ali Jaunpuri (1800–73), a former 'Wahhabi'-turned-'loyalist' Islamic reformer of the nineteenth century, brought the syncretistic Bengali Muslims, mainly peasants, into the fold of shari'a-based, orthodox and puritan Islam. The 'Wahhabi' and Faraizi leaders mobilised Bengali Muslim masses against British colonial rule as well as against the local exploiting classes of (Hindu) *zamindars* (landlords), *bhadralok* (professionals) and *mahajans* (moneylenders). The first step towards the mobilisation process was through the extensive Islamisation of the masses. Karamat Ali and his hundreds of successors, who adopted a pro-British loyalist attitude out of pragmatism after the failure of the Indian Mutiny of 1857–8, not only Islamised the bulk of the Bengali Muslims but also created a strong sense of belonging to a Muslim community in the subcontinent.[11] In the absence of a powerful modern Muslim leadership in nineteenth-century Bengal, the ulema emerged as the leaders of the Muslim community both in the arenas of politics and religion. The Hindu revivalist movements and the anti-Muslim socio-economic and political stand of the bulk of the Hindu elites and middle classes in the nineteenth and twentieth centuries further strengthened the hold of the ulema and their patrons, the *ashraf* (aristocratic, upper-class Muslims), on the Bengali Muslim masses. The Hindu opposition to legislative and other government measures to benefit the Bengali Muslims, such as the Bengal Tenancy Act of 1885, its amendments, the enactment of the Bengal Free (rural) Primary Education Bill and the establishment of the Dhaka University in Muslim majority East Bengal, further antagonised Muslim leaders.

The re-emergence of the ulema in the arena of Bengal politics in 1919 spearheaded the pervasive anti-British Khilafat (Caliphate) movement. Islam and ulema continued to play very important roles in the political mobilisation of the Bengali Muslims up to the partition of 1947. The Muslim elite, the *ashraf–ulema–jotedar* triumvirate, representing Muslim aristocrats, clergy and rich peasants/petty landlords, successfully mobilised Bengali Muslims against the dominant Hindu *zamindar–bhadralok–mahajan* triumvirate. This mobilisation in the name of a separate Muslim identity, by 1947, led to the transformation of East Bengal into the eastern wing of Pakistan. The arousal of Muslim communal solidarity among the bulk of Bengali Muslim masses as an alternative to class solidarity demonstrated that religion and ethnicity had the potential to become more important than class differences.[12]

It is interesting that despite the constant harping on the themes of Islamic solidarity and Muslim separatism under the aegis of the Pakistani ruling classes during 1947 and 1971, the bulk of the East Bengali Muslims distanced themselves from 'communal Islam'. Not long after the Partition of 1947 they showed a preference for secular institutions for the sake of their Bengali identity. The clash of these two identities, 'Islamic' (Pakistani) and 'secular' (Bengali) ultimately led to the creation of Bangladesh. This was possible after the mass emigration of members of the Hindu *zamindar–bhadralok–mahajan* triumvirate to India and the emasculation of the rest of the hitherto dominant Hindus in East Bengal in the wake of the Partition. Not long after the Partition it dawned upon sections of the East Bengali Muslim elites that Pakistan, the promised utopia of Muslim separatist leaders, was nothing but a mirage – the 'promised land' of South Asian Muslims was a deception to exploit the eastern wing as a colony of the western wing of Pakistan.

Islam, secularism and Bengali nationalism, 1972–5

Bengali Nationalism, more precisely, East Bengali Nationalism, had been the guiding principle of Sheikh Mujib's Awami League, which eventually formed the first government in independent Bangladesh. The exclusion of the Indian Bengalis (mostly Hindus, who opted to live as citizens of the Indian state in the wake of the partition of 1947) as members of the Bengali nation as defined by the Awami League, practically indicated that the Muslim majority Bengalis of the erstwhile East Pakistan wanted to secede from the dominant and exploiting non-Bengali West Pakistan out of sheer economic, political and cultural differences. Here by 'culture', the top leaders and the bulk of the followers of the movement for Bengali nationalism only meant linguistic and other aspects of culture, not religion. This means, they were (are) Bengalis but nevertheless they remained (remain) Muslims at the same time. They never conceived, let alone fought for, a secular/socialist Bangladesh. Had the Pakistani ruling elite in 1971 accepted Sheikh Mujib, the leader of the majority party, Awami League, as the prime minister of Pakistan, 'Bengali Nationalism' would have taken a totally new meaning. However, the rulers of the new nation of Bangladesh for various reasons,

Islamic resurgence and politics in Bangladesh 109

mainly political, adopted the four-pronged state ideology of 'Bengali nationalism', 'socialism', 'secularism' and 'democracy', *a la* Nehruvian 'democratic socialism' (often touted as 'Mujibism').

The abysmal failure of Mujibism to alleviate poverty and restore law and order eventually led to the Islamisation of the polity. The failure of the 'welfare state' forced a large section of the underdogs to cling to Islam either as a means to escape from the harsh reality or to achieve their cherished golden Bengal through piety, Islamic justice and egalitarianism. Without having substantial changes in living conditions – around 50 per cent of the population still living below the poverty line – the tide of globalization in the post-Cold War period has not reduced Islamic fervour. The obsolence of socialism/communism as an alternative to 'illiberal democracy' and autocracy in the Third World since the early 1990s and the sudden rise in the intensity of Islamic resurgence and 'Islamic' terror globally in recent years have further intensified Islamism in Bangladesh.

The overall situation of the country in the wake of the liberation of 1971 was simply unbearable for the bulk of the people. Although they were relieved of the nine-month-long reign of terror under the Pakistani occupation army, the liberation did not bring an end to suffering and exploitation. Fellow Bangladeshis, genuine and pseudo freedom fighters, mostly donning the Awami hat, started a reign of corruption, nepotism and lawlessness throughout the country. While Awami leaders in the name of socialism were busy plundering the nationalised industries, banks and insurance companies and the 'abandoned' non-Bengali properties, previously owned by Urdu-speaking refugees from Bihar, Gujarat and Uttar Pradesh, the bulk of the Bengalis were soon turned into disillusioned, hungry and angry masses. By 1974, Bangladesh had already become 'the basket case' of Henry Kissinger. The floods and subsequent famine of 1974 killed thousands and impoverished the bulk of the population. The price of consumer goods rose ten to twenty times in the mid-1970s. Hyperinflation, corruption and a general scarcity of basic goods turned the average Bangladeshi against India and the Awami League.

Disenchantment swelled the ranks of the opposition groups and parties, including the leftist National Socialist Party (JSD) and the clandestine Maoist Sarbahara Party of Siraj Sikdar. A large number of them, including many erstwhile collaborators of the Pakistani occupation forces, joined hands with Mawlana Bhashani (the champion of 'Islamic Socialism') who soon after the liberation started a vitriolic anti-Awami, anti-Indian campaign. Bhashani's popularity and the sharp decline in that of Prime Minister Mujib paved the way for the rise of various Islamic groups not long after the assassination of the latter in 1975. Mujib had a complicated approach to Islam. On the one hand he promoted the idea that secularism 'did not mean the absence of religion' and offered generous state patronage to madrasa education, while on the other hand, he saw religion as 'a shadow, the ghost of the past one did not know how to deal with'.[13]

By early 1975, the Mujib Government had crushed both the JSD and the Sarbahara Party, the secular and leftist opposition groups. While the bulk of the JSD leaders were behind bars, in January 1975, Siraj Sikdar was killed in police custody. The straw that broke the camel's back was the introduction of the one-party government under Sheikh Mujib, in the name of the so-called Bangladesh Peasants' and Workers' Awami League (BKSAL). This act established a Soviet style government where top ranking bureaucrats, university teachers, and even the chiefs and deputy chiefs of the armed forces, had to join the BKSAL. This act in January 1975, on the one hand killed the remnants of democracy, and on the other turned both secular and Islamic politics underground – the only option for the people.[14]

Islam and Bangladeshi nationalism, 1975–81

In the long run, the Islamic parties outpaced the various secular/leftist parties in the wake of the overthrow of the BKSAL regime in August 1975. Henceforth, both the military and civil governments of the country promoted Islam to contain the militant one promoted by the grassroots-based, well organised Jamaat-i Islami and other groups. It is noteworthy that General Zia's Government (1975–81) withdrew the ban imposed on all Islam-oriented political parties by the Mujib Government for their active collaboration with the Pakistani occupation forces in 1971. Zia and his successors promoted Islam and Islamic parties, including the Jamaat and Muslim League, for the sake of legitimacy and for containing the Awami League.[15]

From the rapid success of President Zia in popularising his ideals, programmes and most importantly, his regime, among the bulk of Bangladeshis, it appears that Islam fetched him rich dividends. Curiously, what 'soldier' Zia grasped, namely that the country was not prepared for 'socialism' and 'secularism', was simply beyond 'politician' Mujib's comprehension. His associates, mostly sycophants and half-educated political agitators from the countryside and small towns, were too naïve to understand the reality. Moreover, the rich dividends from the nationalised industries and financial institutions for them, acquired in the name of socialism, were too lucrative to lose. The collective failure of the Awami leadership was also with regard to their failure to grasp the implications of discarding the Islamic character of the polity. One may point out the way the Mujib Government replaced a Qur'anic inscription, 'Read in the name of thy Lord' with 'Knowledge is Light' from the emblem of Dhaka University. With hindsight, one may mention how the Communist Party, stigmatised as the promoter of a 'Godless' and 'un-Islamic' order, failed to breakthrough in the peasant and worker fronts in the 1940s and afterwards. The bulk of the Bengali Muslims, including peasants and workers, whole-heartedly supported the Muslim separatist Pakistan movement in the 1940s. Sheikh Mujib and his overzealous associates were not clear about how to implement 'socialism' and 'secularism' in Muslim majority Bangladesh, where the bulk of the population were both religious and in favour of private property. The people had never been prepared to work for these alien concepts during the Liberation War. They fought for independence, not for secularism and socialism.

The subsequent governments gradually leaned towards the oil-rich Muslim countries of the Middle East and the West for the sake of sustained growth and legitimacy. Significantly, the Saudi recognition for Bangladesh came only after the assassination of Sheikh Mujib and the overthrow of his government. Meanwhile Bangladesh's transformation into a quasi-Islamic state by discarding 'socialism' and 'secularism' went unhindered because the West, especially the US, preferred pro-Western Islamists to pro-communist social democrats during the peak of the Cold War in the 1980s. Meanwhile, President (General) Zia amended the constitution replacing 'socialism' and 'secularism' with 'social justice' and 'absolute faith in God Almighty', respectively. He also had 'In the name of Allah, the Beneficent, the Merciful' in Arabic, inserted at the beginning of the constitution.[16]

Islam, military rule and legitimacy

In May 1981, Zia died in an abortive military takeover. In March 1982, General Ershad, the army chief, toppled the successive, elected government. He had neither the charisma nor the popularity of Zia. He is widely known for his promiscuity and corruption. Consequently with a view to legitimising his rule, in June 1988, he amended the constitution by introducing Islam as the 'state religion'. In this he was supported by obscure Islamic groups and, quite surprisingly, the secular Bangladesh Teachers' Federation.[17]

One may argue that Ershad played the Islamic card with a view to containing the so-called fundamentalist forces and his secular opponents by appealing to the majority of Bangladeshi Muslims who, according to one study, favour non-cleric, English-educated, 'anti-Indian' and Islam-oriented politicians as their leaders.[18] Ershad introduced the *Zakat* Fund to raise poor-tax in accordance with the teachings of Islam. He also declared Friday as the weekly holiday and frequently visited mosques, shrines and the Muslim holy places in Mecca and Medina. Ershad played the 'India card' quite well. After having diplomatic problems with India in 1982, he bitterly criticised India for the construction of the Farakka barrage across the Ganges and told his people: 'It is being said today that if we do not get water from Farakka the northern and southern regions of Bangladesh will turn into deserts. *I want to remind everybody concerned that Islam was born in desert, but Islam did not die. Islam could not be destroyed'*.[19]

Ershad also befriended influential *pirs*, those of Atrashi, Charmonai and Sarsina for example, and some 'Anglo Mohammedan' leaders who congratulated him for the 'State Religion' Act. But he was challenged as insincere by the Jamaat-i Islami and pro-Iranian Mawlana Muhammadulla (Hafizjee Huzur), an influential cleric who condemned the Act as sham and inadequate. Curiously, 'Anglo Mohammedan' Kazi Qader (Muslim League leader) felt that the Act was aimed at suppressing the movement of the God-fearing Muslims. He demanded the immediate declaration of Bangladesh as an 'Islamic Republic'.[20]

Although various feminist and human rights NGOs bitterly criticised the 'State Religion' Act in Bangladesh, the bulk of Bengali Muslims have accepted the provision. So far no subsequent government has gathered enough courage to alter the amendment. Two women's organisations, Naripakhyo and Oikyobaddho Nari Samaj, protested against the act. They argued that the 'sovereignty of the country' and 'the spirit of the freedom struggle' were in danger because of the Act. However, many men jeered at them for holding rallies, asking them to observe *purda* (seclusion of women from public view), presumed to be a requirement for Muslim women. Many men were even happy about an Islamic state of Bangladesh where women would not compete with them in the job market.[21]

Not long after the enactment of the 'State Religion' Act, several liberal democrats and women's organisations started a campaign to rekindle the 'spirit of the liberation war' or 'secularism' to contain Ershad's autocracy. Several NGOs, funded by overseas donors, came forward in support. After failing to repeal the act, a section of left-oriented intellectuals under the leadership of Ahmed Sharif, a retired Dhaka University professor, and Colonel (retired) Nuruzzaman (freedom fighter) lent support to the anti-Ershad movement. Under the banner of the Muktijuddho Chetona Bikash Kendro (Centre for the Development of the Spirit of the Liberation War), they spoke at some of the women's rallies. Stressing the virtues of democracy, socialism and secularism, Ahmed Sharif urged that 'the right to be fed be incorporated in the constitution' instead of Islam as the state religion.[22]

While the various Islamic groups including the Jamaat-i Islami condemned Ershad as an 'Indo-Soviet agent and enemy of Islam', they did not join hands with the 'secular', 'socialist' and 'liberal democrats', or the women's groups. The latter had been avowedly anti-Jamaat for its 'fundamentalist' tilt and collaboration with Pakistani rulers in 1971. By the late 1980s, a Bengali book published a long list of the 'killers and collaborators of 1971'. The polity since then has been sharply polarised between the so-called 'pro-' and 'anti-Liberation' forces. The former represents the so-called secular and liberal

Islamic resurgence and politics in Bangladesh 113

parties and individuals that are soft on India and harsh on Pakistan. The latter, the so-called 'Islam-loving' groups and individuals, have strong anti-India and pro-Islam commitments. The 'secular' groups, including the Awami League, use the 'liberation-in-danger' slogan to mean that Pakistani machination is at work to subjugate Bangladesh, while to the Islamists, including the BNP and the Jamaat-i Islami, independence is at stake because of Indian 'expansionism'. The parliamentary elections of 1991, held after the overthrow of Ershad in December 1990, contrary to the expectations of the Awami League, brought Khaleda Zia, the widow of President Zia, to power.

Her party, the Bangladesh Nationalist Party (BNP) came to power with the support of the Jamaat-i Islami and she became the Prime Minister. It is interesting that most political parties, including the Communist Party of Bangladesh, used Islamic slogans for their success in the elections of 1991. While the 'Islam-loving' parties attracted 54.13 per cent of votes, despite their Islamic rhetoric, slogans and banners, the Awami League-led eight-party alliance managed to poll only around 34.81 per cent of votes in the elections.[23] One may again deduct more than ten per cent minority (mainly Hindu) votes from the total votes polled by the Awami League-led alliance, as traditionally the minorities have been voting for the Awami League. This means, in 1991, around 75 per cent Bangladeshi Muslims did not vote for the Awami League.

The Jamaat-i Islami factor

The Jamaat-i Islami was formed in the 1940s in northern India. Mawlana Mawdudi, the founder, who had earlier strongly opposed the concept of Pakistan, later migrated to Pakistan from northern India and worked for the establishment of an Islamic state, based on shari'a law. The Jamaat throughout the Cold War maintained a pro-Western and anti-communist policy. The party collaborated with the Pakistani occupation army in Bangladesh and is despised by many liberal democrats and others for its role in 1971. Not long after the overthrow of the Mujib government in 1975, the Jamaat emerged as a legitimate organisation in Bangladesh. Unlike its counterparts in India and Pakistan, the Jamaat in Bangladesh is led and followed mostly by upper-class peasants and the lower middle classes. It is widely believed that the Jamaat, having several NGOs, clinics and charitable organisations across Bangladesh, has been gaining ground, emerging as an alternative to secular organisations.[24] Of late, sections of Jamaat workers have adopted an anti-US stand, especially in the wake of the US war in Afghanistan in 2001–2.

Although the Jamaat had faced a three-pronged attack from the Ershad government, 'secular/socialist/liberal' groups and from a section of the orthodox ulema, mostly belonging to the conservative Deoband school, the party was gaining ground. While the 'secular/liberal' groups condemn the Jamaat for its obscurantism and 'war crimes', a section of the ulema regard Mawlana Mawdudi a heretic, and the Jamaat a heresy. The 1980s and the early 1990s had been the golden era for the Jamaat. By then their student wing had captured student unions at Chittagong and Rajshahi universities by defeating the combined groups of their opponents. This was the period when the party enjoyed the blessings of Saudi Arabia and, most importantly, the United States.[25] In the 1991 parliamentary elections the Jamaat captured eighteen seats and more than 12 per cent of the votes (more than four million votes), compared to ten seats and slightly more than a million votes in the elections of 1986.[26]

The emergence of the Jamaat as the third largest party in terms of its share in the total votes cast in the 1991 elections alarmed its rivals. In March 1992, the proponents of the Spirit of the Liberation War, under the leadership of Colonel (retired) Nuruzzaman (and with the blessing of Ahmed Sharif) organised a 'public trial' of Jamaat leader Ghulam Azam, an alleged war criminal, for his active collaboration with Pakistan during the Liberation War. No sooner had Ghulam Azam been elected as the chief of the Jamaat in Bangladesh, than the organisers of the 'trial' formed the Killer-Collaborator Elimination Committee (*Ghatak-Dalal Nirmul Committee*). The Awami League lent its support to the Elimination Committee to gain political leverage.[27] The 'trial' was embarrassing both for the Jamaat and its allies, the BNP Government. Curiously, the Awami League, which had earlier supported the physical attack on Jamaat leader, Matiur Rahman Nizami, by some Dhaka University students in May 1991, later asked the Jamaat leaders to 'forget the past and look forward to the future'. And in early 1991, the Awami League had no qualms about soliciting Jamaat parliamentary support for their presidential candidate. At the time the Jamaat had twenty members in the parliament with unflinching loyalty towards Ghulam Azam.[28]

Islamists in Bangladesh also started facing a hostile West not long after the Gulf War of 1991. The West must not have relished the way large numbers of Bangladeshi Muslims, including leading politicians from the so-called liberal democratic parties like the BNP and Awami League, expressed solidarity with Saddam Hussein. Some candidates during the parliamentary elections of 1991 even identified themselves as 'Saddam's candidates', displaying life-size portraits of the Iraqi dictator.[29] The Jamaat, however, opposed Saddam Hussein's Kuwait invasion, which, according to a Jamaat leader, cost them dearly as most Bangladeshi Muslims were supporters of Saddam and bitter critics of the West.[30] However, the Jamaat's poor performance in all the previous and successive elections belies this assertion. Nevertheless, the fact remains that by the 1990s the Jamaat had not only regained its lost image despite its anti-Liberation role in 1971, but it also started playing the role of 'king maker', as evident from the results of the parliamentary elections since 1991 vis-à-vis the formation of government by the two major political parties, the BNP and Awami League.

The late 1980s and the early 1990s also witnessed the gradual transformation of the Cold War between the Islamists (mainly the Jamaat) and the so-called secular/liberal forces into open confrontation. The latter, the 'pro-India' and 'pro-Western' lobbies, respectively represent the Awami League (and its allies belonging to the erstwhile pro-Soviet political parties) and the various NGOs/human rights groups. They have been opposing the Jamaat in the name of championing the cause of liberation, women's rights, human rights, minority rights and secularism. The Taslima Nasrin episode (see below), the NGO–mulla conflict and the mutual mud-slinging between the mulla and Awami–NGO lobbies were parts of the play called the 'Public Trial of Ghulam Azam' in 1991. While the mullas have been vilifying the Awami–NGO lobby as the 'enemies of Islam', 'Indian agents' and 'agents of neo-imperialism', the latter have been portraying the former as 'anti-liberation/Pakistani agents', 'fundamentalist/Taliban' and 'communal (anti-Hindu and anti-minority fascist)'. One may cite scores of scurrilous writings against the so-called Islamic fundamentalist-cum-communal forces, especially the Jamaat.[31] The 'secular/liberal' groups own most of the well-circulated Bengali and English newspapers in the country. The Reliance Group of India owns the widely-circulated *Janakantha*.

It is common to portray the Jamaat as 'communal' and 'anti-liberation' in the post-liberation period, let alone as pro-Taliban. Jimmy Carter felt that Islamic parties who believed in election, despite having 'fundamentalist' belief and support for shari'a law could not be classified as 'extremist'.[32] And those among them who have accepted the reality of Bangladesh cannot be simply rejected as 'anti-liberation' either. Nevertheless, the fact remains that some powerful Jamaat leaders do not believe in the democratic ethos – some do not rule out 'other means' or armed insurrection as a means to power.[33] Jamaat workers' militancy and their occasional armed encounter with 'liberal democrats', mainly the Awami Leaguers, have alarmed many concerned about an eventual Jamaat takeover of the country. Many Bangladeshi intellectuals feel that the BNP–Jamaat coalition government that came to power in October 2001 has been too soft on the Jamaat. Even the banning of a movie, *Matir Moina*, for its negative portrayal of the madrasa system of education, by the government in May 2002 is interpreted by many not as a fear of the Awami League by the BNP, 'but of Jamaat-i Islami deserting BNP'.[34]

Popular Islam, fatwa, women and NGOs in the village community

The writings and comments by Taslima Nasrin (b. 1962), a medical doctor turned feminist writer on Islam, patriarchy and society in Bangladesh in the early 1990s brought her (and eventually her country) to the limelight. She is another member of the so-called secular-liberal-democrat group in Bangladesh with a strong anti-Islamic, pro-Indian and anti-male bias in her writings. She was a controversial figure and very unpopular both among Islamists and others in Bangladesh for advocating free sex and other maverick ideas including the merger of Bangladesh with the Indian state of West Bengal. In early 1993 she published *Lajja*, a fictional portrayal of the Hindu minority in Bangladesh, paradoxically in the wake of the killing of thousands of Muslims in India during and after the demolition of the Babri Mosque in late 1992. This endeared her to the Hindu militants in India. This novelette, soon translated into English and several other Indian languages, grossly exaggerated the plight of Hindus in Bangladesh by singling out the Jamaat-i Islami workers as members of the killer-rapist-abductor gangs.[35] Not long after the publication *of Lajja*, a couple of obscure mullas from the periphery issued the so-called fatwa-to-kill against the author. Despite later denial of such a fatwa, the Indian and Western media publicised the so-called death threat portraying Bangladesh as another 'Islamic' country with all its negative attributes, turning Nasrin into their Salman Rushdie and the two mullas into the protégé of Ayatollah Khomeini.[36] Her alleged remarks made to the Indian media in 1994 suggesting 'rewriting the Qur'an' enraged the bulk of Bangladeshi Muslims and this finally led to her expulsion from the country. The wide coverage of the Taslima Nasrin episode in Indian and Western media has convinced many that Bangladesh is no different from other intolerant and obscurantist 'Islamic' countries.

While the Taslima Nasrin episode had been drawing world attention, persecution of rural women was going on in the name of Islamic justice. The cruel and illegal acts of the traditional village courts or, *salish* had been very disturbing to human rights activists and others. The public trial of poor women by village elders and mullas, which led to several deaths of the victims, convinced many of the 'impending' ascendancy of Islamic extremism in Bangladesh. Meanwhile, the proliferation of Western-funded NGOs in the country, advancing micro credit to rural women (albeit at very high rates of interest, the average rate being around 32 per cent), running schools and generating jobs, mainly for women, polarised the polity between pro- and anti-NGO groups. Broadly speaking, the former represents the so-called secular-liberal-democrat groups (often the beneficiaries of the NGOs) and the latter mainly Islam-oriented and anti-West/anti-globalization groups and individuals. The controversial and extortionist modus operandi of NGOs, especially the way the Grameen Bank, BRAC and Proshika operate, preferring women to men as their clients in the name of female empowerment and alleviation of poverty, has alienated village elders and others from the NGOs. In the common parlance of the villagers the various powerful local and foreign NGOs are described as: '*CAREer gari, BRACer bari, Grameener nari, aar Proshikar barabari*' (CARE [An American NGO] is known for its vehicles, BRAC for its buildings, Grameen for its women and Proshika for its excesses). Purportedly mullas' and village elders' dislike for the NGOs was due to activities which were seen as 'anti-Islamic': bringing women to the close proximity of unrelated men and the alleged promotion of Christian missionaries. The conflict may be explained as another dimension of the age-old conflict between the dominant urban and weak rural elites. NGO preference for women to men as their clients has hit patriarchy and the well-entrenched village elders and mullas by posing the threat of taking away their traditional clients. The NGO lobby's projection of the mullas as 'fundamentalists', 'anti-women' and 'anti-liberation' led to the proliferation of anti-NGO fatwas and a backlash toward NGO workers in the countryside. Mufti Fazlul Haq Amini, an influential cleric, in a public meeting demanded the execution of NGO activist Kazi Faruq Ahmed, for his 'anti-Islamic' activities.[37]

The fatwa controversy came to the limelight in the 1990s after the local media, NGOs and donors took exception to the persecution of rural women in the name of Islam. Poor rural women, often victims of rape by influential villagers or those alleged to have cohabited with their former husbands after being divorced are punished for committing adultery. Sometimes influential village elders force them to remarry someone as penance for committing adultery through the *salish*. The village mullas, totally dependent on village elders for sustenance, play the vital role in justifying the 'judgments' in the name of shari'a law. In late 2000 a village woman at Naogaon district in northern Bangladesh, fell victim to a *salish* verdict and was forced to commit suicide. Wide publicity of the incident led to the High Court verdict declaring the dispensing of fatwas illegal on 1 January 2001.[38] The influential Jamaat-i Islami, several Islamic groups and hundreds of ulema condemned the judgment as un-Islamic and the judges as *murtads* (apostates).[39] While Mawlana Fazlul Karim, the influential *pir* of Charmonai, the chief of the Islamic Constitution Movement condemned the judgment, Mufti Amini threatened to launch a 'Taliban-style Revolution' in Bangladesh to counterpoise the 'enemies of Islam'.[40] Islamic zealots were on the rampage at Brahmanbaria, Chittagong and certain other places, chanting anti-government and pro-Taliban slogans: 'Amra sabai Taliban, Bangla habe Afghan' (We are all Taliban and will turn Bangladesh into another Afghanistan).[41]

Although most liberal-democrats favoured the anti-fatwa judgment, the government, being apprehensive of a backlash, was thinking in terms of reviewing the judgment in 2001.[42]

Soon the polarised polity witnessed the showdown between pro-fatwa clerics and anti-fatwa, pro-NGO *Nagorik Andolon* (Citizen's Movement). Among others, the *pir* of Charmonai, Mufti Amini and Mufti Azizul Haq organised a grand pro-fatwa rally in Dhaka on 2 February 2001. Declaring the NGOs 'number one enemy' of Islam and Bangladesh, the clerics blamed the Awami League government for appointing judges with bias against Islam.[43] The pro-NGO and anti-fatwa *Nagorik Andolon* confronted the clerics and asked the government to ban all religiously motivated political parties.[44]

Meanwhile the government was considering the formation of a shari'a board to issue fatwas in accordance with Islam and on behalf of the state.[45] Liberal-democrats and leftists opposed any such move to institutionalise fatwa through the state machinery.[46] However, one may set aside the liberal-democrats' reservations about the mullas' authority to issue fatwas as they represent a minority view, mainly belonging to the urban middle and upper classes. The Muslim community, especially at the grassroots level, favours fatwa as the fastest and cheapest way of getting justice. The average mulla's revulsion for the NGOs is shared by Bangladeshi Muslims at the grassroots level. This is reflected in the popularity of scores of mulla-cum-demagogue, including Mawlana Delwar Hussein Saidi (a Jamaat MP since 1996), Pir Fazlul Karim, Mufti Fazlul Haq Amini and Mufti Ubaidullah and others. Saidi's video and audiocassettes containing rustic speeches and extreme views, reflecting the little traditions of Islam in Bangladesh, sell in thousands throughout the country.[47] One year after the controversial anti-fatwa judgment, he felt that 'fatwas should guide the judiciary and not the other way round'.[48]

Islamic militancy: real or imaginary?

Urban mullas with rural backgrounds and links have been campaigning against the NGOs and their urban patrons and associates, mainly professionals and intellectuals; often portraying them as *murtads*, enemies of Islam and agents of neo-imperialist West.[49] And, as per Islamic law, apostates are liable to capital punishment. Death warrants and bomb attacks on some of the enlisted '*murtads*', presumably by Islamic militants, became quite common during 1991 and 2001. The ongoing conflict between the pro-NGO 'civil society' and the anti-NGO Islamists in early 2001 alarmed the US State Department and various donor agencies, including the Asian Development Bank. Pointing out its adverse effects on the economy of Bangladesh, they condemned the 'violation of human rights'.[50]

Bangladesh has had its share of political violence associated with Islamic radicalism. The little known *Harkatul Jihad al-Islami*, an 'Islamic militant' group, is reported to have been involved in terrorist activities in 2001. There have also been calls for jihad and a 'Taliban-style revolution in Bangladesh', providing a wealth of material for sensational media coverage. However fears of an 'impending' collapse of law and order, are not grounded in reality. A cover story by the *Far Eastern Economic Review* [*FEER*] in April 2002 is a reflection of this alarmist view.[51] The *FEER* story does not comfort liberal-democrats and secular people. According to Bertil Lintner, the Thailand-based Swedish journalist:

> A revolution is taking place in Bangladesh that threatens trouble for the region and beyond if left unchallenged. Islamic fundamentalism, religious intolerance, militant Muslim groups with links to international terrorist groups, a powerful military with ties to the militants, the mushrooming of Islamic schools churning out radical students, middle-class apathy, poverty and lawlessness – all are combining to transform the nation.

The report has also suggested that Western donors and diplomats, more concerned with the problems of governance and development than the rise of Islamic militancy in Bangladesh 'seem to have paid scant attention to the deeper long-term danger' of Islamic resurgence in the country. Citing the indifference and complacence of the Bangladeshi middle classes and government about the 'impending threat' of Talibanisation of the polity, the report considers ominous the electoral success of the Jamaat-i Islami, having seventeen seats in the three-hundred-member parliament and two ministers in the cabinet of the BNP-led coalition government. According to the report, more extremist Islamic clerics and groups in Bangladesh, such as Mawlana Ubaidul Haq and the 'shadowy' Harkatul Jihad, having connections with their Pakistani, Afghan, Chechen, and Southeast Asian counterparts with blessings from Osama bin Laden, have been active in the region. The January 22 attack (in 2002) on the American Cultural Centre in Calcutta has been imputed to Harkat gunmen. The report has cited how the Jamaat supporters in general and Ubaidul Haq in particular took part in anti-US protests during the Afghan War in late 2001. According to the report, while addressing thousands of Muslims, including the President and several cabinet ministers of Bangladesh at the Eid congregational prayer in Dhaka in December 2001, Ubaidul Haq publicly condemned the US President as 'the most heinous terrorist in the world'. 'America and Bush must be destroyed. The Americans will be washed away if Bangladesh's 120 million Muslims spit on them', the cleric exhorted.[52]

It seems the report has nothing to do with reality. One is not sure if there are any hidden agenda of individuals or groups behind such reporting. Soon after the excerption of the Internet version of the story in local newspapers, the BNP–Jamaat coalition government under Khaleda Zia condemned the report as baseless, imposing a ban on the circulation of the April 4 issue of the periodical in Bangladesh. However, no sooner had Sheikh Hasina of the opposition Awami League blamed the BNP–Jamaat coalition government for the 'prevalent terrorist image' of Bangladesh than Prime Minister Khaleda Zia blamed Hasina's party for 'planting' the *FEER* story.[53] A similar sensational report came out in the *Wall Street Journal* (April 2, 2002) entitled, 'In Bangladesh, as in Pakistan, a Worrisome Rise in Islamic Extremism'. 'Militant groups with links with international terrorists' and 'powerful military with ties to militants' are said to have mobilised Islamic militants in the country. One wonders if there is a link between such sensational writings and what Sheikh Hasina and her party has been doing, vilifying the BNP and its allies as 'Islamic fundamentalists' and as local agents of Osama bin Laden. Curiously, the report portrays the Awami League as 'left-leaning and secular', ignoring how the party since the early 1990s has been projecting itself as a champion of Islam and how Sheikh Hasina donned the Islamic *hijab* on the eve of the 1996 parliamentary elections. The pro-Awami League sympathy of the reporter is further reflected in his corroboration of Sheikh Hasina that the BNP-led coalition government, which came to power after 'ousting', not 'defeating' the Awami League, has established 'a reign of terror across the country'. He blamed the BNP-led government as 'anti-Hindu' and 'pro-fundamentalist'. It is curious that he has blamed the Harkatul Jihad behind the threats against Taslima Nasrin in 1993 and for 'the attempted murder' of popular poet Shamsur Rahman in 1999. One has every reason to agree with Enayetullah Khan, the editor of weekly *Holiday*, that the so-called attack on the poet was a sham and that he has 'lost his face as a tool of propaganda'. Khan points out Bertil Lintner's 'Indian connection' for embellishing his article 'with Indian intelligence quotes as credible evidence of the Harkatul Jihad nexus between Pakistan and Bangladesh through the intermediation of the Inter-Services Intelligence (ISI) of Pakistan'.[54]

It is interesting that while the BNP-led government sued the *FEER* for damages to the tune of one billion dollars for tarnishing the country's image[55], liberal democrats and the media also condemned the *FEER* reports for its anti-Bangladesh stand. The *Daily Star* of Bangladesh (a 'liberal democrat' daily, soft on the Awami League) in an editorial mentions 'regular and credible elections', the freedom of expression, the existence of private TV channels, women's impressive turnout in elections, the rise in the literacy rate, women's representation in the armed forces and their gradual empowerment process in Bangladesh to portray a liberal democratic image of

Bangladesh. The editor considers the *FEER* article prejudiced, one-sided and highly irresponsible.[56] The countrywide condemnation of the article (with the exception of the Awami League corroborating the story) was soon followed by its rebuttal by foreign reporters, diplomats and others familiar with Bangladesh. According to Philip Bowring, former editor of the *FEER*, Western 'Islam-bashers' have been responsible for this type of 'media demonisation of Islamic nations'. He blames the avidly pro-US Dow Jones, who own the periodical, for the sensational story, in line with the Western media in the wake of September 11. 'For sure, some nasty extremists do exist in this as in all other countries, but the nation's secular polity and the precedence of Bengali over Islamic identity is rooted in its independent history', Bowring reiterates. To him, there is no point in going after 'make believe enemies' in countries like Bangladesh, as the real terrorists live elsewhere, including some of the major Western cities. He is critical of alienating hundreds of millions of Muslims, who he thinks, 'are far more moderate than Christian fundamentalist zealots such as Attorney General John Ashcroft in the Bush Government'.[57] Among several Western observers, Mary Anne Peters, the US ambassador to Bangladesh, was very critical of the *FEER* and the *Wall Street Journal* for publishing such biased articles on Bangladesh, 'a liberal Muslim' nation. She felt that investigation was essential to find out the truth behind the story.[58]

Despite claims by Sheikh Hasina and other Awami League leaders, in tune with the *FEER* report that there are Taliban elements in the country and in the BNP-led coalition government formed in October 2001, the allegations do not make any sense, as the Jamaat-i Islami is not a pro-Taliban organisation at all. To Hasina, two cabinet ministers belonging to the Jamaat and one of her contenders in the election represent the Taliban. She told this to a BBC reporter in the US. Another Awami League leader, former foreign minister Abdus Samad Azad, told the same thing to the visiting British Prime Minister Tony Blair in Dhaka.[59] And the BNP cannot be singled out as an ally of the Jamaat either. The Jamaat and Awami League were both opposed to the BNP government of 1991–6.

Conclusions

The mutual vilification of the two parties indicates how the country is sharply polarised between the pro- and anti-Awami League camps, the former representing 'liberal democracy' and 'pro-Liberation forces' and the latter, 'pro-Islam' and 'anti-Indian' viewpoints. The Awami League tries to get dividends by projecting the BNP as 'anti-liberation' for its electoral alliance with the Jamaat. This was evident in the aftermath of September 11 (on the eve of the parliamentary elections of October 2001) when the Awami League government pasted posters on city walls in Dhaka, portraying BNP leaders as 'pro-Taliban' and 'friends' of Osama bin Laden. Both major parties adopt expedient slogans and policies to secure power. The Awami League has no qualms about using the Islamic card for political leverage, just as the BNP does not hesitate to portray itself as the champion of liberal democracy and nationalism. However, nothing would be more simplistic than explaining the rise of Islamism as a mere by-product of the perennial conflict between the Awami League and its adversaries.

It is of course not possible to reject totally the presence of Islamic militants, fanatics, 'fundamentalists' and even pro-Taliban activists in the country. In the changed post-Cold War environment of globalization and market economy, which is forcing the less-developed countries like Bangladesh to adopt World Bank and IMF recommendations, at the expense of state subsidies and welfare, Islamism has emerged as an alternative order. Very similar to Pakistan, Afghanistan, Algeria and Egypt, among other Muslim countries, the Bangladesh polity has been divided between the Western and 'vernacular elite', to paraphrase Olivier Roy;[60] the latter representing the underdogs, forced to adopt alternative ideologies in order to survive. Leaders belonging to the upper classes have often espoused radical ideas in the name of establishing an Islamic 'welfare state'. Mujib for example, promoted 'national socialism' as a version of the 'welfare state'. In the post-Cold War era, Islamism has replaced the earlier doctrines with certain modifications albeit retaining the same mass appeal – to empower the underdogs representing the peasantry and the 'vernacular elite' from the lower middle classes. This is in part the result of a population movement from the rural to urban centres, which has made an imprint on the political culture of cities. Uprooted rural migrants tend to have close links with the clergy and the countryside. And as V.S. Naipaul points out, it takes more than one generation 'to change a village way of thinking'.[61]

Again, contrary to conventional wisdom, Islamism is no longer the monopoly of the mulla. In Bangladesh, the bulk of the Jamaat-i Islami cadres, if not the leaders, are not madrasa-educated mullas, but are from the various petty bourgeois classes representing the middle and poor peasantry, small businessmen and shop-keepers, school teachers and other under-employed and unemployed classes.[62] Many of them can be classified as members of the peripheral 'vernacular elite' or graduates from Bengali medium institutions – the least preferred in the private sector job market. They nourish a tremendous sense of deprivation and have the potential to turn very violent and anarchical. Their madrasa-educated counterparts – even poorer and almost totally unemployable in both the public and private sectors other than in some low paid teaching positions or as employees of mosques – are also angry and frustrated with anything that goes by the name of secularism and

Islamic resurgence and politics in Bangladesh

modernism. Historically, the replacement of Hindu landed and professional elites in the wake of the Partition, non-Bengali elites after the Liberation of 1971 and English-educated elites in the name of Bengali nationalism by relatively inferior and unskilled people has been responsible for social disorder, political chaos and economic mismanagement. The ongoing triangular conflict among modernists in line with globalisation, Bengali nationalists and Islamists in the country is reflective of the situation.

The people of Bangladesh have lost faith in the prospect of the 'welfare state'. The fatalist peasant masses are resigned to their pathetic fate. They are not posing a serious threat to law and order, as peasants 'never make history' and are incapable of leading themselves other than organising short-lived 'pre-political' uprisings reflecting their 'class-in-itself' mentality. The real danger comes from the disgruntled lower middle classes and the various lumpen elements in society. The broken promises of successive governments since independence, coupled with corruption, unemployment and misery, are adversely affecting the loyalty of the petty bourgeoisie. The fast disappearing middle classes can turn to the Jamaat as the alternative of the so-called liberal-democratic and secular parties. This, however, would not signal the ascendancy of Islamic militants and anti-Hindu communal forces. It is highly unlikely that the Jamaat and its allies would pose any threat to India once in power. Despite the alarmist views of some Western analysts, governments and their local adherents in Bangladesh, who seemingly have been influenced by Huntington's 'clash of civilizations' thesis, the ascendancy of Islam to political power in Bangladesh would not destabilise the region. However, the persecution and suffering of Muslims, for example in the Middle East and India, continue to provoke sympathy for their coreligionists and anger against their persecutors.

Notes

1 *Bangladesh Observer* and *Daily Star*, October 3, 4, and 5, 2001.
2 James C. Scott, *The Moral Economy of the Peasant: Rebellion and Subsistence in Southeast Asia* (New Haven: Yale University Press, 1976), pp. 5, 9, 13–55; Taj I. Hashmi, 'Moral, Rational and Political Economies of Peasants: An Appraisal of Colonial Bengal and Vietnam', *Second International Conference on Indian Ocean* Studies (Proceedings), Perth, 1984.
3 Taj I. Hashmi, *Pakistan as a Peasant Utopia: The Communalization of Class Politics in East Bengal, 1920–1947* (Boulder: Westview Press, 1992), pp. 4–20.
4 Asim Roy, *Islamic Syncretistic Tradition in Bengal* (Princeton: Princeton University Press, 1983); Taj I. Hashmi, *Women and Islam in Bangladesh: Beyond Subjection and Tyranny* (London: Macmillan Press, 2000), pp. 60–74.
5 Taj I. Hashmi, 'Islam in Bangladesh Politics', in Hussin Mutalib and Taj I. Hashmi (eds), *Islam, Muslims and the Modern State* (London: Macmillan

Press, 1994), pp. 103–5; Razia Akter Banu, 'Jamaat-i Islami in Bangladesh: Challenges and Prospects', in H. Mutalib and Taj I. Hashmi (eds), *Islam, Muslims and the Modern State*, pp. 80–96; K.M. Mohsin, 'Tabligh Jama't and the Faith Movement in Bangladesh', in Rafiuddin Ahmed (ed.), *Bangladesh: Society, Religion and Politics* (Chittagong: South Asia Studies Group, 1985).

6 Maulana Mansurul Haq (ed.), *Mr Mawdudir New Islam*, (Dhaka: Jamia Qurania Arabia, Lalbagh, 1985); *Jamaat Unmasked: The True Colour of a Fundamentalist Party* (Dhaka: The Council of National Religious Scholars – Jatiyo Olama Parishad, 2001). These publications reflect the views of the anti-Jamaat Muslim clerics; mainly belonging to the Deoband School of thought who run the Qaumi *madrasas* in the subcontinent.
7 Taj Hashmi, *Pakistan as a Peasant Utopia*, chapters 5, 6 and 7.
8 Basant Chatterjee, *Inside Bangladesh Today: An Eye-Witness Account* (New Delhi: S. Chand & Co., 1973), p. 155.
9 Chatterjee, *Inside Bangladesh Today*, p. 143.
10 Richard Eaton, *The Rise of Islam and the Bengal Frontier, 1204–1760* (Berkeley, CA: University of California Press, 1993), chapters 5 and 8.
11 See A.R. Mallick, *British Policy and the Muslims in Bengal, 1757–1856* (Dhaka: Bangla Academy, 1977), chapters 3, 4 and 5; Muin-ud-Din Ahmad Khan, *History of the Fara'idi Movement* (Dhaka: Islamic Foundation, 1984), *passim*; Taj I. Hashmi, 'Karamat Ali and the Muslims in Bengal, 1800–1873', *Dacca University Studies*, vol. XXIII (June 1976).
12 Rafiuddin Ahmed, *The Bengali Muslim 1871–1906: A Quest for Identity* (New Delhi: Oxford University Press, 1981), pp. 84–95, 160–5, 190; Taj I. Hashmi, *Peasant Utopia*, chapter 7.
13 Syed Jamil Ahmed, 'Bengali Nationalism Through Sociology of Theatre', in A.M. Chowdhury and Fakrul Alam (eds), *Bangladesh on the Threshold of the Twenty-First Century* (Dhaka: Asiatic Society of Bangladesh, 2002), p. 301.
14 Zillur R. Khan, *Martial Law to Martial Law: Leadership Crisis in Bangladesh* (Dhaka: University Press Ltd, 1984), chapter 4.
15 Taj I. Hashmi, 'Islam in Bangladesh Politics', pp. 110–13.
16 'The Proclamation [Amendment] Order, 1977', *Bangladesh Observer*, April 23, 1977.
17 Talukder Maniruzzaman, 'Bangladesh Politics: Secular and Islamic Trends', in S.R. Chakravarty and Virendra Narain (eds), *Bangladesh: History and Culture, Vol. I* (New Delhi: South Asian Publishers, 1986), p. 46.
18 Razia Akter Banu, *Islam in Bangladesh* (Leiden: E.J. Brill, 1992), chapter 9.
19 T. Maniruzzaman, 'Bangladesh Politics', p. 71.
20 Taj I. Hashmi, 'Islam in Bangladesh Politics', pp. 114–16.
21 *Holiday* (18 April 1988) and *Sangbad* (17 April 1988).
22 *Holiday* (18 April 1988).
23 Taj I. Hashmi, 'Islam in Bangladesh Politics', pp. 125–7.
24 Zohair Hossain, 'Mawlana Sayyid Abul A'la Maududi: An Appraisal of His Thought and Political Influence', *South Asia*, 1 (June 1986); M.S. Agwani, 'God's government: Jamaat-i Islami of India', R.A. Banu, 'Jamaat-i Islami in Bangladesh', in H. Mutalib and Taj I. Hashmi (eds), *Islam, Muslims and the Modern State* and my interview with Professor Ahmed Sharif over the telephone from Melbourne, Australia (15 June 1994).
25 Taj I. Hashmi, 'Islam in Bangladesh Politics' pp. 120–2.

Islamic resurgence and politics in Bangladesh 125

26 Jamaat-i Islami Bangladesh, *Bulletin: Jamaat-i Islami Bangladesh*, Dhaka, April 1991, p. 8.
27 Badruddin Umar, 'Why Has Ghulam Azam's Trial Emerged as an Issue?', *Ajker Kagaj*, 1 April 1992.
28 *Bichitra*, Annual Number, January 1992, p. 39.
29 Taj I.Hashmi, 'Islam in Bangladesh Politics', p. 127.
30 Jamaat-i Islami, 'Nizami Analyses Election Results', *Bulletin*, p. 7.
31 Ahmed Sharif *et al.* (eds), *Ekattarer Ghatak O Dalalra Ke Kothay*, Mukti Juddho Chetona Bikash Kendra, Dhaka, 1987; Borhanuddin Khan Jahangir, *Bangladeshe Jatiyatabad Ebong Moulobad* (Dhaka: Agami Prakashani, 1993); Aman-ud-Daula, *Ghulam Azamer Nagarikatta Mamla* (Dhaka: Dibya Prakash, 1993); Mawlana Abdul Awwal, *Jamaater Asal Chehara* (Dhaka: Agami Prakashani, 1993); Shahriyar Kabir (ed.), *Bangladeshe Shampradayikatar Chalchitra*, (Dhaka: Pallab Publishers, 1993); Shahriyar Kabir (ed.), *Ekattarer Ghatak Jamaat-i Islami: Atit O Bartaman* (Dhaka: Muktijuddho Chetona Bikash Kendra, 1989); Bangladesh Hindu Buddhist Christian Unity Council, *Communal Discrimination in Bangladesh: Facts and Documents* (Dhaka, 1993); Taslima Nasrin, *Lajja* (Dhaka: Pearl Publishers, 1993) and *Lajja: Shame* (London: Penguin Books, 1994).
32 *Daily Star* (5 August 2001).
33 My interview with Mawlana Abbas Ali Khan, the acting chief of the Jamaat, Dhaka (21 May 1991).
34 Afsan Chowdhury, 'Is "Islam in danger" slogan back in circulation?' *Daily Star* (21 May 2002).
35 Taslima Nasrin, *Lajja*.
36 Taj I. Hashmi, ' Women and Islam: Taslima Nasreen, Society and Politics in Bangladesh', *South Asia*, 18, 2 (Dec.1995) and *Women and Islam in Bangladesh*, chapter 6.
37 *Daily Star* (4 April 2001).
38 *Prothom Alo* (2 January 2001).
39 *Daily Star* (2, 3 and 4 January 2001).
40 *Janakantha & Jugantar* (6 January 2001).
41 *Prothom Alo* (6 February 2001).
42 *Prothom Alo* (9 January 2001).
43 *Daily Star* and *Prothom Alo*, (3 February 2001).
44 *Holiday*, (9 February 2001).
45 *Prothom Alo* (15 February 2001).
46 *Prothom Alo* (18 February 2001).
47 Taj I. Hashmi, *Women and Islam in Bangladesh*, pp. 88–9.
48 *Jai Jai Din* (15 January 2002).
49 Taj I. Hashmi, *Women and Islam in Bangladesh*, p. 204.
50 *Dainik Dinkal* (28 February 2001); *Holiday* (2 March 2001).
51 'Beware of Bangladesh – Bangladesh: A Cocoon of Terror', *Far Eastern Economic Review* (4 April 2002).
52 *Prothom Alo* (20 December 2001).
53 *Prothom Alo* (4 April 2002); *Daily Star* (4, 11 and 12 April 2002).
54 'O' Secularism!', *Holiday* (5 April 2002).
55 *Holiday* (5 April 2002).
56 '*FEER*'s prejudiced and one-sided cover story', *Daily Star* (5 April 2002).
57 'West's Islam-bashers playing into bin Laden's hands', cited in *Holiday* (12 April 2002); *Daily Star* (16 April 2002).

58 *Daily Star* (14 April 2002).
59 *Prothom Alo* (1 and 5 January 2001).
60 Olivier Roy, *The Failure of Political Islam* (Cambridge, MA: Harvard University Press, 1994).
61 V.S. Naipaul, *Beyond Belief: Islamic Excursions Among the Converted Peoples* (New Delhi: Penguin Books, 1998), pp. 257–8.
62 Razia Akter Banu, 'Jamaat-i Islami in Bangladesh', pp. 84–95.

8 Islam and political legitimacy in Malaysia

Osman Bakar

The nature of Malaysian Islam

Malaysia is a multi-ethnic and multi-religious country with Muslims forming only slightly more than half (55 per cent) of its population of 22 million. But it has the reputation of being a predominantly Islamic country that has been relatively successful in achieving political stability and inter-ethnic harmony. Undeniably, Islam's influence and impact on Malaysian society and national life has been pervasive and appears to be steadily growing, much to the dismay of many non-Muslims, due in no small measure to the active role of the state.[1]

Malaysian Muslims are to be found among all of the country's ethnic groups. However, the majority of them are Malays, the indigenous people of the country. There are only small numbers of ethnic Chinese and Indian Muslims, either as recent converts to Islam or as descendants of Muslim immigrants from China and India respectively. There are also non-Malay *bumiputera* Muslims both among the *Orang Asli* ('the original people') in Peninsular Malaysia, and among the numerous ethnic groups in the states of Sabah and Sarawak. Given the fact that Islam in Malaysia is predominantly the religion of the Malays, understandably it has assumed a distinctive Malay character as defined and shaped by the Malay worldview and cultural values. Not surprisingly also many non-Malays have tended to view it as a Malay religion, and not as a universal religion that is open to all races and ethnic groups. The mere social fact that all Malays are Muslims, a reality non-Malays experience in their daily life, has helped to reinforce the communal perception that Islam is basically a Malay religion.

Malay politics, religious attitudes and behaviour have generally tended to fortify this communal perception.[2] However, things are slowly changing. Positive changes in the direction of a more universal Islam are discernible in at least three main areas. The first significant domain of change is at the intellectual level of discourse. The idea of a global and universal Islam began to make a significant impact on Malay intellectuals, especially the younger ones, in the 1970s. The spread of the idea in a religious and political climate dominated by a Malay-oriented Islam was an important aspect of Malaysian Islamic resurgence that started at the beginning of the decade. The main force behind this intellectual and universal approach to Islam was the Malaysian Muslim Youths Movement (ABIM).[3] The second significant domain of change that has the effect of broadening the boundaries of Malaysian Islam is the Malay involvement in inter-religious dialogues and their overall interest in other religions. More Malays are showing a genuine interest in Islam's encounter with other religions and the propagation of Islam among non-Malays.[4] A major breakthrough in Malaysian inter-religious understanding occurred in March 1995 when the widely publicised International Seminar on Islam–Confucianism Dialogue was held at the University of Malaya.[5] The main aim of the dialogue was to explore and to highlight the common spiritual and moral teachings of the two religions. This and other dialogues that followed between Islam and Confucianism presented a new and encouraging chapter in the history of ethnic relations in the country, especially as far as the Malays and the Chinese are concerned. For various reasons the small Chinese Muslim community was particularly elated and responsive to the dialogues.[6]

The third domain of positive change is that of Islamic political discourses and practices. A new openness is discernible in certain segments of the Malay-Muslim community in the last decade or so. The opposition Islamic Party (PAS) under the present leadership is pursuing a political Islam that is ideologically oriented rather than ethnic-based as it used to be. Its 'universal Islam' approach has allowed for the admission of non-Malay Muslims as party members. In the past few general elections, PAS has chosen a few Chinese Muslims as candidates. This 'liberalisation' move towards a multi-ethnic PAS, which has been welcomed by proponents of a multi-racial national politics, has posed a kind of psychological challenge to the ruling United Malays National Organisation's (UMNO) ethnic-based politics. But more challenging to UMNO is PAS' stand on special Malay privileges. PAS leaders have often said Malay privileges based purely on ethnic considerations are against the teachings of Islam, which stands for justice for all irrespective of race and religion. PAS appears to be more willing than UMNO to abolish Malay privileges, a constitutional provision, on Islamic grounds. PAS is also prepared to accept a non-Malay as the Prime Minister as long as he is a Muslim. Although there is nothing in the Federal Constitution to prevent a non-Malay, even if not a Muslim, from becoming prime minister, Malay political dominance grounded in the structure of the political system ensures that in practice the nation's most powerful post will always go to a Malay. The idea of a non-Malay Prime Minister is an affront to the doctrine of Malay supremacy (*ketuanan Melayu*) championed by UMNO. But PAS political stance on the issue has forced Prime Minister Mahathir Mohamad to respond by saying it is a matter of time before a non-Malay becomes the nation's political leader. Regardless of their political motives, such statements by top Malay leaders on both sides of the political spectrum will have the important effect of opening up and liberalising the Malay political mind.

Even more significant are recent developments in the public discourse on the ever-controversial issues of the Islamic state and the right to interpret Islam.[7] The issue of the Islamic state in Malaysia is not a recent one. PAS has been harping on the issue for decades. But UMNO has rejected PAS' Islamic state as unsuitable and impracticable for Malaysia's multi-racial and multi-religious society. Recently though, Mahathir proclaimed Malaysia an Islamic state,[8] generating a fresh and even more heated debate on the issue. It is difficult for non-Muslims not to get involved and to take a stand in an issue of such national importance. In the process of making their position on the Islamic state known, either opposing or defending, it is inevitable that at some point the views of these non-Muslims will clash with those of some Muslim groups if not of the whole Muslim community. Recent events go to show that the majority of the Malay-Muslims does not seem to be prepared yet to tolerate the idea of non-Muslims participating in a public discourse on Islam.[9] Those few non-Muslims who dared to be a part of this new openness in discoursing Islam, and their Muslim sympathisers, have found out the hard truth that in Malaysia an open and freer discussion of Islam is still a thing of the future.

Generally speaking, Malay conservatism in religious matters has a lot to do with the nature and character of Islam with which they have been associated for centuries. Malay Islam is, from the very beginning of its history, homogeneous. Theologically speaking, the Malay-Muslims have known only one school of thought, namely the Sunni Ash'arite, especially as interpreted and articulated by the famous eleventh/twelfth century Sufi-theologian al-Ghazali. In the interpretation and practice of Islamic law, all of them belong to the Shafi'ite school of thought. Intra-religious pluralism is thus something entirely foreign to the Malays. Until modern times, when Muslims of ethnic Chinese and Indian origin began to be found in Malaysia, all Malays have been Muslims and all Muslims Malays. Thus the Malays had not experienced ethnic diversity within Islam either. This partly explains the suspicious attitude of many Malays to any attempt to liberalise the Malay religious mind so as to embrace a wider Islamic pluralism, especially if such an attempt comes from outside their community. Moreover, due to reasons connected with Malay political power and institutions like the monarchy, Malaysian Islam has become very much regulated by the state. The state's rigid control of all activities having to do with Islam is not helpful in speeding up the realisation of a universal Islam.

Relations of the state with Islam and the ulema

The Malaysian state's relationship with Islam is quite unique in the Muslim world. This evolving and dynamic relationship began at the time of Malaysia's independence when it adopted a constitution that made certain provisions concerning the position of Islam. The constitutional provision that 'Islam is the religion of the Federation'[10] makes Islam an integral component of the state. By virtue of this constitutional provision, Malaysia already possesses a certain Islamic character that makes it inappropriate to be labelled a 'secular state'. This provision also means that the state has a certain responsibility towards Islam. Since it is stated in the same provision 'but other religions may be practised in peace and harmony in any part of the Federation', the state has also a responsibility in ensuring freedom of religious worship for all religions.

The idea of Islam as the state religion and the character of the state such an idea implies have aroused much controversy in the days leading to independence from British rule. Prior to the adoption of the constitution of the new nation, there were three major contending positions on the place and role of Islam. Perhaps most important was the position taken by the Alliance Party, led by Tunku Abdul Rahman, considering the fact that the multi-ethnic and multi-religious party had been chosen to lead the country into independence following its landslide victory in the first general elections in 1955. The party proposed to the Reid Constitutional Commission[11] that 'the religion of Malaysia shall be Islam', but 'the observance of this principle shall not impose any disability on non-Muslim natives professing and practising their religions and shall not imply that the state is not a secular state'.

The next important position was that of the Sultans and Rulers, who had been traditionally the heads of Islam in their respective states during the colonial period, and an embodiment of institutional Islam in the context of Malay culture. The Sultans and Rulers at first opposed the idea of making Islam the religion of the Federation.[12] 'They were told by their constitutional advisors that if the Federation had an official religion, the proposed Head of the Federation would logically become the Head of the official religion throughout the Federation.' Consequently, 'this would be in conflict with the position of each of the Rulers as Head of the official religion in his own state'. Their initial opposition was understandable, since the only real powers and prerogatives left with them is over religious matters. Still, what has survived of the state Islamic establishment headed by the state monarchy is to be counted as a public institution of great importance to the Muslim community. This traditional Malay-Islamic institution together with its official ulema and religious administrators gives the state its Islamic character.[13]

Then there was the position of PAS under the leadership of Dr Burhanuddin Al Helmy, which clearly wanted to establish an Islamic state. Accordingly, PAS favoured inserting the declaration of Islam as the official religion of the Federation, but insisted 'Islam shall be the official religion in the real sense of the word, based on the teachings of the Qur'an and the Prophetic Sunna'. In a speech just a week before independence, Dr Burhanuddin emphasised that 'independence is meaningless unless and until the Islamic law has governed the life of the individual, the society, and the state.'[14] PAS' position on Islam then was no less significant for the nation, even though the party won only one parliamentary seat in the 1955 general election, the sole seat for the opposition. Its goal to establish Malaysia as an Islamic state had a strong appeal among certain sectors of the Malay community. As the results of subsequent general elections have shown, PAS has continued to grow in strength and influence to emerge as the Malays' traditional alternative to UMNO.

What came to be adopted finally is the now famous Article 3, Clause 1 of the constitution. The part of the Alliance Party's proposal on the secular character of the Federation was deleted. However, in interpreting the meaning of Islam as the official religion, Tunku as the first Prime Minister had consistently maintained the secular character of the Malaysian state.[15] The Alliance Party's intention in making Islam the official religion, as was explained to the Rulers, was primarily for ceremonial purposes, for instance to enable prayers to be offered in the Islamic way on official occasions. Satisfied with the explanation, the Sultans and Rulers gave way to the move for a Federal position of Islam as the official religion. They obtained a constitutional guarantee that their 'rights, privileges, prerogatives and powers' they have traditionally enjoyed as heads of Islam in their respective states will remain unaffected and unimpaired.

PAS, which prior to independence claimed that both the independence deal and the constitution were British-imposed, did not expect to see its demand for an Islamic state based on the Qur'an and the Prophet's Sunna met by the Constitutional Commission. The party promised to remain faithful to its interpretation of 'Islam the official religion': the state, it insisted, must abide by the teachings of the Qur'an and the Prophet.

Islam and the state under Tunku and Razak

The role of the state in the promotion and implementation of Islamic programs has been expanding steadily over the decades. The first Prime Minister of Malaysia, Tanku Abdul Rahman, while repeatedly saying that Malaysia was a secular country, allowed his Muslim-dominated administration was spending a considerable amount of public money on the building of mosques, including the first national Mosque, and religious schools throughout the newly independent nation in the name of the advancement of Islam. Muslim critics of Tunku's policy on Islam accused him of being contented with promoting symbols rather than the substance of Islam.[16] He might not have done enough for Islam, certainly falling short of the expectations of many Muslims, but what he did was quite significant especially in the context of his times, before the 1970s emergence of the Islamic revival movement, known as *dakwah* in Malaysia. PERKIM (Malaysian Islamic Welfare Association), The Annual Qur'an Recital Competition, and Tabung Haji (The Pilgrimage Fund) are Tunku's legacies that also happen to be imposing symbols of Malaysian Islam.[17] All these religious landmarks are at the top of the list of achievements that have made Malaysia well known in the Muslim world. PERKIM can still boast of itself as the nation's leading Muslim missionary body working among the non-Malays. The Qur'an Recital Competition has become a religious festival with a worldwide Muslim audience. Tabung Haji is Malaysia's best proof that Islamic economic principles based on the Qur'an can be implemented successfully in the modern world. The overall contributions of Tunku's Government to Islam are much more significant than what many Muslims are usually prepared to concede. It is his public image in the Muslim community as a secularist opposed to Islamic law that has tended to obscure the significance of his achievements.

Under his successor Tun Razak, the role of the state in the development of Islam expanded and intensified. More new mosques, prayer rooms in public places, and religious schools at all levels were built throughout the country, especially in rural areas where the majority of Muslims live. There was a greater emphasis on religious knowledge in the national educational curriculum, as the subject of Islam became compulsory for all Muslim students in government-funded schools. More significantly, under the directive of the Ministry of Education, Islamic studies programs were introduced and expanded at institutions of higher learning. Furthermore, Razak intensified institutional building related to the administration of religious affairs.[18]

However, from the point of view of the future relations of Islam and the state, the real significance of the Razak Administration lies in its major and far-reaching policies in the political and socio-economic domains centred on the Malay-Muslim and other *bumiputera* communities. We may point to four major areas of significance. First, to forge a new Malaysian identity out of its ethnic and religious pluralism, Razak proclaimed the *Rukunegara* ('national ideology'), formulated in universal terms was acceptable to all. The *Rukunegara* was criticised by some Muslims as not Islamic since it was not formulated in Islamic terms and as a reaffirmation of the secular basis of state and society. But the government leaders and other Muslims argued the

Rukunegara was fully in accord with Islam's universal teachings. Second, to address the socio-economic imbalances among its ethnic groups, especially the deep grievances of the Malays, he launched the New Economic Policy (NEP).[19] Again, the NEP was not short of Muslim critics eager to label it as incompatible with Islam. In response, Razak argued that the objectives of the NEP to eradicate poverty among all Malaysians irrespective of race, to restructure Malaysian society with the view of eliminating the identification of race with economic function, and to advance the cause of Malay-bumiputera ownership could not be opposed to Islam. The NEP would be in conformity with the need to strengthen Islam.

Third, to ensure political stability, Razak created the *Barisan Nasional* ('The National Front'), a broad coalition of ethnic-based political parties to rule the country. The coalition was representative of all ethnic groups in the country. In 1974, he even succeeded in luring PAS into the coalition, thus reducing political tensions and animosity in the Malay community. PAS' entry into the coalition boosted the Razak Administration's Islamic credentials, but it also gave an opportunity to the party to put an Islamic stamp on many of the state programs, not to mention the opportunity to expand its influence in the Malay community. Fourth, Razak's rule took off to coincide with the beginning of Islamic resurgence in the country. The state's increasing need to accommodate Islam during this period was partly in response to the challenge posed by Islamic resurgence.[20] An alternative Islamic opposition had emerged to replace PAS from among non-governmental and non-political organisations. Islamic resurgence in Malaysia as in other parts of the Muslim world was from the very beginning partly political in nature. Its rallying cry 'Islam is a complete way of life' was to drive home the message that Islam is not just a private religion concerned with rituals but also a public religion concerned with how a society and a state should be ordered and organised. In short, political Islam was an overriding concern of Islamic resurgence. The massive role of the state in the formulation and implementation of the *Rukunegara* and the NEP could hardly be pursued in a predominantly Muslim society on the principle of the separation of religion from politics. Thus, between the state and the Islamic resurgence movement, they contributed significantly to the expansion of public space for political Islam. A political process was set in motion for a broader Islamic transformation of Malaysia and a more engaging relationship between Islam and the state.

Islam and the state under Mahathir

It was perhaps under Prime Minister Mahathir, who took office in July 1981, that we witnessed the biggest and most significant Islamic transformation of the country. He sought to effect that transformation through what has been known as his 'Islamisation Policy.'[21] Clearly, his idea of Islamisation is comprehensive, one that would appeal to Islamic resurgence activists but strongly opposed by many non-Muslims, and he sought to put this idea into practice in almost every aspect of Malaysian public life. His 'Islamisation' program, both short and long term, embraces the transformation of the Malay mind and attitudes to be in line with the requirements of Islam and modernity, the inculcation of Islamic values in economic development and in the government machinery, and the creation of a national administration guided by Islam. He has also been concerned with the Islamic identity of his own party, UMNO, in the face of PAS accusation that UMNO is a secular party. In the domain of law, however, he took the stand that 'Islamic laws are for Muslims and meant for their personal laws, but laws of the nation, although not Islamically-based can be used as long as they do not come into conflict with Islamic principles.'[22]

In line with his Islamisation policy and with this stand on Islamic law, Mahathir established the *Shariah and Civil Technical Committee* with the objectives of upgrading the status of shari'a courts and ensuring all laws of the country will be in conformity with Islam.[23]

Mahathir's pet program, however, is economic development. His political aim is 'to make Islam in Malaysia synonymous with economic progress and modernisation.'[24] So obsessed has he been with the nation's economic progress and modernisation that one could almost say that even his Islamisation policy has been conceived and pursued in quest of that goal. For him, it is only through Islam, and thus his Islamisation policy that the Malays can successfully arise to the call of economic progress and modernisation. As a whole, over the last two decades, the Mahathir government had introduced numerous financial and commercial legislation, institutions, schemes, and projects that were aimed at elevating the socio-economic status of Malays and making them a competitive race.[25]

That Malaysia had undergone a very significant Islamic transformation over the last four decades is difficult to refute. But has the transformation been sweeping enough to enable Malaysia to be regarded as an Islamic state? The answer seems to hinge on what one means by Islamic state. Apparently, Mahathir feels Malaysia's Islamic transformation has been substantial enough to entitle it to be called an Islamic state even if one judges its credentials by the criteria used in classical Islamic political theories.[26] In September 2001 Mahathir proclaimed Malaysia an 'Islamic state'. That proclamation has received mixed reactions from the public. It is still too early for anyone to assess its impact on Malaysian politics and its implications for the future development of Islam. Indications are that the 'Islamic state' debate is set to dominate the nation's political discourse for the rest of the decade, and possibly beyond.

The state and the ulema

As true elsewhere in the Muslim world, the ulema had always been an influential force in the Malay-Muslim community both before and after independence. Before independence, the ulema had played a pivotal role in the nationalist struggle to liberate the country from colonial rule. After independence, they continue to play a significant societal role with some actively engaged in political life and others making their impact outside politics. To the extent that societal life is governed by religious principles and there is a need for interpreters of the religion in various spheres of life, the ulema's services are in constant demand. The influence and standing of the ulema in society usually fluctuates in proportion to the level of religious consciousness and observance in the community. Clearly, Islamic resurgence of the last three decades has elevated their influence and standing to new heights. Political leaders can only ignore this reality to their own detriment.

On its part, the state duly recognises the importance of the ulema and their political support, and accordingly makes efforts to develop policies and programs that would accommodate their interests and their societal role in the service of the state. The ulema officially in the service of the state are mostly associated with the religious establishment in each of the thirteen states in the Federation and the federal territory. These are the muftis, qadis, and other religious officials whose functions are to formulate and administer policies, programs and activities pertaining to the various religious laws and regulations, needs, and welfare of the Muslim community, including religious education, in their respective states. Following the gradual expansion of the religious bureaucracies at the federal level over the years, the state ulema have grown in numerical strength and influence. In theory, these ulema as servants of the state are supposed to be above partisan politics. In practice, however, the majority either voluntarily or otherwise often find themselves lending support to the ruling party.

Ever since democratic elections were held nationwide in 1955, UMNO and PAS have been fiercely competing against each other for the support of the ulema. It is a competition in which PAS clearly has the edge over UMNO whose political support among the ulema is secured mainly from segments of the state religious bureaucracies. The strong ulema support PAS has enjoyed, especially in the rural areas, is understandable given the Party's unequivocal political stand to struggle for the implementation of the shari'a, the creation of an Islamic government, and the establishment of an Islamic state, all of which are emotive issues for Muslims. Moreover, PAS has a historic link with the ulema given their instrumental role in its formation in 1951.[27]

Throughout the party's history, its ulema have provided the main source of leadership and political strength for it. Many of them are religious teachers influential in the rural community, because they own and run practically all of the popular traditional religious schools (*pondoks*). However, the 1979 Iranian Islamic Revolution marked a major turning point in the history of the Party's relationship with the ulema. Many members became attracted to the idea of Islamic political rule under an ulema leadership. The party's youth wing took an increasingly radical stance towards the UMNO-led government in their determination to establish an Islamic state. In 1982 the movement for an ulema leadership grew strong enough to force the resignation of its president, Mohd Asri Hj Muda who was regarded as not Islamic enough and as lacking the ulema credentials to lead the party to victory.

PAS' choice to succeed Asri was his deputy, Haji Yusuf Rawa (1922–2000), an Islamic reformist identified with the ranks of the ulema. Credit must be given to Haji Yusuf for having succeeded during his six-year leadership in transforming the controversial idea of an ulema leadership into an important element of PAS' new political ideology, giving practical shape to the idea, and popularising it in the Muslim community and even beyond.[28] Under his leadership the Ulema Consultative Council (*Majlis Syura Ulema*) was formed to ensure that 'the role of the ulema as leaders of the *umma* becomes more meaningful, and under their guidance all Party policies and decisions will always be guided by Islamic teachings and in conformity with them'.[29] He also broadened the concept of the ulema to include the religiously learned Muslim intellectuals regardless of their earlier educational backgrounds.

A continuity of ulema leadership begun by him seemed to be assured, at least for quite some time.[30] The party today is clearly in the firm hands of the ulema. In recent years, however, there has been a steady influx of intellectuals and professionals into the party, a phenomenon that reflects the growing appeal of Islam, especially the promises of political Islam to modern-educated Muslim intelligentsia, mostly graduates of Western universities. A number of them have been brought into the party leadership at both the state and central levels. Although it is possible that the inclusion of more intellectuals and professionals in the leadership will influence and even moderate the views of the traditionally trained ulema, that 'intellectual opening-up' has been done within the framework and in the name of the supremacy of the ulema leadership. The intellectual interaction going on inside PAS between the ulema, intellectuals and professionals may well lead to what has been termed in discourses on Islam familiar to Islamic movements in the country as the process of 'turning ulema into intellectuals, and intellectuals into ulema.'

This kind of cross-fertilisation of ideas between groups with differing educational backgrounds is not without precedents in the history of Islamic resurgence in the country. When ABIM was at its height of influence in the 1970s one of its successes that has had much impact on Malaysian society was the meeting of minds it brought about between its intellectuals and its ulema. Thanks to its progressive leadership and comprehensive Islamic programs, ABIM was then able to lure many non-partisan ulema into the organisation as well as PAS ulema disillusioned with Asri's leadership and his decision to bring the party into the ruling coalition. It was the combined strength of the intellectuals and the ulema with their common approach to Islam and various societal issues that has helped ABIM to emerge as a formidable force and the most dominant non-political Muslim organisation during the decade.

Besides ABIM, there are a few other religious and *dakwah* groups with their own ulema. In particular, we may mention the *Persatuan Ulamak Malaysia* (Malaysian Association of Ulema), the *Darul Arqam* and the *Jamaat Tabligh*, all of which are non-governmental.[31] The ulema association has the potential of turning into an influential organisation independent of political affiliations, but in practice its impact on society and the government has been minimal primarily because of a lack of dynamic leadership and attractive programs. In recent years, members of the association are more inclined to support PAS, thus causing the government to view them in an unfavourable light. The *Darul Arqam*, a neo-Sufi brotherhood with spiritual links to a Javanese Sufi was headed by the charismatic Ustaz Ashaari Muhammad, a former ABIM state leader. With several ulema in its leadership, the organisation was gaining popularity in the Malay community including among university students, public servants, and even UMNO members when the authorities banned the organisation in 1991 on charges of deviationist teachings. But many believe that the government had other motives in banning the organisation. Having a vision of a uniform Islam in which males were required to wear long robes and turbans and females veils covering their faces, and a simplistic approach to the problems of the *umma*, *Darul Arqam* was hardly the kind of religious movement that Mahathir would like to see flourishing in a Malaysia that he wants to fashion into a progressive, modern and powerful Islamic state. Similarly, the *Jamaat Tabligh*, a branch of the world-wide network known under the same name with its spiritual centre in India was severely criticised by the authorities in the *dakwah* decade of the 1970s for its *dakwah* practices perceived as obstacles to Muslim progress.

As previously mentioned, religious activities are very much controlled and regulated by the state, certainly much more than what we find say in Indonesia. Both religious and political considerations have motivated the government to impose various forms of restrictions on religious activities. Religiously, the state seeks to preserve the theological and legal orthodoxy and uniformity of official Malay Islam. Thus the Shi'a doctrine is not allowed to be propagated in the country and religious authorities are on the constant lookout for clandestine Shi'a activities. The monitoring of suspected Shi'a activities was at its peak in the first few years of the Iranian Islamic revolution. There had been cases of detention under the Internal Security Act of individuals including university lecturers accused of propagating Shi'ism. Interestingly Shi'a Iran is a regular participant in the country's annual International Qur'an Recitation emerging several times as champions. The state has also been active in monitoring and clamping down on what it considers deviationist interpretations and practices of Islam, especially those associated with Sufism and Sufi brotherhoods. Sufism is in fact viewed with great suspicion in official circles and practically all the Sufi *tariqas* in the country operate secretively.

Politically, the government seeks to prevent the politicisation of religion and its exploitation for sectarian political goals. In particular, it is duly worried that a greater freedom in religious expression would only result in more voices critical of the government with PAS gaining political influence at the expense of UMNO. The primary target of the government's strict regulations of Islam is individuals and groups highly critical of it, particularly PAS. Every program in the name of Islam, be it public presentation or religious instruction, study circles or media discussion has to be referred to the religious establishment for its clearance. As an opposition party that UMNO feared most, PAS finds itself greatly constrained in its movements, programs and access to the public by the state's rules and regulations. The government on the other hand has an unlimited access to its controlled media and mosques for the propagation of its interpretations of Islam. Despite the fact that the state's rules and regulations favour UMNO, the voice of Islamic opposition has grown surprisingly louder.

Islam and issues of political legitimacy

In Malaysian politics, there has long been the recognition that Islam is the most important source of political legitimacy for the state.[32] When the British colonial rulers were making moves to grant political independence to Malaya, they knew they had to grapple with the issue of the Islamic legitimacy of the nation to be born and to resolve it to the satisfaction of the Malays. The British were fully aware that Islam meant a great deal to the Malays being an integral part of their own ethnic identity. The Malays would not consider as legitimate an independent Malaya that failed to provide a respectable place and role for Islam in the new state and to guarantee their political dominance.[33] Of course, the British did not want to see an Islamic Malaya as insisted by PAS and earlier by *Hizbul Muslimin*, and in fact they used repressive measures against politically oriented Islamic groups to ensure that the movements for a Malay-Islamic independent state would not succeed. Their preference was for a secular and democratic Malaya that would appear to be accommodating Islam as well. They found in UMNO and the Alliance it led a more than acceptable political leadership that would help them to secure an independent Malaya. As discussed earlier, the alliance made the significant proposal to the Reid Commission to make Islam the country's official religion while maintaining its secular character. The two seemingly contradictory positions betrayed the Alliance's policy of political compromise, between appeasing Islam and remaining faithful to secularism.

The Muslim opposition perception of Islamic legitimacy was different. Its demand was to make Islam the official religion in accordance with the teachings of the Qur'an and the Sunna. A lesser goal would be considered as illegitimate and a failure to provide a respectable place and role for Islam in the new state. Given the wide support such a religious view enjoyed among the Malays, including UMNO's rank and file, it was understandable why the Tunku's Alliance persisted in making Islam the official religion. The exclusion from the Federal Constitution of any reference to a secular character of the new nation would only help to confer a greater Islamic legitimacy to the state in the eyes of the Muslims.

If the issue of Islamic legitimacy of the state was sought to be addressed by the various parties to the independence deal through securing acceptable constitutional provisions on Islam and the rulers as heads of the religion in their respective states, the issue of political legitimacy of the national government to lead an independent Malaya was sought to be resolved through the ballot box. The legitimacy of the Alliance to lead the nation into independence was decisively settled. The Party won the pre-independent general elections in 1955 with a landslide. Moreover, it garnered support from the majority of the Malay-Muslim electorate. The Alliance victory was, however, not without criticisms. The opposition complained that the elections were far from being democratic and fair, with the colonial authorities exploiting various instruments of the state including the draconian Internal Security Act in favour of the Alliance.

Ever since multi-party democracy was introduced in the country, the practice of democracy itself is often an issue of contention between UMNO and PAS as both parties seek to legitimise their respective positions on the issue by appealing to Islam. PAS would criticise what it considered as the undemocratic policies and practices of the UMNO-led government, especially arrests of its leaders without trial under the Internal Security Act, as repugnant to Islamic teachings on freedom, justice and fairness. The UMNO-led government would justify its practice of democracy, while admitting its more restricted form in comparison with Western democracy, in the name of public interest to which it says Islam gives due regard befitting Malaysia's pluralist society that is troubled by ethnic and religious sensitivities and prejudices.

Notwithstanding these opposition criticisms, with the kind of electoral victory the Alliance had won, not only had the party fulfilled an important criterion of political legitimacy in the eyes of Western democracy, but also in the sight of Islamic democracy. In traditional Islamic political thought, the legitimacy of a ruler to govern depends among other things on whether or not he commands the support of the majority of the people. However, securing the popular support of the populace is just an instrument to serve a higher moral purpose for the state, namely the just implementation of Islam's divine law, the shari'a. As for the Alliance it did not interpret Islam as the official religion in the same religious terms as PAS had done nor did it define the legitimacy of the government in terms of its obligations to the shari'a. But it was quite aware that it had to be seen progressively doing more for Islam and the Malay-Muslim community if it were to remain in power. Only with pro-Islam policies could it ever hope of securing the broad support of the Malay-Muslims. PAS in particular was always around to put political pressure on UMNO into doing more for the development of Islam and the Malay-Muslim community.

From the point of view of Malaysian Islam, the history of the nation's independence may be described as the history of the state's attempts to accommodate as much of Islam as possible with the primary intention of preserving and enhancing the Islamic legitimacy of the state. In practice the interests of the state and the government that runs it almost coincide with those of the ruling party, namely UMNO. Having ruled the nation since independence, the party has behaved as if it alone is capable of safeguarding the Malay-Islamic character of the state. Many Malaysians are wondering if it would be willing to respect a democratic verdict at the ballot box were it to lose a general election at the federal level.[34] Sceptics who doubt UMNO's willingness to play the role of the opposition in the nation's political democracy would readily point to the fact that the party has often behaved in ways that give the strong impression that it is determined to stay in power at all costs.

However, one notable thing about UMNO's success in maintaining its position as the dominant partner in the ruling coalition, notwithstanding its reckless use of state power, is its ingenuity in adapting itself to new realities and new moods in the political thinking of the people, particularly the Malays. UMNO has shown time and again that it is capable and willing to launch new political initiatives and undertake bold political ventures especially when its power base is severely eroded and its legitimacy to rule is seriously challenged.[35] The first big shock to the UMNO-led government was registered in the 1959 general elections. Only two years after UMNO's triumphant celebration of national independence, the party lost to PAS the control of Kelantan and Terengganu. PAS' fast-growing popularity within such a short

Islam and politics in Malaysia 141

span of time clearly showed that the twin issues of Islam and Malay nationalism on which it had passionately campaigned had a broad appeal among the Malays. Seeing its Malay power base undermined and thus its legitimacy to be the protector of Malay and Islamic interests threatened, UMNO quickly responded with various corrective measures to win back Malays who had switched support to PAS.

The formation of Malaysia in September 1963 was an event of a major political significance even when viewed within the context of our discussion of Islamic political legitimacy. It gave rise to new political realities and developments that forced the Malays to perceive their political dominance in a new light and thus with important consequences for UMNO–PAS rivalry. PAS and leftist groups had opposed the formation of Malaysia on constitutional grounds, viewing it as a British imperialist imposition on the will of the people in the territories involved. Regionally, neighbours Indonesia and the Philippines also opposed the new political entity with the former declaring it 'a neo-colonialist plot' and the latter laying territorial claims to the state of Sabah. Indonesia's Sukarno even launched his *konfrontasi* to contain the new nation resulting in armed clashes between the two brother nations. The *konfrontasi* provided the UMNO-led government with a golden opportunity to blow the trumpet of patriotism to its political advantages and to tighten its control on the nation. Although PAS opposed the proposal to establish Malaysia, it accepted as a *fait accompli* the newly born nation to which it swore allegiance. In contrast, leftist groups like the Partai Rakyat (the People's Party) refused to recognise the legitimacy of the new Federation, declaring it legally non-existent and that defiance did not come to an end until the 1970s. Several leaders of PAS and Partai Rakyat were detained under the Internal Security Act on charges of complicity with Indonesia to destroy the new Federation, which both Parties denied. With many opposition leaders under detention, and the country in a patriotic mood, UMNO and its coalition partners were well placed to lead the 1964 general elections into a resounding victory.

In a sense, in the formation of the new Federation was also sown the seeds of contention between two visions of political legitimacy and the seeds of a racial conflict that was to burst into actual bloodshed in May 1969. The inclusion of Singapore, Sabah and Sarawak had drastically altered the ethnic makeup and imbalances of the population to the disadvantage of the Malays and significantly favouring the ethnic Chinese. Coupled with this fact was the growing impact that Singapore's Lee Kuan Yew's dynamic personality and charismatic leadership had on the Chinese community not only in his island home base but throughout the Federation. Lee's vision of a 'Malaysian Malaysia' that in effect called for an end to Malay privileges and dominance electrified the non-Malays but angered the Malays who viewed the nascent movement for multi-racialism as a great threat to their rights and the survival of the Malay-Islamic character of the nation. Lee's People's Action Party (PAP) quickly spread its wings across the causeway to major Malaysian cities and towns where most of the Chinese live.

The great appeal that the 'Malaysian Malaysia' slogan had to the Chinese community needs to be understood in the light of splits within the community over issues of its legitimate political representation in the national government and attitudes towards the UMNO-led government. Lee's charisma aside, there were deep-seated reasons that explain the enthusiastic Chinese response to the 'Malaysian Malaysia' concept. The whole nation had often been reminded by the Tunku that as far as UMNO was concerned the MCA was the sole legitimate representative of the Chinese community just as the MIC was the sole legitimate representative of the ethnic Indian community. These two parties were considered as UMNO's trusted friends and permanent partners in power sharing. The problem was that many Chinese perceived the MCA as a party that was only concerned with the business and economic interests of the more wealthy Chinese and as too supportive of UMNO as long as those interests were protected. Those who questioned the MCA's legitimacy to represent the interests of the Chinese community either voted for the opposition or abstained from voting. If Lee's 'Malaysian Malaysia' concept had galvanised Chinese support, it was because they thought they had found a political vehicle that could effectively air their ethnic grievances and fight for their interests.

On the Malay side, both UMNO and PAS strongly opposed Lee's 'Malaysian Malaysia' concept. A verbal war broke out between Lee and other PAP leaders and UMNO leaders some of whom the PAP dubbed as 'ultra-Malays'. Ethnic tensions and polarisation increased as a result, with Malay–Chinese clashes even occurring in Singapore. Sensing that the PAP was becoming a big threat to the Alliance, the 'Malaysian Malaysia' idea fast becoming a divisive force in the country, and his international image eclipsed by Lee's, Tunku expelled Singapore from the Federation in 1965. But the political assertiveness of the non-Malays in hostility to the Alliance had gained momentum. The struggle for a 'Malaysian Malaysia' was carried on by the Democratic Action Party (DAP), PAP's successor in the Federation. Meanwhile, the Malays became more disillusioned with the Tunku's policies and leadership, after seeing that he had failed to remedy the economic imbalances that put them well behind the Chinese in material prosperity. They registered their frustration at the Tunku and UMNO by shifting their support to PAS. The anti-Alliance attitudes among both Malays and non-Malays but for different reasons clearly manifested themselves in the 1969 general elections when UMNO lost many seats to PAS and its non-Malay partners to DAP and Gerakan. The May 13 ethnic violence erupted following the Malays backlash against the Chinese over their provocative processions in the capital city in celebration of their election victory.

The May 13 tragedy forced UMNO to broaden its view of political legitimacy required for the peaceful and just governance of a multi-ethnic and multi-religious country like Malaysia. The Razak Administration had to address both Malay grievances that questioned UMNO's legitimacy to govern and non-Malay grievances over their legitimate representation in the government that raised the question of the meaning of a legitimate power sharing in a democratic ethnic pluralism. The NEP and the National Front were hailed nationally as the most appropriate remedial formula to address the various political and socio-economic issues that the tragedy had raised. The Chinese in the Peninsula were no longer represented in the government by the MCA alone but also by the then popular Gerakan, while those in East Malaysia were represented by other parties. With PAS joining the National Front, the Malay-Islamic legitimacy of the Razak government became more enhanced. With all factors of legitimacy considered, ethnic, religious and political, the UMNO-led government under Razak emerged as the most broad-based and the most representative in the nation's history. Malaysians endorsed the new power sharing arrangement and the legitimacy that went with it by voting the Barisan Nasional to power with one of its best performances in the nation's electoral history. Many groups had benefited from the post-May 13 political realignment, but clearly it was UMNO that had emerged as the greatest beneficiary.

Perceptions of legitimacy to rule, however, may change with time depending on several factors. In the case of Islamic legitimacy, one important factor that brings about changing perceptions of it among Muslims is the dynamic nature of Islam, the religion itself. The teachings of the Qur'an and the prophetic hadith may be understood and interpreted in conformity with the needs of the time. Changing political and socio-economic conditions can inspire fresh understandings and interpretations of Islam. Islamic resurgence beginning in the early 1970s was precisely a new Muslim response, especially of the young, to both domestic and global changes in society that had raised profound issues of cultural identity, social justice and so on. Its impact on the country among others was to raise societal issues that were to have important consequences on the meaning of political legitimacy from the Islamic point of view. The state then thought that a broad consensus had been reached on all societal issues of importance, leaving little room for criticism and opposition. Even PAS became an integral part of that consensus although it did make clear that it had a mission to accomplish within the *Barisan Nasional*, namely to help infuse Islamic values into government policies and projects. But the ABIM-dominated decade of Islamic resurgence in the 1970s challenged that consensus with its more comprehensive vision of Islam and society that proved too progressive and radical even for PAS.

ABIM's Islamic critique of the NEP and its increasing popularity among intellectuals, ulema and students clearly showed that although well thought out and formulated, the NEP has its shortcomings which could not be ignored. In ABIM's assertive view, the shortcomings were not minor but major and these pertain to the lack of a spiritual and ethical dimension in economic development. This missing dimension had to be brought in not just because Islam insisted on it but also because it would help to guarantee Muslim success in socio-economic development. As a strong believer in an Islamic approach to economic development as well as its Islamic content, ABIM went beyond the infusion of Islamic values policy advocated by PAS to pressure the government to establish Islamic economic institutions directly based on the teachings of the Qur'an. In questioning the Islamic legitimacy of many government policies and projects in education, law, culture, economic development and others, ABIM had also helped to cultivate in the Muslim mind a new consciousness and appreciation of the meaning of political legitimacy in an Islamic society. Generally speaking, Islamic resurgence had helped to create a social and intellectual environment in which more and more Muslims were acquiring the religious conviction that a government deserves to receive Muslim support only if its policies and projects are legitimated by Islam.

Mahathir became the nation's leader after a decade of Islamic resurgence had passed when such a political impact was being felt in the community much to the worry of UMNO. He was deeply aware of its long-term implications for UMNO and its legitimacy to rule in the sight of the Malay-Muslims whose Islamic consciousness was clearly on the rise. In a 1982 interview early in his administration, Mahathir did not rule out the possibility of Islamic rule in Malaysia.[36] In saying so he was not simply making a prediction of what is yet to come but he seemed to be working toward realising that political goal. What he did for Islam was more than just a response of a secular leader under intense pressure from his Muslim constituency as is often the case among contemporary Muslim leaders. It was also out of his personal conviction informed by his newly acquired knowledge of Islam. A thinker and an avid reader, he had showed an intellectual leaning toward Islam even when he was still the deputy Prime Minister. As a result of Islamic resurgence he had come to believe that secularism, the implementation of the shari'a and revival of Muslim glory would be the centre-stage issues of Malay politics for many years to come. His approach to Islam and his Islamisation policy clearly reflected his determination to address those issues in accordance with his modernist philosophical attitudes towards those issues. His wooing of Anwar Ibrahim and ABIM was a calculated strategy on the one hand to strengthen the Islamic credentials of his government and on the other to 'out-Islam' PAS in its Islamic challenge. Mahathir with the help of Anwar succeeded to a large extent in both.[37]

But Anwar has his own vision of Islam and his own political agenda. The cornerstone of his Islamic agenda is social justice that he strongly believes is the core of Islam's social teachings. His commitment to social justice that went back to his student leader days had been consistently strong. As the second most powerful man in the country, he was able to have an intimate knowledge of corruption in high places. Corruption was perhaps the main issue that brought Mahathir and Anwar into sharp political differences made worse by their conflicting responses to the 1997 Asian financial crisis and several other issues. Mahathir's sacking of Anwar from both the government and UMNO on alleged moral grounds but which many believed was politically motivated undermined the Islamic legitimacy of his government as well as the Islamic credentials of UMNO. Anwar's supporters who constituted the core of UMNO's Islamic constituency left the party either to join PAS or the newly formed Justice Party (Parti Keadilan).[38]

But where Mahathir's leadership suffered most was in the Malays' perception of its moral character as they critically questioned the legitimacy of Anwar's shocking treatment at the hands of the state. The more Anwar's deficient moral worth was sought to be exposed by the authorities, the greater was Mahathir's loss in the moral stature of his leadership. In the 1999 general elections dominated by the Anwar issue, PAS and Keadilan dealt a severe blow to UMNO. In the context of our discussion, however, more important than the Anwar issue in the long run will be the broader and more fundamental issues of Islamic political legitimacy that it had raised. The meanings of an Islamic leadership, an Islamic government, an Islamic state, and an Islamic legal system are likely to gain new importance in Malaysian politics with PAS possibly making greater impact on the Malay-Muslims. Mahathir's main task right now is to rehabilitate himself and his party in Islamic terms to meet the growing challenge of PAS. His 'Islamic state declaration' appeared to be a move with that goal in mind.

The declaration is likely to raise a number of issues that will invite critical responses from many individuals and groups. The first issue is whether the constitution is secular or Islamic. For a start, the DAP has challenged the constitutionality of Mahathir's declaration arguing all along that the constitution is basically secular. PAS leaders are of the view that the constitution is basically Islamic although they reject the claim that Malaysia is already an Islamic state.[39] If the same constitution is considered secular by some groups and Islamic by other groups, then clearly there is an urgent need to have a national dialogue on the meanings of 'secular' and 'Islamic' with the view of establishing whether these meanings are reconcilable or not. Secondly, there is the issue of the shari'a. Whoever hopes to establish an Islamic state will have to address the traditional Islamic view that the *raison d'être* of such a state is the implementation of the shari'a. Both UMNO and PAS have to present their positions on the shari'a in a more concrete manner and to allay fears of the non-Muslims concerning its implementation. Thirdly, the declaration helps to bring home the message to Malaysians that there is not just one model of the Islamic state. Some non-Muslims feel that to the extent an Islamic state in Malaysia is inevitable given Islam's dominance in the country, and to the extent that Malaysia is a democracy, they have to exercise their freedom of choice, either in favour of *Barisan Nasional*'s Islamic state or that of PAS.[40] Fourthly, a more substantive discourse can be expected on the place and role of democracy and religious pluralism in an Islamic state. The issue of the responsibility of the state toward religions other than Islam has in fact begun to be discoursed. The PAS governments of Kelantan and Terengganu have lately been paying more attention on the religious needs of its non-Muslim population. Non-Muslims have also raised the question of their rights as citizens to participate in the nation's discourse on the Islamic state.

Conclusion

It may be asserted that relations between Islam and political legitimacy as they pertain to Malaysia have undergone a profound transformation over the four and a half decades of independence, made possible by a combination of domestic and global changes that had impacted the nation. As appreciation of Islam becomes more widespread and deepens, so the parameters of those relations become progressively widened. Until the 1970s issues of Islamic political legitimacy had been defined primarily in terms of ethnic Malay and *bumiputera* interests to whom Islam appeared to be subordinated. With Islamic resurgence, Islam interpreted in more universal terms has become the central factor in influencing issues of political legitimacy in the country. At the heart of these issues in contemporary Malaysia is the contention between UMNO and PAS on the meaning and the legitimacy of the Islamic state, while attempting to remain faithful to the nation's original constitution and democratic framework.

Notes

1 A detailed study of the relations of Islam and the state in the Malaysian experience is yet to be undertaken. For existing discussions of the subject, see Osman Bakar 'Islam and the state in Malaysia', paper presented at the Tun Abdul Razak Chair of Southeast Asian Studies, Ohio University Conference: Malaysia in the 21st Century, Washington, DC (2–4 April 2002). See also Hussin Mutalib, *Islam in Malaysia: From Revivalism to Islamic state*

Islam and politics in Malaysia 147

(Singapore: Singapore University Press, 1993) and Norhashimah Mohd Yasin, *Islamization/Malaynization: A Study on the Role of Economic Development of Malaysia, 1963–1993* (Kuala Lumpur: A. S. Noordeen, 1996).

2 Hussin Mutalib, *Islam and Ethnicity in Malay Politics* (Singapore: Oxford University Press, 1990). See also Chandra Muzaffar, 'Malayism, Bumiputeraism, and Islam', in Ahmad Ibrahim, Sharon Siddique and Yasmin Hussain (compilers), *Readings on Islam in Southeast Asia* (Singapore: Institute of Southeast Asian Studies, 1985), pp. 356–61.

3 There are many writings available on Malaysian Islamic resurgence of the 1970s. For example, see Zainah Anwar, *Islamic Revivalism in Malaysia: Dakwah Among Students* (Kuala Lumpur: Pelanduk Publications, 1987); Chandra Muzaffar, *Islamic Resurgence in Malaysia* (Petaling Jaya: Penerbit Fajar Bakti, 1987); Judith Nagata, *The Reflowering of Malaysian Islam: Modern Religious Radicals and Their Roots* (Vancouver: University of British Columbia Press, 1984).

ABIM, founded in 1971 by Anwar Ibrahim has helped to lay the foundation of a universal Islam in contemporary Malay society through its numerous programmes dealing with ideas. It disseminated writings on Islam authored by leading Muslim thinkers mostly associated with the world-wide Islamic movements like the Jamaat-i Islami in Pakistan and the al-Ikhwan al-Muslimun in the Arab world.

4 A growing number of Malay academics and Islamic activists have turned to the study of Christian theologies and the history and development of Christian communities in Malaysia. See, for example, Ismail Abdul Rahman, *Gerakan Gereja Katolik di Malaysia* (Bangi: National University of Malaysia, 2000); Ghazali Basri, *Christian Mission and Islamic Da'wah in Malaysia* (Kuala Lumpur: Nurin Enterprise, 1992).

5 See Osman Bakar (ed.), *Islam and Confucianism* (Kuala Lumpur: University of Malaya Press, 1979).

6 Rosey Ma, 'Difficulties Faced by Chinese Muslim Converts in Malaysia', Master's thesis presented to the International Islamic University of Malaysia, 1996.

7 In Malaysia, the issue of the right to interpret Islam concerns both Muslim intellectuals who are not ulema and the large non-Muslim community. The ulema insist on restricting public discourse to the religiously competent but the non ulema seek to universalise the right. The right of non-Muslims to discourse on Islam is also being debated.

8 The proclamation was made on 21 September 2001 at the annual general assembly of the Gerakan Party, a component of the ruling coalition, the National Front (Barisan Nasional).

9 The recent case of Patricia Martinez, the first Malaysian non-Muslim scholar of Islam, is one in point. She was accused together with several Muslims by the Ulema Association of disparaging or insulting Islam for her remarks touching on Muslims which many considered as blameless.

10 See the Federal Constitution, Article 3, Clause 1.

11 For a discussion of the Alliance Party's constitutional proposal, see Ahmad Ibrahim, 'The Position of Islam in the Constitution of Malaysia', in Ibrahim, Ahmed, Siddique and Hussain (compilers), *Readings on Islam in Southeast Asia* (Singapore: Institute of Southeast Asian Studies, 1985) pp. 213–20.

12 Ibrahim, 'The Position of Islam in the Constitution of Malaysia', p. 214.

13 Even if Islam had not been made the religion of the Federation, Malaysia would still be a country in which nine of its states possess this traditional Islamic character aided by the position of Islam as the official religion in each of these states.
14 Kamarudin Jaffar, *Dr Burhanuddin Al Helmy: Pemikiran dan Perjuangan* (Kuala Lumpur: IKDAS, 1980), p. 215.
15 In 1984, in response to a question, Tunku reiterated his conviction that 'this country is a secular state' meaning 'it is not a Muslim state.' See Tunku Abdul Rahman, Tan Chee Khoon, Chandra Muzaffar and Lim Kit Siang (eds), *Contemporary Issues on Malaysian Religions* (Petaling Jaya: Pelanduk Publications, 1984), p. 25. In a 1992 interview Tunku again defended his secular interpretation of the Malaysian state. See Mutalib, *Islam in Malaysia*, pp. 94–6.
16 Tunku is well known for his criticism of certain aspects of the shari'a. See Mutalib, *Islam in Malaysia*, p. 95.
17 See Mohd Yasin, *Islamization/Malaynization*.
18 Significantly, in 1974 he elevated the Secretariat for the National Council of Islamic Affairs to the status of a full-fledged Division of Islamic Affairs in the Prime Minister's Office headed by a Deputy Minister.
19 On Islamic critiques and responses to the NEP and its impact on political Islam, see Chandra Muzaffar, *The NEP: Development and Alternative Consciousness* (Penang: Aliran, 1989) also his *Islamic Resurgence in Malaysia: Mutalib, Islam and Ethnicity in Malay Politics*, and Mohd Yasin, *Islamization/Malaynization*, pp. 178–9.
20 For example, as early as 1972, the Government had begun to embrace *dakwah* programmes. In 1974 the Malaysian Islamic Propagation Foundation was established and calls to prayer were broadcast on the government-controlled Malaysian Radio and Television (RTM).
21 For discussions of Mahathir's Islamisation Policy, see, for example, Diane K. Mauzy and R. S. Kline, 'The Mahathir Administration in Malaysia: Discipline through Islam', *Pacific Affairs*, 56, 4 (1983/4), pp. 617–48 and Mohd Yasin, *Islamization/Malaynization*, chapter 5.
22 See interview with Mahathir: *Utusan Melayu*, 26 and 27 October 1984 quoted in Mutalib, *Islam in Malaysia*, p. 30.
23 For a discussion of the committee's objectives, tasks and achievements in revising the laws of the nation in conformity with Islamic laws, see Mohd Yasin, *Islamization/Malaynization*, pp. 218–20.
24 See International Herald Tribune, 6 May 1991. For a critical discussion of Mahathir's economic policies, see Jomo K. Sundaram, *Mahathir's Economic Policies* (Kuala Lumpur: INSAN, 1988). Mahathir has also frequently emphasised the importance of Muslim industrialisation not only in Malaysia but throughout the Muslim world. On his thoughts on Islam and industrialisation, see Hashim Makaruddin (ed), *Islam and the Muslim Ummah: Selected Speeches of Dr Mahathir Mohamad* (Subang Jaya: Pelanduk Publications, 2001), pp. 263–8.
25 Among Mahathir's achievements are the establishment of the Islamic Bank, the Malaysian Islamic Economic Development (YPEIM) and the Islamic Insurance Company.
26 Ulema in UMNO have argued Malaysia has met the minimum requirements of an Islamic state stipulated by some classical religious thinkers. See Wan Zahid Wan Teh, *Malaysia is an Islamic State* (Kuala Lumpur: Malaysian Ministry of

Information, 2001). Patricia Martinez, perhaps the first to have analysed the theological arguments advanced in Wan Teh's booklet, was perfectly right in saying that 'it merits analysis because it is the most concrete explanation or envisioning of the Islamic state that the government has proclaimed'. For her critical analysis of the booklet, see her article 'The Islamic state or the state of Islam in Malaysia', *Contemporary Southeast Asia*, 23, 3 (December 2001), pp. 474–503.
27 See N.J. Funston, 'The Origins of Partai Islam Se Malaysia', *JSEAS*, 7, 1 (1976), pp. 58–73.
28 On the life, thoughts and leadership of Yusuf Rawa, see Kamarudin Jaffar, *Memperingati Yusuf Rawa* (Kuala Lumpur: IKDAS, 2000).
29 Jaffar, *Memperingati Yusuf Rawa*, p. 9.
30 Yusuf was succeeded by Fadzil Nor, a former university lecturer in Islamic studies and deputy president of ABIM under Anwar Ibrahim. Fadzil who died on 23 June 2002 is likely to be succeeded by Haji Hadi Awang, currently the Chief Minister of Terengganu and the deputy president of the party.
31 For references to these *dakwah* movements, see for eample M. L. Lyon, 'The Dakwah Movement in Malaysia', *Review of Indonesian and Malayan Affairs*, 13, 2 (1979), pp. 34–45, Mohammad Abu Bakar, 'Islamic Revivalism and the Political Process in Malaysia', *Asian Survey*, 21, 10 (October 1981), pp. 1040–59, Judith Nagata, 'Religious Ideology and Social Change: The Islamic Revival in Malaysia', *Pacific Affairs*, 53, 3 (Fall 1980), pp. 405–39.
32 For a good discussion of the major issues related to legitimacy in Malaysia, see William Case, 'Malaysia: Aspects and Audiences of Legitimacy', in Muthiah Alagappa (ed), *Political Legitimacy in Southeast Asia: The Quest for Moral Authority* (Standford: Stanford University Press, 1995).
33 For an extensive treatment of this general theme, see T.N. Harper, *The End of Empire and the Making of Malaya* (Cambridge: Cambridge University Press, 1999).
34 Although the UMNO-led coalition has never lost control of the federal government since independence, it has already experienced electoral defeats at the hands of the opposition in the states of Kelantan, Terengganu and Penang.
35 Case, 'Malaysia: Aspects and Audiences of Legitimacy'.
36 Mauzy and Milne, 'The Mahathir Administration in Malaysia', p. 643.
37 For a discussion of Anwar's early role and contributions in the Mahathir Administration, see Mauzy and Milne, 'The Mahathir Administration in Malaysia', pp. 636–40.
38 Keadilan headed by Anwar's wife, Wan Azizah Wan Ismail, was formed in 1999. It participated in the general elections that year winning five parliamentary seats including one by Wan Azizah.
39 In July 2001 in our conversation with Tuan Guru Haji Hadi Awang, we posed the question as to whether the Federal Constitution presents a major obstacle to the realisation of a PAS Islamic state. He replied 'just a few amendments to the existing constitution are needed'.
40 The DAP has rejected both versions of the Islamic state. But non-Muslim component parties of the *Barisan Nasional* appear to have no choice but to support Mahathir's Islamic state.

9 Divided majority
Limits of Indonesian political Islam

Greg Fealy

On the afternoon of 20 October 1999, cries of *Allahu Akbar* (God is Great) rang through the chamber of Indonesia's paramount political institution, the People's Consultative Assembly (MPR). As the final votes of the ballot to elect the nation's fourth president were recorded on a large whiteboard, the victory of Abdurrahman Wahid over Megawati Sukarnoputri was assured. Triumphant Muslim politicians punched the air in delight and hugged colleagues. Onlookers in the crowded balconies began singing the traditional Muslim anthem, the 'Salawat Badr'. Never before in Indonesia's 54-year history had an MPR session been marked by such an overtly Islamic atmosphere. The jubilation of Muslim politicians and their supporters was due in part to a conviction that Islam had won a telling victory over secular-nationalism and minority dominated politics.

Abdurrahman's election appeared to show Islam's power as legitimating force in Indonesian politics. He was the first genuine Islamic leader to hold the presidency. A religious scholar, he was the chairman of Indonesia's largest Islamic organisation, Nahdlatul Ulama, and the grandson of one of the country's most revered ulema (Islamic scholar), Hasyim Asy'ari. Although all preceding presidents had been Muslim, none had serious credentials as an Islamic leader. Abdurrahman's nomination as presidential candidate had, moreover, won the support of all major Islamic parties. His rival, Megawati, herself a Muslim, was the leader of the main secular nationalist party and was portrayed by her Muslim detractors as antipathetic to Islam. Many Islamic groups also opposed her presidential nomination on the grounds that Islamic law forbade a female from becoming head of state.[1]

The euphoria of Muslim politicians at the 1999 presidential election tells us much about the national history of Islamic politics. Despite Indonesia having the world's largest Muslim community, defeats for political Islam have far outnumbered victories. Islam, though the avowed religion of a large majority of Indonesians, has rarely been the dominant element in the nation's politics. In fact, from the late 1950s to the mid-1990s, Islam was politically marginalised and subject to state repression under Sukarno's Guided Democracy and Soeharto's New Order regimes. Hence, Abdurrahman's election was seen as marking not just a resurgence in Islamic politics, but a new high point of Islamic influence in national affairs. Some Muslim politicians and observers went so far as to predict a new era of Indonesian politics dominated by a united, purposeful alliance of Muslim parties. As will be seen later, such hopes were soon dashed.

In the following discussion, I will focus on the role of Islam in providing political legitimacy in Indonesia. Drawing on Lipset's work, legitimacy can be defined as the capacity of a political system to engender belief that existing political institutions and leaders are the most appropriate ones for society.[2] A government is legitimate when those subject to its rule accept its right to make decisions. Legitimacy derives from the primary values held by a community and citizens are likely to accept a government's decisions or the outcomes of a political system if they satisfy those primary values. Islamic legitimacy concerns the role of Islamic values, concepts and symbols in shaping the nature of the state as well as its political culture. Therefore, a central question for this discussion is: 'to what degree have Islamic criteria moulded the Indonesian political system and validated leaders, movements and governments?'

In considering this, two broad points need emphasis. First, the discourse of Indonesian Muslims on politics and state is not monolithic. There have been a wide range of views about the role Islam should play in national life. At one end of this spectrum, Muslims have used Islamic principles to justify armed rebellion and the establishment of a breakaway Islamic state. At the other end, they have drawn on the precepts of their faith to sanction pluralist or even secular positions regarding the role of Islam in the state. Thus, there is not one set of values and symbols wielded by Indonesian Muslims but many. This diversity of aspiration and expression is important to understanding not only the cultural richness of Indonesian Islam but also its frequent lack of unity and coherence as a political force. Second, Islam, while seldom a determining factor in national affairs, has nevertheless been a consistently significant legitimating force. All Indonesian governments, including those which have tightly controlled Islamic parties, have been wary of alienating the Islamic community and have carefully cultivated Muslim support. Both Sukarno and Soeharto devoted considerable effort and expense to co-opting Muslim leaders to their cause or, at the very least, gaining Muslim approval for government policies.

As part of the discussion of Islamic legitimacy in Indonesia, I will look at the main variants within Indonesian Islam and the ways in which these have been played out in politics, before discussing the relationship between Islam and the state and the role of Islamic parties during the Sukarno and Soeharto eras. To conclude, I will survey the developments in the post-Soeharto period.

Characterising Indonesian Islam

According to the 1990 census, 87 per cent of the population are Muslim.[3] On 2002 population estimates, this would mean an *umma* (community of believers) of about 185 million, by far the largest of any nation in the world. But there are several grounds for regarding these figures with caution. To begin with, all Indonesian citizens must profess adherence to one of five officially recognised faiths: that is, Islam, Catholicism, Protestantism, Hinduism and Buddhism. A significant number of those who describe themselves as Muslim are only nominally so, or may not be Muslim at all. Many 'unrecognised' religious minorities find it less troublesome to be regarded as Muslims rather than as adherents of an official minority faith.

The picture becomes more complex if one looks at the major sub-cultures within Indonesian Islam. Historically, scholars have drawn a distinction between the devout and less pious Muslims. The most widely used typology was that of *santri* and *abangan*, popularised by the American anthropologist, Clifford Geertz, in the early 1960s to describe Javanese Islam.[4] *Santri* were the pious Muslims, those who adhere strictly to the tenets of the faith such as praying five times daily, fasting during the holy month of Ramadan and giving alms as well as avoiding alcohol or gambling. *Abangan* covered a broad category of Muslims ranging from the nominal or lax to the religiously active but syncretistic. The distinguishing quality of the *abangan* was that they practiced their faith either irregularly or in a way which deviates from ritual prescriptions set out in scripture. Though aware of the basic principles and devotions of the faith, *abangan* may choose not to pray or fast or are unconcerned about breaching the proscriptions of Islamic law on such matters as eating pork or drinking wine. The more syncretistic *abangan* can have highly developed religious lives in which a variety of Hindu, Buddhist or autochthonous practices are blended with Islamic ritual. *Abangan* do not necessarily see themselves as less pious than their *santri* counterparts, even though this is the way they are portrayed in much of the scholarly literature. Importantly, when considering their political orientations, *santri* of the 1950s and 1960s would usually vote for Islamic parties and endorse explicitly Islamic agendas, whereas *abangan* supported nationalist, socialist and communist parties and opposed concepts such as an Islamic state. One historical indicator of the size of the *santri* community was Indonesia's first general election in 1955, at which the total vote for Islamic parties was 16.6 million or 43.9 per cent of votes cast.

Within *santri* Islam, two major sub-variants exist: traditionalism and modernism (or reformism).[5] Doctrinally, traditionalists are to be distinguished from modernists largely by their strict adherence to one of the four main Sunni law schools (*mazhab*) – almost invariably the Shafi'i school – and also by their more eclectic approach to non-Islamic religious and cultural practices. Traditionalist ulema see themselves as the legatees of centuries of accumulated Islamic scholarship as well as being sensitive to the rich local tradition of religious life. Traditionalists are inclined to tolerate or adopt non-Islamic practices provided they are not specifically prohibited by Islamic law. Modernists tend to base their Islamic law and ritual on the Qur'an and Sunna (compendia of the example of the Prophet Muhammad) and reject non-Islamic religious and cultural practices. They do not adhere solely to any one law school but allow selective adoption or rejection of *mazhab* teachings. In addition there is often a socio-economic and demographic divide between traditionalists and modernists. Traditionalists predominate in rural areas, tend to be poorer and less educated, with many working as farmers, labourers or small traders; modernists are concentrated in urban areas, are better educated and more likely to be professionals, public servants or well-to-do private entrepreneurs.

The main traditionalist organisation is Nahdlatul Ulama (NU) or Revival of the Islamic Scholars. Established in 1926, NU now claims a membership of over 35 million, based predominantly in East and Central Java. As its name implies, ulema play a central role in the organisation. Prominent ulema, who are usually heads of large Islamic boarding schools or *pesantren* ('place of *santri*'), command reverence and loyalty from their *santri* followers and have extensive decision-making power within NU at both the national and regional levels. Formally, ultimate power within NU is held by the Shura (Religious Consultative Council), membership of which is limited to respected ulema. An executive board or Tanfidzia manages the organisation and can comprise both ulema and *awam* or 'lay' people. A number of smaller traditionalist organisations such as al-Jamiyatul al-Wasylia and Persatuan Tarbiya Indonesia or Perti (West Sumatra), Mathlaul Anwar (West Java) and Nahdlatul Wathan (Lombok) enjoy localised support but none has the national stature or political clout of NU.

The largest modernist organisation is Muhammadiya, which boasts a membership of 25 million. Founded in 1912, Muhammadiya's membership is more widely distributed than that of NU, with a strong branch structure in 'outer islands' such as Sumatra, Kalimantan and Sulawesi as well as across the towns and cities of Java. Muhammadiya has a Majelis Tarjih comprising experts in Islamic law, whose function is to issue fatwa providing guidance to members on shari'a-related matters. In general, however, ulema are less dominant than in the NU and professionals, academics and public servants have traditionally been prominent in the organisation's leadership. Other important, though numerically much smaller, modernist bodies include Persatuan Islam and al-Irsyad.

The contemporary value of the *santri–abangan* and traditionalist–modernist dichotomies is much debated by scholars of Indonesian Islam. To begin with, it is widely accepted that the proportion of *santri* Muslims, particularly in urban areas, has increased markedly since the late 1970s. This process, often referred to as *santri*-isation is evident in the increasing prevalence of Islamic attire such as headdresses and flowing gowns for women, the greater number of Muslims praying at mosques and taking the pilgrimage to Mecca, the growth in Islamic publishing, and the proliferation of programs with Islamic themes on television and radio. The result is that far greater numbers of Muslims appear devout in their practise of the faith and Islamic symbols and idioms now feature more prominently in social and political discourse than ever before. At the same time, the number of *abangan* has fallen sharply, leading some observers to question whether the category is any longer valid.[6] There seems also to have been a convergence of traditionalism and modernism in recent decades. Many of the doctrinal and devotional differences that once sharply divided the two streams are no longer problematic. Indeed, traditionalists and modernists commonly now pray together and co-operate on a wide range of religious and social projects. Some differences persist, however, such as attitudes towards the dead: praying at gravesites to seek spiritual intercession with God from deceased holy persons remains an integral part of traditionalist practice; modernists, in general, continue to disapprove of the practice.[7] Despite the easing of doctrinal disputes, political and cultural divergences remain a source of tension between the two streams. For example, during 2000 and 2001, NU groups attacked Muhammadiya buildings and leaders in several areas of East Java in retaliation for perceived modernist undermining of Abdurrahman's presidency.

The doctrinal, cultural and demographic fault lines which produced distinct traditionalist and modernist streams have also cut across politics. Traditionalists and modernists have proven to be uneasy allies and have often been direct rivals. Indeed, when it came to politics, each stream had major differences over ideology, policy and leadership style, and each used different aspects of Islamic thought and tradition to legitimate their particular approach to politics.

Islam and the state

Indonesia is often described as a secular state but formally it is a state based on religion. The first principle of the five-part national ideology, Pancasila, enshrines 'belief in Almighty God' (*KeTuhanan yang Maha Esa*). This was, in effect, a compromise between those wanting a secular state and those favouring an Islamic state. While there is no official state religion or formal acknowledgement of the authority of religious law in the constitution, the use of the term 'Almighty God' implies monotheism, a concession to Muslim sentiment.

The issue of the formal role of Islam in the state has been one of the most divisive issues in Indonesia's political and constitutional history. In particular, bitter debate surrounded the question of whether to recognise the shari'a in the constitution. This issue created complex fissures in the political elite. Most non-Muslims and *abangan* secular nationalists were staunchly opposed and *santri* politicians were also divided. While the majority backed constitutional recognition of the shari'a, some prominent *santri* favoured a religiously neutral state. Much of this debate focused on the so-called Jakarta Charter, an agreement struck between Muslim and nationalist leaders on 22 June 1945 as part of the preparations for Indonesia's independence. The most controversial part of the charter was a seven-word clause which translates as: 'with the obligation for adherents of Islam to practise Islamic law' (*dengan kewajiban menjalankan syari'at Islam bagi pemeluk-pemeluknya*). The legal implications of the clause were ambiguous. The minimalist interpretation was that the obligation to follow Islamic law lay with individual Muslims, not the state; the maximalist position held that the state must ensure adherence to the shari'a and that the charter would provide the constitutional basis for extensive legislation giving effect to Islamic law. Although often portrayed as an attempt to make Indonesia an Islamic state, the inclusion of these seven words in the constitution would not, of itself, have had this effect. After all, there was no proposal for Islam to become the official state religion; the seven words were intended as an adjunct to Pancasila, not a replacement. Furthermore, it remained to be seen whether Islamic parties would have the will and numbers in parliament to push through the shari'a-based legislation needed for the state to enforce Islamic law. In addition to the shari'a issue, Islamic leaders also succeeded in having a stipulation inserted into the draft constitution that the president be a Muslim.

The committee charged with finalising the constitution initially agreed to the Jakarta Charter's inclusion as the preamble, but at a meeting on 18 August 1945, the day after independence was proclaimed, pro-charter Muslim leaders came under strong pressure from 'secular' Muslims, nationalists and religious minorities to drop the seven words. The main argument was that the predominantly non-Muslim regions in Indonesia's east might break away from the republic if an Islamically inclined state was declared. Reluctantly, Muslim leaders agreed to exclude the charter in the interests of national unity. They also dropped the clause requiring the president to be Muslim. The omission of the charter drew a bitter reaction from many sections of the Islamic community. They felt that the charter's opponents had been alarmist and that Muslims had been forced into making greater sacrifices in establishing the new state than had non-Muslims. Islamic political leaders consoled themselves with the expectation that they would later win large majorities in the parliament and Constituent Assembly and could implement the shari'a through legislation and constitutional amendments.[8]

The Jakarta Charter re-emerged as a polarising issue in the late 1950s. The popularly elected Constituent Assembly, which began drafting a new constitution in 1956, became deadlocked in early 1959 over the issue of whether or not the charter should form the preamble. Nationalist and non-Muslim parties, with the backing of President Sukarno and the increasingly influential Army leadership, opposed the charter's inclusion. Muslim parties forced the matter to a series of votes in May and June 1959 but fell well short of the necessary two-thirds majority. On 5 July, Sukarno dissolved the Assembly and decreed the return of Indonesia's founding 1945 Constitution without the charter. The only concession to Muslim sentiment was the insertion of an imprecise clause stating that the charter 'gave soul' (*menjiwai*) and 'connecting totality' (*rangkaian-kesatuan*) to the constitution. This was little more than a gesture. The word shari'a was not mentioned in the body of the constitution and the vague acknowledgement of the charter carried no legal force. The charter was effectively buried as a serious political issue for the next forty years. Sukarno discouraged further debate on the matter and the New Order stigmatised efforts to implement shari'a as contrary to Pancasila and inimical to national stability.

Despite the exclusion of the Jakarta Charter, the state has nonetheless played an active role in the religious life of the nation, and Islam in particular. This has been evident in the existence and functions of the Department of Religious Affairs, in the statutory recognition of shari'a in specific areas of law affecting Muslims, and the special state funding allocated to a variety of overtly Islamic purposes.

Since January 1946, Indonesia has had a Department of Religious Affairs to administer matters of religious law, ritual and education. The decision to establish the department was in part an attempt to appease Muslim groups aggrieved at the omission of the Jakarta Charter.[9] Though formally serving Indonesia's five officially recognised religions, the department is largely devoted to Islamic affairs. Its Islamic orientation is evident in its logo, which depicts a Qur'an resting on a *rehal* (folding book stand), and its Arabic motto: *ikhlas beramal* (sincere commitment to service). The department is currently responsible for over 40,000 Islamic educational institutions, administers marriage law for Muslims, oversees the organisation of pilgrimages to Mecca, and manages ritual issues such as the timing of '*id al-fitr* and other major celebrations in the Muslim calendar. The department presently has over 200,000 staff, making it the third-largest government department.[10] Historically, it has been a bastion of Islamic patronage and the major employer of ulema within the bureaucracy. For most of the 1950s and 1960s, the department was controlled by NU and much of its funding and recruitment during that period favoured traditionalists. From 1971, however, the Soeharto regime appointed a succession of modernist intellectuals and retired military officers with modernist inclinations to head the ministry, effectively breaking NU's hold. Not until 1999 did NU regain the portfolio.

Several areas of the department's activities warrant special mention. A major element of its educational program is administering the network of State Islamic Institutes (IAIN). First established in 1960, there are now fourteen IAIN spread across Sumatra, Java, Kalimantan and Sulawesi offering undergraduate and postgraduate studies in a range of Islamic-related sciences to over 30,000 students. There is no equivalent state-run institution for any of the other four 'official' religions. Although academic standards at IAINs are generally lower than at state universities, the institutes have also produced a good deal of innovative scholarship in recent years, particularly on liberal interpretations of Islam. The department's authority in matters of marriage and family law also had an impact on the personal lives of Muslims. Department officials register marriages and disputes over marriages, divorces, inheritance and religious bequests (*waqf*) involving Muslims can be brought before religious courts. Until the late 1980s, however, the power of these courts was limited: their decisions were neither binding upon the petitioners nor recognised by civil and military courts.[11]

The Council of Indonesian Ulema (MUI) provides a similar example of state sponsorship of Islamic institutions, though MUI's role has often proved controversial. It was established in 1975 under the aegis of the Department of Religious Affairs, ostensibly to issue fatwa and advise government on Islamic issues as well as to promote good relations among Islamic groups. It has representatives from all major Islamic organisations on its board and it claims its decisions reflect the broad diversity of opinion within the *umma*.[12] In reality, MUI decisions have limited impact on the broader Islamic community, and most Muslims would pay greater heed to fatwa issued by their own ulema or by the organisations to which they are affiliated, such as Muhammadiya, NU or al-Irsyad. Many traditionalist ulema, for example, complain that MUI is dominated by doctrinaire modernists. Furthermore, MUI gained a reputation in many Muslim circles during the Soeharto era of being a tool of the government. A succession of decisions were seen as reflecting the regime's wishes rather than considered jurisprudential interpretation. The most notorious were several fatwa declaring that state lotteries in which senior regime figures had a financial interest were not prohibited for Muslims. Also, senior MUI officials were closely associated with the regime's electoral vehicle, Golkar, and frequently campaigned for the party during elections.

Defeat, repression and accommodation: Islamic politics, 1945–1980s

Muslim political leaders of the 1950s and 1960s, when viewing the manifold failures of Islamic parties, were given to regretting that Indonesia's *umma* was a 'majority with a minority mentality'.[13] As has been discussed above, however, the assumption that Indonesians who shared the same Islamic faith also had the same political views was badly amiss. Indeed, the ideal of a politically united *umma* has been often invoked in Indonesian Islam, but seldom realised. The starting point to understanding why Islam has not enjoyed greater power as an autonomous legitimating force lies in an examination of the internal disagreements and rivalries which have riven the *umma* for much of the past century.

Arguably, the only period of genuine political union and thus, unity of legitimation, came in the first years of Indonesian independence. In 1945, acting on the principle of Islamic solidarity, almost all politically active Islamic organisations came together in one party, Masyumi (Majelis Syuro Muslimin Indonesia; Indonesian Muslim Advisory Council).[14] Tensions emerged between modernists and NU from the late 1940s, however, which eventually resulted in NU seceding from Masyumi and forming its own party in 1952.[15] From this time on, NU and Masyumi were, more often than not, political adversaries and relations between them were frequently acrimonious.

There were several elements underlying this contrasting political behaviour of traditionalists and modernists. To begin with, both parties tended to see themselves as direct competitors for a similar *santri* constituency and both vied for control of the Department of Religious Affairs with its lucrative patronage opportunities and capacity to influence grassroots Islamic activities. Religious affairs was especially critical to NU as it was the only section of the bureaucracy accessible to ulema and party cadre with a traditional Islamic education. Modernists tended to have state or modern Islamic educational backgrounds and thus were better able to compete for positions across the public service. Ideologically, modernists had a technocratic and economically rationalist approach. Problems were analysed and solutions formulated with only limited reference to public opinion; professional expertise and 'rationality' were seen as the key ingredients to solving problems. Traditionalists were more populist in orientation. They saw themselves as representing the interests and values of ordinary Muslims and believed that the community had the spirit and instincts needed to solve the nation's problems. Policies that caused suffering among grassroots communities were resisted, regardless of their 'technical' merit.

Finally, traditionalists tended to adopt a more pragmatic and accommodatory approach to politics than did modernists. NU used politics as a means of securing or protecting its sectional interests, particularly insofar as access to government patronage and the religious bureaucracy were concerned. In pursuing these interests, flexibility, moderation and a capacity for compromise became defining features of NU's behaviour. Traditionalist ulema drew on classical Sunni principles of political quietism in support of this approach, often citing jurisprudential maxims such as: 'avoiding danger takes precedence over seeking benefit' and 'one danger cannot be eliminated by recourse to another'. Underlying this was a view that upholding the authority of (traditionalist) ulema and the schools of law as well as ensuring order and piety in the *umma* were paramount.[16] The modernists, by contrast, emphasised resoluteness and consistency in their approach to politics. They were reluctant to compromise on core matters of policy and frequently quoted passages from the Qur'an and hadith enjoining steadfastness and commitment to what is deemed right.

In practical politics, these differences inclined NU and Masyumi towards alliances with non-Islamic parties rather than with each other. NU was drawn to the Indonesian Nationalist Party (PNI), with its populist, Java-centric orientation; Masyumi found co-operation with the technocratic Socialist Party (PSI) and outer islands-based Christian parties more congenial. Importantly, neither NU's nor Masyumi's non-Muslim partners stood in the way of their gaining control of the Department of Religious Affairs. Only on overtly Islamic issues such as the Jakarta Charter did NU and Masyumi co-operate closely.

The lack of solidarity between NU and Masyumi became a major element in the political dynamic from the late 1950s, when Sukarno and the army were pushing Indonesia towards the authoritarian Guided Democracy. Masyumi was implacably opposed to the dismantling of parliamentary democracy, arguing that it was not only a breach of the community's democratic rights but also contrary to the Islamic principle that there be consultation and deliberation (*shura*) between the ruler and ruled. NU reluctantly agreed to Guided Democracy, fearing that its own interests as well as those of the broader *umma* would be jeopardised if it refused to participate. NU's acquiescence was crucial to the success of the Guided Democracy forces. Sukarno portrayed his new regime as uniting the diverse strands of Indonesian politics but this claim was only credible once one of the major Islamic parties was involved. The president later coined the acronym Nasakom (i.e. Nasionalis–Agama–Komunis or Nationalist–Religion–Communist) to describe the supposed integration of disparate elements. NU became the main representative of the 'religion' element and, in return for keeping control of the Department of Religious Affairs, provided a measure of Islamic legitimacy to the regime. NU leaders intoned that Guided Democracy was consistent with Islamic precepts as it provided both strong leadership and consultation. Despite Sukarno's concern to garner Islamic endorsement, the central legitimating theme of the regime was 'revolution'; Islam was, at best, only a secondary element.

The authoritarian shift marked the start of more than thirty years of state repression of political Islam. Sukarno banned Masyumi in 1960 and two years later senior Masyumi leaders were arrested and detained until 1967. The representation of Islamic parties in the restructured parliament was just 25 per cent, down from 45 per cent in the previous democratically elected parliament. NU's influence over the direction of government was much reduced. Arguably, the disunity of Islamic parties in facing the threat of Guided Democracy, paved the way for Islam's political marginalisation.

The New Order regime that came to power in 1966 proved even more antagonistic towards Islam as a political force. Soeharto, himself, was strongly *abangan* and innately suspicious of *santri*, as also were most of the key figures in the regime. Few *santri* enjoyed high office, and Christians and *abangan* commanded disproportionate influence within government. In its early years, the regime embarked on a determined program to depoliticise Islam. It refused to allow the rehabilitation of Masyumi in 1967, but did permit the formation of a new Masyumi-based party, Parmusi (an acronym for the Indonesian Muslim Party), on condition that no leaders from the banned party held senior positions in the new one. During the 1971 election campaign, the first of the New Order period, Parmusi and particularly NU were subjected to widespread intimidation and abuse from the security forces and government officials. In 1973, the regime forced the amalgamation of the four legal Islamic parties to form the United Development Party (PPP). From the outset, the New Order undermined the party's effectiveness by manipulating rivalries between its NU and Parmusi components. It also restricted PPP's ability to appeal to Muslim voters by imposing a succession of electoral restrictions, including bans on the use of the Arabic language and Islamic symbols. Despite this, the party succeeded in attracting almost 30 per cent of the vote in the 1977 and 1982 elections though this was still less than half of the vote for the regime's party, Golkar. The New Order's most bitterly resisted move came in 1984–5, when it ordered all social and political organisations to have Pancasila as their sole ideological foundation (*asas tunggal*).[17] Although most Islamic organisations eventually complied, they did so only after immense pressure and the threat of dissolution from the regime.[18]

In contrast to its repression of Islam as an independent political force, the regime was a generous patron of 'religious' Islamic activities and infrastructure. For example, in the mid- to late 1980s, over US$30 million was allocated to mosque construction, leading to an increase in the number of mosques from 507,175 in 1985 to 550,676 in 1990.[19] Soeharto, himself, established the Pancasila Muslim Service Foundation (YAMP) in 1982, for the stated purpose of developing socio-religious resources for the *umat*.[20] By 1991, YAMP had raised over US$80 million and built more than 400 mosques. Undoubtedly, these activities had a political objective: through such beneficence the regime could parry accusations that it was anti-Islamic.

The New Order was especially magnanimous towards Muslim leaders and groups which directly supported Golkar or one of its many affiliates. A number of special Golkar affiliate organisations were established with the purpose of attracting and mobilising Islamic support for the party. These included an Islamic education wing (GUPPI), a proselytisation council (MDI), an ulema corps (Satkar Ulama) and a sufi order (PTI). Involvement in such organisations brought access to power and patronage as well as an obligation to campaign for Golkar at elections and endorse government policies. Soeharto's corporatist agenda allowed Golkar-affiliated Muslim groups little genuine influence over government decisions. The regime wanted Islamic legitimation with only token concessions to Muslim political sentiment. As with Guided Democracy, the New Order used Islam as a secondary validating tool; its primary legitimacy rested upon 'development' and 'order'.

Islamic reform and political revival, 1980–2001

At the height of the New Order's political repression of Islam during the late 1970s and early 1980s, new patterns of thinking emerged in the *umma*, particularly among younger intellectuals, which would have a major impact on the nature of Islamic legitimation. This phenomenon, which was initially called the 'reform movement' (*gerakan pembaruan*) and more recently 'cultural Islam' (*Islam kultural*), would consciously reject much of the political agenda pursued by Islamic parties since independence and seek to redefine Islam's relations with and role in the state. Key figures in this movement included Abdurrahman Wahid and Nurcholish Madjid.

Cultural Islam's critique of political Islam contained several key elements. The first is that Islamic parties had succeeded in few of their goals. They had failed to have the Jakarta Charter inserted into the constitution, had been unable to unite Muslims politically, had not gained a majority of votes at general elections, and had rarely been able to get Islamic inspired laws into the statutes. Therefore, they argued, Muslims needed to find other ways of achieving their aspirations. This is perhaps best summed up in Nurcholish Madjid's 1972 dictum: 'Islam yes; Islamic parties no'. Second, political Islam's confrontation with the New Order had been misguided and counter-productive, resulting in greater suspicion towards and marginalisation of the Muslim community. The coercive might of the Soeharto regime far exceeded the power of the Islamic parties and hence, Islam would always be the loser in any confrontation. Third, the preoccupation of Islamic leaders with politics had led to a neglect of the intellectual and cultural dimensions of religious life. Too many Muslim politicians had become consumed with winning seats in parliament and had failed to foster new thinking and approaches to enriching and strengthening the faith.[21]

The solution to these problems, according to the proponents of cultural Islam, was to revitalise the faith through cultural, intellectual and social means rather than through purely political means. Instead of seeking to create a pious society through state-enforced Islamic law, far better, they argued, for Muslims to become more devout through a deeper understanding of Islamic principles and thought. In other words, inner religious life counted for more than external politico-legal conditions. The cultural Islam movement called on Muslims to bring intellectual fervour to their faith and particularly espoused an Islamically based liberal agenda. It wanted Muslims to be critical and creative, questioning old beliefs and producing challenging new approaches to applying the faith in contemporary society. The movement has produced much new scholarship in which Islam was used as a basis for developing concepts regarding such issues as the environment, human rights, gender equality, democratisation, civil society and scientific advancement. Many of these thinkers were set on demonstrating that Islam was not an inherently conservative religion, but in fact could be a 'progressive' and 'transformative' force.

Cultural Islam's attitudes towards the formal role of the shari'a in the state were especially controversial. Many younger intellectuals repudiated the concept of an Islamic state, arguing that the Qur'an contains no prescription for the structure of the state. Nurcholish Madjid and Abdurrahman Wahid, for example, argued that the case for an Islamic state rested on faulty exegesis and that the concept had wrongly been sacralised by successive generations of Muslim politicians. They supported the religiously neutral Pancasila as the basis of the Indonesian state, asserting that the pluralism and religious equality inherent in this were consistent with Islamic principles. They furthermore questioned the assumption, widely held in Islamic political circles, that good Muslims should only support Islamic parties. They contended that pluralist, 'deconfessionalised' parties were not a priori less virtuous for Muslims than an exclusively Islamic party.

The values of this reform movement took concrete form in variety of ways. In the vanguard was Nurcholish's Paramadina Foundation which he formed in the early 1970s. It aimed to promote Islamic values which were inclusive and tolerant, through research projects, publications and seminars. In contrast to most other Islamic organisations, it targeted educated, well-to-do urban Muslims by holding seminars at luxury hotels and establishing up-market, academically selective schools and religious training courses. It also enjoyed considerable success at engaging senior civilian and military officials of the regime. Groups such as Paramadina helped to break down middle-class wariness of Islam. In the traditionalist community, NU under Abdurrahman's leadership also did much to popularise the cultural Islam agenda. In 1984, NU decided to leave party politics and return to its original socio-religious form. It withdrew from PPP and gave members the freedom to join or support the party of their choice. Many younger NU intellectuals became involved in civil society activities, such as forming NGOs engaged in fields as diverse as grassroots empowerment, interfaith dialogue, conflict resolution and gender awareness.

The New Order's own stance towards Islam began to change from the late 1980s. A series of legislative and institutional concessions to Islamic sentiment provided tangible evidence of this. Prominent among them were the expansion of the authority of religious courts in 1989, the establishment of the Indonesian Muslim Intellectuals Association (ICMI) in 1990, lifting of a ban on female state school students wearing headdresses (*jilbab*) in 1991, the upgrading of government involvement in alms collection and distribution, the founding of an Islamic bank (BMI) in 1992, and the abolition of the state lottery (SDSB) in 1993. ICMI proved especially significant. Led by Soeharto favourite and then Minister for Research and Technology, B. J. Habibie, it became a major vehicle for patronage and rapid career advancement for senior Muslim bureaucrats, intellectuals and professionals. In contrast to the preceding two decades, Soeharto now appeared set on pursuing a 'proportionality' policy whereby the number of Muslims in cabinet and senior military and bureaucratic positions would roughly reflect the percentage of Muslims in society. In his own personal behaviour, Soeharto appeared also to embrace a more *santri* form of Islam. He took the pilgrimage to Mecca in 1991 and began appearing regularly thereafter at events to mark major Islamic celebrations. The media also began carrying accounts of the president's interest in and knowledge of the Qur'an and prominent ulema became increasingly frequent visitors to the palace.

The reasons for this change of heart are open to some dispute. Many of the Muslims who benefited from this rapprochement asserted that Soeharto had (belatedly) realised the error of his previous repression of Islam. Some also believed it reflected a genuine awakening of interest in Islam for the ageing president. Political analysts believed, however, that Soeharto's relations with the armed forces were under growing strain and that he was cultivating Islamic support in order to counterbalance the declining loyalty of the military.[22] Many Muslims were aware of Soeharto's probable political agenda, but were unconcerned provided the Islamic community enjoyed the opportunity to consolidate itself within the nation's power structures.

Soeharto's downfall in May 1998 led to the dismantling of most of the repressive structures imposed by the New Order. Restrictions on political parties, the media and freedom of speech and association were lifted and democratic elections were scheduled for June 1999. For the first time in almost four decades, Muslims had substantial freedom in expressing their political aspirations. Their subsequent behaviour has provided a revealing indicator of changing attitudes and priorities. Two developments in particular deserve close attention: the fragmentation of Islamic politics; and the rise of pluralist Islam.

When the government allowed the registration of new parties, more than forty Islamic parties applied. Of these, twenty-one eventually contested the 1999 election out of a total of forty-eight parties. This proliferation of parties reflected a complex fissuring within the *umma*, which none of the major streams and organisations were immune. There were four NU-based parties and significant numbers of Muhammadiya supporters spread across at least five major parties. Another four parties used variants of Masyumi's distinctive crescent and star symbol. Never before had political Islam been so divided.[23]

In addition to this, psephological analysis suggests that probably more than two-thirds of Muslim voters in the 1999 election chose either non-Islamic parties, such as Golkar and Megawati's PDIP, or pluralist Islamic parties rather than Islamist parties. Pluralist Islamic parties were those which took Pancasila as their ideological basis but which nonetheless relied heavily on an Islamic identity or leadership to attract votes. On the basis of this, it would seem that Muslim support for a multi-religious rather than an Islamically based state has never been stronger. Arguably, cultural Islam has contributed to this commitment to pluralism but it may also be true that the New Order's unrelenting stigmatising of the 'Islamic state' issue has played a role as well.

Despite their electoral setbacks, the more Islamist parties remain committed to the Jakarta Charter. At the 2000, 2001 and 2002 annual sessions of the MPR, the PPP and Crescent-Star Party (PBB) proposed the reinclusion of the 'seven words' in the constitution but the motions attracted support from only a small minority and were emphatically rejected by mainstream Muslim organisations such as NU and Muhammadiya.[24] There would appear little prospect of the charter gaining the necessary two-thirds majority in the MPR in the foreseeable future.

At the regional level, however, the campaign for the implementation of shari'a is having some success. The north Sumatran province of Aceh has provided the most concrete example of this. Shari'a was promulgated under special autonomy laws in early 2002, though there is intense debate within the local Islamic community over the scope of the laws and details of

Limits of Indonesian political Islam 165

implementation. The shari'a issue has also attracted strong support from Muslim groups in South Sulawesi, West Sumatra and Banten, but is still well short of majority support. In a number of districts in West Java, shari'a has been implemented in a de facto fashion by local Muslim groups, often in concert with district government officials and ulema. Commonly in such areas, bands of Muslim youths patrol the streets enforcing the wearing of 'modest' Islamic garb for women, closing shops and offices during Friday prayer time and attacking nightclubs and red-light districts. At the time of writing, it is difficult to say how much momentum the pro-shari'a movements might gain. Presently, many Islamic parties see the promotion of shari'a as electorally advantageous and are likely to continue their campaigns in the future. But resistance within many sections of the *umma* to state imposition of Islamic law remains a major hurdle and will probably deny the pro-shari'a forces the support they need to enact the necessary laws in many of the provinces where such demands are heard.

The developments within Islamic politics since 1999 suggest that its long history of internal rivalry and disunity continues, despite ephemeral periods of solidarity such as that which resulted in Abdurrahman Wahid's election as president. Abdurrahman proved an inept and erratic leader and was eventually dismissed by the MPR on 23 July 2001 and replaced by Megawati, his vice-president. Many of his erstwhile Muslim allies led the charge against him and shifted their support to Megawati, conveniently putting aside their earlier objections to her secular nationalism and gender. Megawati, for her part, was careful to curry Muslim favour prior to her election by appearing regularly at Islamic celebrations, by taking the pilgrimage to Mecca and by casting herself as a product and patron of the Islamic education system. Despite her deeply held secular nationalist views, Megawati, like Sukarno and Soeharto before her, understood the legitimating power of Islam.

Conclusion

The central questions underlying this discussion have been: first, to what extent has Islam shaped the nature of the Indonesian state and political system, and second, what role has Islam played in legitimating national political leaders and governments? The answer to the former is that Islam has been a contributory factor in moulding the state but hardly a decisive one. It is important to note that most Islamic groups in Indonesia never sought to establish a full Islamic state, as was the case in Pakistan or Saudi Arabia. The great majority of Muslim leaders accepted that Indonesia would be a religiously neutral state based on Pancasila, though, historically, Islamic opinion has also favoured constitutional recognition of the obligation for Muslim citizens to uphold the shari'a . The failure of Islamic parties in the

1940s and 1950s to achieve acknowledgement of shari'a was a major blow to those seeking formalisation of Islam's role in the state. Similarly, the inability of Islamic parties to win more that 44 per cent of the vote at any general election has deprived them of the parliamentary majorities needed to drive through legislation reflecting Islamic values and interests; only a handful of statutes mention shari'a.

These constitutional and electoral failures are a product of the major divergences of view within the Islamic community. The segmentation of the *umma* into *abangan* as well as traditionalist and modernist *santri* groupings has given rise to markedly different political interests and agendas. Although Muslim leaders frequently use the rhetoric of Islamic solidarity, in reality they have only been united when confronted with a serious common threat or responding to fundamental matters relating to the practice of the faith. In general, none of the major Muslim groups trusts the other to represent its political and religious interests, with the result that intra-*umma* competition rather than brotherhood has become a chief characteristic of the Islamic struggle.

Political Islam has, nonetheless, won important concessions regarding Islam's role in the state. There is a large religious bureaucracy run through the Department of Religious Affairs which is predominantly given over to serving the Islamic community. Successive governments have also channelled extensive resources to Islamic groups. There is also de facto recognition across the political elite of the need to respect Islamic sentiment. For example, although there is no constitutional requirement for a president to be Muslim, in practice, it would be almost impossible for a non-Muslim to become head of state.

With regard to the second question, Islam has been an ever-present factor in legitimating national leaders and governments. During the four decades of Sukarno and Soeharto rule, however, this legitimacy was usually delivered in return for financial rewards and limited opportunities for advancement within the regime rather than for political influence within government. In the early 1950s and, more recently, since Soeharto's fall, Islamic parties have often won a significant share of power, though their policy differences have restricted their impact upon government decision making. Thus, Islam has seldom acted as an independent, cohesive or determining force in Indonesian politics.

Notes

1 For an account of the controversy regarding Islamic law and a female president, see Bernhard Platzdasch, 'Islamic Reaction to a Female President', in Chris Manning and Peter van Diermen (eds), *Indonesia in Transition: Social Aspects*

of Reformasi and Crisis (Singapore: Research School of Pacific and Asian Studies, 1999), pp. 226–49.

2 S. M. Lipset, *Political Man* (Baltimore: Johns Hopkins University Press, 1981).

3 Biro Pusat Statistik, *Penduduk Indonesia: Hasil Sensus Penduduk 1990*, series S2, (Jakarta: BPS, 1992), p. 24. This is the most recent published census containing figures on religious belief. Statistics for the other faiths were: Protestant, 6 per cent; Catholic, 3.6 per cent; Hindu, 1.8 per cent; and Buddhist, 1 per cent.

4 Clifford Geertz, *The Religion of Java* (Chicago: University of Chicago Press, 1964). Although Geertz's *abangan–santri* dichotomy has been the most widely used, other scholars have developed typologies with similar features. The Javanese anthropologist, Koentjaraningrat, used the terms 'Agami Jawi' and 'Agami Islam Santri' *Javanese Culture* (Singapore and London: Institute of Southeast Asian Studies and Oxford University Press, 1984).

5 The term 'modernism' is commonly used in the literature on Indonesian Islam to mean both 'reformism' (that is, the movement to internally reform Islam as a faith by, among other things, purging it of impure practices) and modernism, the process of making Islam relevant to the modern world.

6 Unpublished article by R. William Liddle and Saiful Mujani, 'The Triumph of Leadership: Religion in the 1999 General Election'.

7 Martin van Bruinessen, 'Traditions for the Future: The Reconstruction of Traditionalist Discourse within NU', in Greg Barton and Greg Fealy (eds), *Nahdlatul Ulama, Traditional Islam and Modernity in Indonesia* (Clayton, Victoria: Monash Asia Institute, 1996), pp. 163–89.

8 The best English-language account of the 1945 Jakarta Charter debates is B. J. Boland, *The Struggle of Islam in Modern Indonesia* (The Hague: Martinus Nijhoff, 1982). See also Endang Saifuddin Anshari, *Piagam Jakarta, 22 Juni 1945* (Jakarta: Rajawali Press, 1981).

9 The government initially considered calling the department the Ministry for Islamic Affairs, but eventually opted for a multi-religious function. For an historical account of the department see Deliar Noer, *The Administration of Islam in Indonesia* (Ithaca, New York: Cornell University Press, 1978); and Boland, *The Struggle of Islam*, pp. 105–12.

10 Zamakhsyari Dhofier, 'The Role of the Department of Religion', in James J. Fox, *Religion and Ritual* (Singapore: Indonesian Heritage Series, Archipelago Press, 1998), pp. 66–7.

11 Daniel S. Lev, *Islamic Courts in Indonesia: A Study in the Political Bases of Legal Institutions* (Berkeley: University of California Press, 1972); and Bachtiar Effendy, *Islam dan Negara: Transformasi Pemikiran dan Praktik Politik Islam di Indonesia* (Jakarta: Paramadina, 1998), pp. 283–90.

12 *10 Tahun Majelis Ulama Indonesia* (Jakarta: Departemen Penerangan RI, 1985) and Majelis Ulama Indonesia webpage <http://www.mui.or.id/index_i.htm>, 15 August 2002.

13 Authorship of this phrase is often attributed to the Dutch scholar W. F Wertheim, but the statement was certainly used by various Muslim leaders well before he popularised it in his book, *Indonesian Society in Transition* (The Hague: W. van Hoeve, 1958).

14 Masyumi was established in 1943 under Japanese auspices as a supposedly non-political organisation. Following the declaration of Indonesian independence, Masyumi converted itself into a political party.

15 Most NU ulema left Masyumi in 1952 and joined the new party. None of the other traditionalist organisations within Masyumi, however, heeded NU's call to secede.
16 Greg Fealy, '"Rowing in a Typhoon": Nahdlatul Ulama and the Decline of Parliamentary Democracy', in David Bourchier and John D. Legge (eds), *Democracy in Indonesia, 1950s and 1990s* (Clayton, Victoria: Centre of Southeast Asian Studies, Monash University, 1994), pp. 88–98.
17 For a good general account of this period, see Adam Schwarz, *A Nation in Waiting: Indonesia's Search for Stability* (Sydney: Allen & Unwin, 1999), chapter 6.
18 The (Secondary School) Islamic Students Association (PII) refused to replace Islam as its ideological basis and was banned by the regime. The Tertiary Islamic Students Association (HMI) split on the issue, with a breakaway section of HMI rejecting Pancasila.
19 'Sujud Syukur', Semoga Mabrur', *Tempo*, 6 July 1991, p. 28.
20 Bachtiar Effendy, *Islam dan Negara*, p. 305.
21 For further discussion of the *pembaruan* and cultural Islam movements, see Robert W. Hefner's, 'Islam, State and Civil Society: ICMI and the Struggle for the Indonesian Middle Class', *Indonesia*, 56 (October 1993), pp. 1–35, and *Civil Islam: Muslims and Democratization in Indonesia* (Princeton and Oxford: Princeton University Press, 2000), especially pp. 113–66 and Greg Barton, 'The Impact of Neo-Modernism on Indonesian Islamic Thought: The Emergence of a New Pluralism' in David Bourchier and John Legge (eds), *Democracy in Indonesia: 1950s and 1990s* (Clayton: Centre of Southeast Asian Studies, Monash University), pp. 143–50.
22 R. William Liddle, 'The Islamic Turn in Indonesia: A Political Explanation', *Journal of Asian Studies*, 55, 3, (August 1996), pp. 613–34.
23 For a discussion of the election results, see Greg Fealy, 'Islamic Politics: A Rising or Declining Force?' in Damien Kingsbury and Arief Budiman (eds), *Indonesia: The Uncertain Transition* (Adelaide: Crawford House, 2001), pp. 119–36. Interestingly, the process of fragmentation has continued since the election, with each of the five largest Islamic parties experiencing internal ructions and the splitting away of dissident factions.
24 No vote was taken on the issue at the annual MPR sessions but in the deliberations on the Jakarta Charter, seemingly less than 20 per cent of members were in favour of its reinsertion.

10 State legitimacy

Shahram Akbarzadeh

Secular leaders in the Muslim world appear to have adopted a two-pronged policy of appeasement and suppression in relation to Islam in order to consolidate their rule and eliminate Islamic contenders to power. The incorporation of Islamic symbols and lexicon in manifestations of state power is justified by reference to the inseparability of Islam and national identity. The adoption of Islamic symbols are designed to bolster the state's legitimacy, complementing its legal, constitutional or dynastic rule. This holds true for all Muslim states. Even in the Islamic Republic of Iran and Saudi Arabia, where Islam is regarded as the primary source of authority, the state relies on a combination of factors (from republican impulses to social welfare) to continually regenerate its legitimacy. This trend has enjoyed a salient rise in the past decades, commensurate with the growth of Islamic opposition movements.[1] The dynamism of the relationship between the ruling elite and political Islam appears to have had a ratchet effect on the public visibility of Islam and its influence in the political domain. In most cases, this is not a desired outcome for the political leadership. But political expediency prevents the leadership from making any bold moves to wind back Islam from the political domain. Instead the state concentrates on controlling the message that is delivered by official members of ulema, favouring the complacent interpretations of Islam. Whether or not this degree of control can be maintained is unclear; it is becoming less and less possible to conceive the Muslim world in secular terms. The temporal and the religious trajectories seem to be converging.

What does this mean for the legitimacy of the secular political leadership and the modern territorial state? Although these two have been historically related, there is increasing evidence that their prospects may diverge. While secularism in its conventional European form of clear demarcation between religion and the state is becoming less and less relevant to, or desired by, Muslim societies, the modern model of statehood (with its claims on demarcated territory and representing a 'nation') has enjoyed an ever-growing popularity. In a historic twist, the secular leadership which was central to the creation of the modern state in the Muslim world is increasingly finding itself under threat and in danger of being marginalised, but the state appears to gather stature and retain its relevance, albeit in an Islamic form. The threat posed by political Islam to the legitimacy of the ruling elite, therefore, should not be interpreted as a threat to the legitimacy of the state.

The history and behaviour of Islamic groups in the past decades attest to the importance of state boundaries in the imagination of political Islam. Three cases may be enumerated to illustrate this point.

- The Muslim Brotherhood is perhaps a pertinent example. Founded by Hassan al-Banna in Egypt (1928), the Muslim Brotherhood (*al-Ikhwan al-Muslimun*) soon inspired other activists in the Arab world. The Brotherhood's message of social justice and strength in (Islamic) unity found resonance in Arab societies, especially in the wake of their crushing defeat in the Arab–Israeli war of 1948–9 – an experience to be revisited in subsequent Arab–Israeli wars. By the 1950s, the Muslim Brotherhood had established a foothold in Jordan, Syria and the Palestinian occupied territories. This impressive expansion seemed to point to the pre-eminence of the ideal transnational community (*umma*), at least within the Arab world. After all, was not it the explicit objective of the Muslim Brotherhood to establish God's sovereignty on earth, unbounded by man-made state boundaries? Yet, as each branch developed, it found itself preoccupied with uniquely national issues and challenges, pushing the ideal of Islamic unity further to the periphery and confined to the realm of abstracts.[2] A case in point is the Palestinian experience. Ahmed Yassin, the leader of the Palestinian Muslim Brotherhood in the 1970s, who later founded the radical Hamas movement in 1987, has exclusively focused on Palestinian liberation, albeit in an Islamic form, as his cause.
- Jamaat-i Islami (The Islamic Society) was formed in 1941 by Mawlana Mawdudi in the Indian subcontinent. Although Mawdudi did not favour the separation of Muslims, which the India–Pakistan Partition entailed, he migrated to Pakistan (Lahore) once that state was born. His political philosophy was influenced by his contemporaries and provided the ideological compass for Jamaat-i Islami. Mawdudi openly questioned the legitimacy of any political system and territorial division in the absence of the primacy of the shari'a. This was the guiding principle for the Jamaat-i Islami fraternity in Bangladesh and Pakistan. It informed the Bangladeshi Jamaat in its 'anti-liberation' stance, as argued in this volume by Taj Hashmi, because it rejected totally the idea of another division of the subcontinent's Muslim population. As in the case of the

India–Pakistan Partition, Bangladesh's break with West Pakistan was seen as a blow against the ideal of *umma*. But being faced with separate, exclusivist states in Pakistan and Bangladesh, the Jamaat-i Islami organisations appear to have made their peace with their respective states. Jamaat-i Islami in Pakistan has been a visible player with strong presence in the legislature. Similarly in Bangladesh, Jamaat-i Islami has worked within the system as a bona fide political party. Jamaat-i Islami leaders may keep the ideal of (eventual) Muslim unity alive in their hearts, but they do not allow the dream to distort their policies and actions within the boundaries of the state. In this they have a pragmatic approach to politics which amounts to acquiescing to, if not endorsing, the legitimacy of the territorial state.

- The history of the Central Asian Muftiyat, with its head office in Tashkent (Uzbekistan), offers another example on the precedence of exclusivist national criteria over inclusive Islamic ideals. Created in 1943 to cover five Central Asian republics, the Muftiyat experienced centrifugal pressures just as the Central Asian republics were emerging from the shadows of the Soviet Union. On the eve of the Soviet collapse, the Kazakh branch of the Muftiyat broke away from the central body and established its own 'autonomous' national office. This experience was repeated in 1992 and 1993 by other regional branches of the Muftiyat, as each republic asserted its independence and gained its own national Muftiyat. This process was no doubt influenced by the desire of the political elite to stamp its mark on all public organisations in the now-sovereign states of Central Asia. Replacing the transnational Muftiyat with national Islamic bodies was congruent with the momentous nation/state-building project. But the ease with which this process was carried out with modest resistance from the ulema, primarily in Tashkent, attested to the wide acceptance of the logic of sovereign statehood. The question, repeatedly raised in justifying the break-up of the Muftiyat, was: how can the Turkmen/Kyrgyz/Kazakh/Tajik Islamic bodies remain relevant and serve their respective national communities if they are accountable to a 'foreign' office, ie. Muftiyat in Uzbekistan?[3]

It may be argued by proponents of the transnational *umma* that pragmatic compromises with existing states do not detract from the ideal of Muslim unity. Pragmatism in this perspective is a necessary measure for survival. But can pragmatism stifle the dream? The case of Saudi Arabia and Iran where the state is ostensibly run on Islamic principles suggest that the imperatives of man-made state sovereignty either override Islamic objectives of Muslim unity and divine order, and/or employ them for the benefit of the state. Saudi financial support for Muslim communities globally is as much about promoting Islam as entrenching an image of benevolence and generosity for Saudi Arabia. The perpetuation of this image is integral to the Saudi claim to leadership in the Muslim world, as evident in its hosting of the headquarters of a number of regional and international organisations, including the Organisation of Islamic Conference and the Muslim World League.

A similar case may be presented against Iran which tends to use a realpolitik compass to find its path in international affairs. The Islamic republic has had a complicated relationship with its Muslim neighbours since its inception, especially after Arab states of the Persian Gulf sided with Iraq in the protracted Iran–Iraq war (1980–8). The ideal of Muslim unity seems to have little practical implications for Iranian foreign policy. This may be related, at least in part, to the Shi'a–Sunni schism that separates Shi'a Iran from the predominantly Sunni Muslim world. Iranian support for Hizbullah in Lebanon and other militant Shi'a groups may be cited as evidence of the commitment to some form of co-operation and unity along sectarian lines. But this support could also point to the importance of religious bonds for irreligious aspirations, namely an entrenched competition with Saudi Arabia for the leadership position in the Muslim world. Noting especially that Iranian–Hizbullah ties were at their peak during the Iran–Iraq war, it is more likely that Iran hoped to influence Muslim public opinion in its favour through sponsoring militancy against Israel, then occupying South Lebanon. The extent of public anger at Israeli aggression and the inaction of governments in the Middle East offered a window of opportunity for Iran to exert pressure on hostile Arab states by appealing to Arab masses. It may, of course, be difficult to assume a coherent foreign policy thinking in Tehran, given the rivalry between the hardliners and the moderates; neither faction appears to have championed the ideal vision of Muslim unity (even a Shi'a unity). In the Transcaucasus, Iran openly sided with Christian Armenia in its war with Shi'a Azerbaijan. To the amazement of some observers, neither the Shi'a connection nor ethnic ties, swayed Iran to support Baku. In fact, ethnic ties between the large Iranian Azeri community and Azerbaijan may have played an important role in Terhran's choice as it feared Azeri separatist incitement from Baku. Political Islam in Iran appears to have completed a full circle, from a force for the supremacy of Islam over the temporal state to a force for the primacy of the state at the expense of the Islamic ideal. Can this be a general pattern awaiting other militant Islamic movements?

If the above is the rule, there are notable exceptions that deserve attention. Hizb ut-Tahrir (Liberation Party) is the most pertinent one as it portends a transnational vision and organisation which promises to transcend state boundaries and unite the *umma* in a truly legitimate order: the caliphate. Founded in 1952 by Taqi al-Din al-Nabahani in Jerusalem the party was initially concerned with the cause of Palestinian liberation. But the logic of pursuing the boundless sovereignty of God, and perhaps the dissemination of the Palestinian diaspora, led Hizb ut-Tahrir to go beyond existing state boundaries and champion the 'recreation of one Islamic state' to incorporate all Muslim societies.[4] The realisation of the Caliphate throughout *dar al-Islam* requires jihad against the prevalent corruption and *kufr* (disbelief) which has replaced the shari'a and the Muslim way of life.[5] But this universalist message needs to be grounded in time and space in order for it to take shape and attain fulfilment:

> Although Islam is a universal ideology, its method does not, however, allow one to work for it universally from the beginning. It is necessary, however, to invite to it universally, and make the field of work for it in one country, or a few countries, until it is consolidated there and the Islamic State is established.[6]

Hizb ut-Tarir has proved a shrewd player, operating in some of the least hospitable political environments. The presence of the party in Egypt, Iraq, Jordan, Libya, Syria, Tunisia and Uzbekistan attest to the effectiveness of its 'Bolshevik' operational philosophy, described as consisting of three phases on its official web-page: (1) establishing a party cadre, reminiscent of the Leninist 'professional revolutionaries', (2) propaganda and interaction with the Muslim community at large, and (3) gaining political power and 'implementing Islam generally and comprehensively, and carrying it as a message to the world'. The success of Hizb ut-Tahrir in gaining a foothold in the above mentioned societies is a result of its ability to address tangible local concerns as well as the more generic aspirations for social justice under Islamic rule. It is in fact more likely that the party's support-base is attracted by the tangible social welfare issues, rather than high-flying ideals about the multinational Caliphate. This is especially true in societies that have a scant knowledge of Islamic history and philosophy. Uzbekistan stands out as one such case. As a result, it appears as though the universalist and transnational objectives of Hizb ut-Tahrir have been modified in practice, but not rhetoric, suggesting that the party is not immune to the gravitational forces of state-base politics.

As contributors to this volume have demonstrated, the aura of legitimacy emanating from Islam is systematically cultivated, setting in motion a process that paradoxically threatens to erode the legitimacy of the ruling elite. The elevation of Islam onto the political plane, formally or informally, confers on it an authority to evaluate government policies that was not tolerated or recognised in 'secular' states. The growing assertiveness of political Islamic organisations is partly the result of their widening public access as a consequence of the acceptability of Islam in politics. This assertiveness presents new challenges to the political elite which is fighting a rearguard battle and finds it either difficult to project sincerity in embracing Islam or to establish its interpretation of Islam as exclusively authentic. The prevalent policy of seeking Islamic credentials for the ruling elite has, in fact, made its public standing more vulnerable. But the challenge of political Islam to the legitimacy of the ruling regimes does not extend to state-bound politics. Territorial delimitation of Muslim societies has made a discernible imprint on their political imagination. Political Islam with its quest for the supremacy of divine sovereignty, appears confined by state boundaries. The ideal of a transnational *umma*, confronting the rest of the world (*dar al-harb*) in a Huntingtonesque fashion, is increasingly irrelevant and devoid of practical utility. Consequently, the ramifications of political Islam, while significant for state politics of Muslim societies, are minimal for the nature of inter-state relations which is governed by self-interest rather than an overriding ideological concern.

Notes

1. Charles Tripp, 'Islam and the Secular Logic of the State in the Middle East', in Abdel Salam Sidahmed and Anoushiravan Ehteshami (eds), *Islamic Fundamentalism* (Boulder, Col: Westview Press, 1996), p. 61.
2. For an extensive discussion of Islamic radicalism from a somewhat different perspective, see Olivier Roy, *The Failure of Political Islam* (Cambridge, MA: Harvard University Press, 1994), especially pp. 107–31.
3. For a more detailed discussion see Shahram Akbarzadeh, 'Islamic Clerical Establishment in Central Asia', *South Asia*, 20, 2 (December 1997), pp. 73–102.
4. For a brief review see Dale F. Eickelman and James Piscatori, *Muslim Politics* (Princeton, NJ: Princeton University Press, 1996), p. 139.
5. Hizb ut-Tahrir's web-page offers a window into its thinking: 'Muslims nowadays live in Dar al-Kufr, because they are governed with laws other than the revelation of Allah (swt)'. <www.hizb-ut-tahrir.org>
6. Hizb ut-Tahrir web-page.

Bibliography

Abdul Rahman, Ismail. *Gerakan Gereja Katolik di Malaysia* (Bangi: National University of Malaysia, 2000).
Abir, Mordechai. *Saudi Arabia: Government, Society and the Gulf Crisis* (London: Routledge, 1993).
Abrahamian, Ervand. *The Iranian Mojahedin* (New Haven: Yale University Press, 1992).
Abu Bakar, Mohammad. 'Islamic Revivalism and the Political Process in Malaysia', *Asian Survey*, 21, 10 (October 1981), pp. 1040–59.
Aburish, Said. *The Rise, Corruption and Coming Fall of the House of Saud* (London: Bloomsbury, 1994).
Agwani, M.S. 'God's government: Jamaat-i-Islami of India', in H. Mutalib and T.I. Hashmi (eds). *Islam, Muslims and the Modern State* (London & New York: Macmillan Press & St. Martin's Press, 1994).
Ahmed, Ishtiaq. *The Concept of an Islamic State* (London: Frances Pinter, 1987).
Ahmed, Rafiuddin. *The Bengali Muslim 1871–1906: A Quest for Identity* (New Delhi: Oxford University Press, 1981).
Ahmed, Syed Jamil. 'Bengali Nationalism Through Sociology of Theatre', in A.M. Chowdhury and Fakrul Alam (eds). *Bangladesh on the Threshold of the Twenty-First Century* (Dhaka: Asiatic Society of Bangladesh, 2002).
Akbarzadeh, Shahram. 'Islamic Clerical Establishment in Central Asia', *South Asia*, 20, 2 (December 1997), pp. 73–102.
Al-Banna, Hasan. *Majmu'at Rasa'il al-Imam al-Shahid Hasan al-Banna* (Cairo: Dar al-Tawzi' wa al-Nashr al-Islamiyya, 1992).
Al-Maktay, Safran et al. 'A-Q-Study of Reactions to Direct Broadcast Satellite Television Programming in Saudi Arabia', *Journal of South Asian and Middle Eastern Studies*, 20, 4 (1997).
Al-Mas'ari, Muhammad. *Muhasabat al-Hukkam* (London: Mu'asasat al-Rafd Linnashr wa al-Tawzi, 1997).
Al-Mawardi, Abu'l-Hasan. *al-Ahkam as-Sultaniyya (The Laws of Islamic Governance)*, Trans. Asadullah Yate (London: Ta-Ha Publishers, 1996).
Almond, Gabriel and Verba, Sydney (eds). *The Civic Culture: Political Attitudes and Democracy in Five Nations* (Princeton, NJ: Princeton University Press, 1963).

Al-Nadawi, Abu al-Hasan Ali al-Husayni. *Madha Khasira al-Alam bi Inhitat al-Muslimin* (Beirut: Dar al-Kitab al-Arabi, 1984).

Amin, Mohammad. *Islamization of Laws in Pakistan* (Lahore: Sang-e-Meel, 1989).

Ansari, Ali M. *Iran, Islam and Democracy; The Politics of Managing Change* (London: Royal Institute of International Affairs, 2000).

Anshari, Endang Saifuddin. *Piagam Jakarta, 22 Juni 1945* (Jakarta: Rajawali Press, 1981).

Anwar, Zainah. *Islamic Revivalism in Malaysia: Dakwah Among Students* (Kuala Lumpur: Pelanduk Publications, 1987).

Bakar, Mohammad Abu. 'Islamic Revivalism and the Political Process in Malaysia', *Asian Survey*, 21, 10 (October 1981), pp. 1040–59.

Bakar, Osman (ed.). *Islam and Confucianism* (Kuala Lumpur: University of Malaya Press, 1979).

Bakhash, Shaul. *The Reign of the Ayatollahs: Iran and the Islamic Revolution* (New York: Basic Books, 1984).

Banu, Razia Akter. 'Jamaat-I-Islami in Bangladesh: Challenges and Prospects', in H. Mutalib and T.I. Hashmi (eds), *Islam, Muslims and the Modern State* (London: Macmillan Press, 1994).

Barton, Greg. 'The Impact of Neo-Modernism on Indonesian Islamic Thought: The Emergence of a New Pluralism', David Bourchier and John Legge (eds), *Democracy in Indonesia: 1950s and 1990s* (Clayton, Victoria: Centre of Southeast Asian Studies, Monash University, 1994).

Basri, Ghazali. *Christian Mission and Islamic Da'wah in Malaysia* (Kuala Lumpur: Nurin Enterprise, 1992).

Biro Pusat Statistik. *Penduduk Indonesia: Hasil Sensus Penduduk 1990*, series S2 (Jakarta: BPS, 1992).

Boland, B.J. *The Struggle of Islam in Modern Indonesia* (The Hague: Martinus Nijhoff, 1982).

Bruinessen, Martin van. 'Traditions for the Future: The Reconstruction of Traditionalist Discourse within NU', in Greg Barton and Greg Fealy (eds), *Nahdlatul Ulama, Traditional Islam and Modernity in Indonesia* (Clayton, Victoria: Monash Asia Institute, 1996).

Buchan, James. 'Secular and Religious Opposition in Saudi Arabia', in Tim Niblock (ed.), *State, Society and Economy in Saudi Arabia* (London: Croom Helm, 1982).

Caporaso, James A. (ed.). *The Elusive State: International and Comparative Perspectives* (New York: Sage, 1989).

Case, William. 'Malaysia: Aspects and Audiences of Legitimacy', in Muthiah Alagappa (ed.), *Political Legitimacy in Southeast Asia: The Quest for Moral Authority* (Standford: Stanford University Press, 1995).

Chatterjee, Basant. *Inside Bangladesh Today: An Eye-Witness Account* (New Delhi: S. Chand & Co., 1973).

Chelkowski Peter J. and Dabashi, Hamid. *Staging a Revolution: The Art of Persuasion in the Islamic Republic of Iran* (New York: New York University Press, 1999).

Dekmejian, R. Hrair. 'The Rise of Political Islamism in Saudi Arabia', *Middle East Journal*, 48, 4 (1994).
—— *Islam in Revolution: Fundamentalism in the Arab World* (Syracuse: Syracuse University Press, 1995).
Dhofier, Zamakhsyari. 'The Role of the Department of Religion', in James J. Fox, *Religion and Ritual* (Singapore: Indonesian Heritage Series, Archipelago Press, 1998).
Dobson, Richard B. 'Islam in Central Asia: Findings from National Surveys', *Central Asia Monitor*, 2 (1994).
Eaton, Richard. *The Rise of Islam and the Bengal Frontier, 1204–1760* (Berkeley, CA: University of California Press, 1993).
Effendy, Bachtiar. *Islam dan Negara: Transformasi Pemikiran dan Praktik Politik Islam di Indonesia* (Jakarta: Paramadina, 1998).
Ehteshami, Anoushiravan. *After Khomeini: The Iranian Second Republic* (London: Routledge, 1995).
Eickelman, Dale F. and Piscatori, James. *Muslim Politics* (Princeton, NJ: Princeton University Press, 1996).
Enayat, Hamid. *Modern Islamic Political Thought* (London: Macmillan Press, 1982).
Esposito, John L. *The Islamic Threat, Myth or Reality?* (Oxford: Oxford University Press, 1992).
Fandy, Mamoun. *Saudi Arabia and the Politics of Dissent* (London: Palgrave, 2001).
Farhi, Farideh. *States and Urban-Based Revolutions: Iran and Nicaragua* (Urbana, IL: University of Illinois Press, 1990).
—— 'On the Reconfiguration of the Public Sphere and the Changing Political Landscape of Postrevolutionary Iran,' in John L. Esposito and R. K. Ramazani (eds), *Iran at the Crossroads* (New York: Palgrave, 2001).
Fealy, Greg. '"Rowing in a Typhoon": Nahdlatul Ulama and the Decline of Parliamentary Democracy', in David Bourchier and John D. Legge (eds), *Democracy in Indonesia, 1950s and 1990s* (Clayton, Victoria: Centre of Southeast Asian Studies, Monash University, 1994).
—— 'Islamic Politics: A Rising or Declining Force?' in Damien Kingsbury and Arief Budiman (eds), *Indonesia: The Uncertain Transition* (Adelaide: Crawford House, 2001).
Foran, John and Goodwin, Jeff. 'Revolutionary Outcomes in Iran and Nicaragua: Coalition Fragmentation, War, and the Limits of Social Transformation'. *Theory and Society* 22, 2 (April 1993).
Forest, Jim. *Religion in the New Russia* (New York: Crossroad, 1990).
Funston, N. J. 'The Origins of Partai Islam Se Malaysia', *JSEAS*, 7, 1 (1976).
Geertz, Clifford. *The Religion of Java* (Chicago: University of Chicago Press, 1964).
Hall, John A. and Ikenberry, John. *The State* (Buckingham: Open University Press, 1989).
Halliday, Fred. (2002) *Two Hours that shook the World* (London: Saqi, 2002).
Haq, Maulana Mansural (ed.). *Mr. Mawdudir New Islam* (Bengali), (Dhaka: Jamia Qurania Arabia, Lalbagh, 1985).

Harper, T.N. *The End of Empire and the Making of Malaya* (Cambridge: Cambridge University Press, 1999).
Hartman, Frederick and Wendzel, Robert. *America's Foreign Policy in a Changing World* (New York: HarperCollins, 1994).
Hashmi, Taj I. 'Karamat Ali and the Muslims in Bengal, 1800–1873', *Dacca University Studies*, 23 (June 1976).
—— 'Moral, Rational and Political Economies of Peasants: An Appraisal of Colonial Bengal and Vietnam', *Second International Conference on Indian Ocean Studies (Proceedings)*, Perth, 1984.
—— *Pakistan as a Peasant Utopia: The Communalization of Class Politics in East Bengal, 1920–1947* (Boulder: Westview Press, 1992).
—— 'Islam in Bangladesh Politics', in Hussin Mutalib and Taj I. Hashmi (eds). *Islam, Muslims and the Modern State* (London: Macmillan Press, 1994).
—— 'Women and Islam: Taslima Nasreen, Society and Politics in Bangladesh', *South Asia*, 18, 2 (1995).
—— *Women and Islam in Bangladesh: Beyond Subjection and Tyranny* (London: Macmillan Press, 2000).
Hefner, Robert W. *Civil Islam: Muslims and Democratization in Indonesia* (Princeton and Oxford: Princeton University Press, 2000).
—— 'Islam, State and Civil Society: ICMI and the Struggle for the Indonesian Middle Class', *Indonesia*, 56 (October 1993).
Heller, Mark and Safran, Nadav. *The New Middle Class and Regime Stability in Saudi Arabia* (Cambridge, Massachusetts: Harvard Centre for Middle Eastern Studies, 1985).
Helms, Christine M. *The Cohesion of Saudi Arabia: Evolution of Political Identity* (London: Croom Helm, 1981).
Hossain, Zohair. 'Maulana Sayyid Abul A'la Maududi: An Appraisal of His Thought and Political Influence', *South Asia*, 9, 1 (June 1986).
Hourani, Albert. *A History of Arab Peoples* (London: Faber and Faber, 1991).
Howarth, David. *The Desert King: A Life of Ibn Saud* (London: Collins, 1964).
Ibn Khaldun, Abd al-Rahman. *Muqaddimat Ibn Khaldun* (Beirut: al-Matba'a al-Adabiyya, 1900).
Ibrahim, Ahmad. 'The Position of Islam in the Constitution of Malaysia', in Ahmad Ibrahim, Sharon Siddique, and Yasmin Hussain (compilers). *Readings on Islam in Southeast Asia* (Singapore: Institute of Southeast Asian Studies, 1985).
International Crisis Group. *Central Asia: Islamist Mobilisation and Regional Security* (Osh/Brussels: ICG Asia Report No.14, 1 March 2001).
Islami, A. Reza S. and Kavoussi, Rostam M. *The Political Economy of Saudia Arabia* (Seattle: University of Washington Press, 1984).
Jaffar, Kamarudin. *Memperingati Yusuf Rawa* (Kuala Lumpur: IKDAS, 2000).
Jahangir, Borhauuddin Khan. *Bangladeshe Jatiyatabad Eborg Moulobod* [in Bengali] (Dhaka: Agami Prakashani, 1993).
Kashi, Mohammad Javad Gholamreza. *Jadouye Goftar: Zehniat-e Farhangi va Nezam-e Ma'ani dar Entekhabat-e Dovom-e Khordad* (Tehran: Ayandeh Pouyan, 1379/2000).

Khan, Muin-ud-Din Ahmad. *History of the Fara'idi Movement* (Dhaka: Islamic Foundation, 1984).
Khan, Zillur R. *Martial Law to Martial Law: Leadership Crisis in Bangladesh* (Dhaka: University Press Ltd, 1984).
Koentjaraningrat. *Javanese Culture* (Singapore and London: Institute of Southeast Asian Studies and Oxford University Press, 1984).
Kostiner, Joseph. 'On Instruments and their Designers: The Ikhwan of Najd and the formation of the Saudi State', *Middle Eastern Studies*, 21, 3 (1985).
Lambton, Ann K.S. *State and Government in Medieval Islam* (Oxford: Oxford University Press, 1981).
Lemercier-Quelquejay, Chantal. 'From Tribe to *Umma*', *Central Asia Survey*, 3, 3 (1984).
Lev, Daniel S. *Islamic Courts in Indonesia: A Study in the Political Bases of Legal Institutions* (Berkeley: University of California Press, 1972).
Levy, Reuben. *Sociology of Islam*, vol. 1 (London: Williams & Norgate, 1933).
Lewis, Bernard. *The Middle East: 2000 Years of History from the Rise of Christianity to the Present Day* (London: Phoenix, 1997).
Liddle, William. 'The Islamic Turn in Indonesia: A Political Explanation', *Journal of Asian Studies*, 55, 3 (August 1996).
Lipset, S.M. *Political Man* (Baltimore: Johns Hopkins University Press, 1981).
Lyon, M.L. 'The Dakwah Movement in Malaysia', *Review of Indonesian and Malayan Affairs*, 13, 2 (1979).
Majelis Ulama Indonesia. *Tahun Majelis Ulama Indonesia* (Jakarta: Departemen Penerengan RI, 1985)
Makaruddin, Hashim (ed). *Islam and the Muslim Ummah: Selected Speeches of Dr Mahathir Mohamad* (Subang Jaya: Pelanduk Publications, 2001).
Malik, Jamal. *Colonialization of Islam: Dissolution of Traditional Institutions in Pakistan* (Lahore: Vanguard Books, 1996).
Mallick, R.A. *British Policy and the Muslims in Bengal, 1757–1856* (Dhaka: Bangla Academy, 1977).
Maniruzzaman, Talukder. 'Bangladesh Politics: Secular and Islamic Trends', in S.R. Chakravarty and Virendra Narain (eds). *Bangladesh: History and Culture, Vol. I*, (New Delhi: South Asian Publishers, 1986).
Martinez, Patricia. 'The Islamic state or the state of Islam in Malaysia', *Contemporary Southeast Asia*, 23, 3 (December 2001).
Mauzy, Diane K. and Kline, R.S. 'The Mahathir Administration in Malaysia: Discipline through Islam', *Pacific Affairs*, 56, 4 (1983/4).
Mohsin, K.M. 'Tabligh Jama't and the Faith Movement in Bangladesh', in Rafiuddin Ahmed (ed.), *Bangladesh: Society, Religion and Politics* (Chittagong: South Asia Studies Group, 1985).
Mumtaz, Khawar and Shaheed, Farida. *Women of Pakistan: Two Steps Forward, One Step Back?* (Lahore: Vanguard Books, 1987).
Mutalib, Hussin. *Islam and Ethnicity in Malay Politics* (Singapore: Oxford University Press, 1990).
—— *Islam in Malaysia: From Revivalism to Islamic State* (Singapore: Singapore University Press, 1993).

Bibliography

Muzaffar, Chandra. 'Malayism, Bumiputeraism, and Islam', in Ahmad Ibrahim, Sharon Siddique and Yasmin Hussain (compilers). *Readings on Islam in Southeast Asia* (Singapore: Institute of Southeast Asian Studies, 1985).
—— *Islamic Resurgence in Malaysia* (Petaling Jaya: Penerbit Fajar Bakti, 1987).
—— *The NEP: Development and Alternative Consciousness* (Penang: Aliran 1989).
Nagata, Judith. 'Religious Ideology and Social Change: The Islamic Revival in Malaysia', *Pacific Affairs*, 53, 3 (1980).
—— *The Reflowering of Malaysian Islam: Modern Religious Radicals and Their Roots* (Vancouver: University of British Columbia Press, 1984).
Naipaul, V.S. *Beyond Belief: Islamic Excursions Among the Converted Peoples* (New Delhi: Penguin Books, 1998).
Nasr, Seyyed Vali Reza. *Mawdudi and the Making of Islamic Revivalism* (Oxford: Oxford University Press, 1996).
Nasrin, Taslima. *Lajja: Shame* (London: Penguin Books, 1994).
Noer, Deliar. *The Administration of Islam in Indonesia* (Ithaca, New York: Cornell University Press, 1978).
Nouri, Abdollah. *Showkaran-e eslah* (Tehran: Tarh-e No, 1378/1999).
Platzdasch, Bernhard. 'Islamic Reaction to a Female President', in Chris Manning and Peter van Diermen (eds). *Indonesia in Transition: Social Aspects of Reformasi and Crisis* (Singapore: Research School of Pacific and Asian Studies, 1999).
Przeworski, Adam. *Democracy and the Market: Political and Economic Reforms in Eastern Europe and Latin America* (Cambridge and New York: Cambridge University Press, 1991).
Quaid-e-Azam Mohammed Ali Jinnah: Speeches as Governor General, 1947–1948, (Karachi: Pakistan Publications, no date).
Qutb, Sayyid. *al-'Adala al-Ijtima'iyya fi al-Islam* (Cairo: Dar al-Shuruq, 1983).
—— *Fi Zilal al-Qur'an* (Cairo and Beirut: Dar al-Shuruq, 1992).
—— *Ma'rakat al-Islam wa al-Ra'smaliyya* (Cairo and Beirut: Dar al-Shuruq, 1993).
Rahman, Abdul. *Gerakan Gereja Katolik di Malaysia* (Bangi: National University of Malaysia, 2000)
Rahman, Abdul, Tan Chee Khoon, Chandra Muzaffar and Lim Kit Siang (eds). *Contemporary Issues on Malaysian Religions* (Petaling Jaya: Pelanduk Publications, 1984).
Rashid, Ahmed. *Taliban: The Story of the Afghan Warlords* (London: Pan Books, 2001).
Rezai, Abdolali and Abdi, Abbas. *Entekhab- e No* (New Choice), (Tehran: Tarh-e No, 1998).
Roy, Asim. *Islamic Syncretistic Tradition in Bengal* (Princeton: Princeton University Press, 1983).
Roy, Olivier. '*Qibla* and the Government House: The Islamic Networks', *SAIS Review*, 21, 2 (Summer–Fall 2001).
—— *The Failure of Political Islam* (Cambridge, MA: Harvard University Press, 1994).

Bibliography 181

Saʻati, Amin. *Al-Shura fi al-Mamlaka al-Arabiyya al-Saʻudiyya* (Cairo: al-Markaz al-Saʻudi li-al-Dirasat al-Istiratijiyya [The Saudi Strategic Studies Centre], 1992).

Said, Edward W. *Orientalism* (London: Routledge & Kegan Paul, 1985).

Sanasarian, Eliz. *Religious Minorities in Iran* (Cambridge: Cambridge University Press, 2000).

Schirazi, Asghar. *The Constitution of Iran: Politics and the State in the Islamic Republic.* translated by John O'Kane (London: I. B. Tauris, 1997).

Schwarz, Adam. *A Nation in Waiting: Indonesia's Search for Stability* (Sydney: Allen & Unwin, 1999).

Scott, James C. *The Moral Economy of the Peasant: Rebellion and Subsistence in Southeast Asia* (New Haven: Yale University Press, 1976).

Sharif, Ahmed et al. (eds). *Ekattorer Ghatak O Dalalra Ke Kothay* (Mukki Dhaka: Mukki Juddho Chetom Bikash Kendra, 1987).

Soroush, Abdolkarim. *Reason, Freedom and Democracy in Islam: Essential Writings of Abdolkarim Soroush*, translated and edited by Mahmoud Sadri and Ahmad Sadri (Oxford: Oxford University Press, 2000).

Sundaram, Jomo K. *Mahathir's Economic Policies* (Kuala Lumpur: INSAN, 1988).

Teh, Wan Zahid Wan. *Malaysia is an Islamic State* (Kuala Lumpur: Malaysian Ministry of Information, 2001).

Tietelbaum, Joshua. *Holier than Thou: Saudi Arabia's Islamic Opposition* (Washington DC: Washington Institute for Near East Policy, 2000).

Tripp, Charles. 'Islam and the Secular Logic of the State in the Middle East', in Abdel Salam Sidahmed and Anoushiravan Ehteshami (eds), *Islamic Fundamentalism* (Boulder: Westview Press, 1996).

Van Bruinessen, Martin. 'Traditions for the Future: The Reconstruction of Traditionalist Discourse within NU', in Greg Barton and Greg Fealy (eds), *Nahdlatul Ulama, Traditional Islam and Modernity in Indonesia* (Clayton, Victoria: Monash Asia Institute, 1996).

Vincent, Andrew. *Theories of the State* (Oxford: Blackwell, 1987).

Watt, W. Montgomery. *The Formative Period of Islamic Thought* (Oxford: Oneworld, 1998).

Weiss, Anita M. 'The Consequences of State Policies for Women in Pakistan', in Myron Weiner and Ali Banuazizi (eds), *The Politics of Social Transformation in Afghanistan, Iran and Pakistan* (New York: Syracuse University Press, 1994).

Wertheim, W.F. *Indonesian Society in Transition* (The Hague: W. van Hoeve, 1958)

Wheeler, Geoffrey. 'The Muslims of Central Asia', *Problems of Communism*, 16, 5 (1977).

Wilder, Andrew. 'Islam and Political Legitimacy in Pakistan', in Aslam Syed, Muhammad (ed.), *Islam and Democracy in Pakistan* (Islamabad: National Institute of Historical and Cultural Research, 1995).

Yasin, Norhashimah Mohd. *Islamization/Malaynization: A Study on the Role of Economic Development of Malaysia, 1963–1993* (Kuala Lumpur: A.S. Noordeen, 1996).

Yasmeen, Samina. 'Islamisation and Democratisation in Pakistan: Implications for Women and Religious Minorities', *South Asia*, 22, Special Issue (1999).

Zaydan, Jurji. *History of Islamic Civilisation*, Trans. D.S. Margoliouth (New Delhi: Kitab Bhavan, 1981).

Index

Abbasid caliphs 18, 19, 20–1
Abd Allah b. Mas'ud 18
Abd al-Malik b. Marwan 17
Abd al-Wahhab, Muhammad ibn 31
Abu al-Hasan al-Nadawi 16
Abdullah, Mukhtarjon 93
Abu Yusuf 18
adultery 78
Advisory Council of Islamic Ideology (ACII) 74
Afghanistan 1, 11, 79, 81, 84, 85, 86
Ahmed, Kazi Faruq 117
al-Azhar 18
al-Banna, Hasan 6, 26
al-Ghazali 2–3
  Politics 3
Al Helmy, Burhanuddin 131
al-Humayd, Salih bin Abdullah 33
al-Qaeda 84
al-Ma'mun 19
al-Mas'ari, Muhammad 42–3
al-Mawardie 2
al-Mu'tasim 19
al-Otaybi, Juhayman 35
al-Qadir 19
al-Sadat, Anwar 1
al-Tirmizi 92
al-Wathiq 19
Amini, Fazlul Haq 117, 118
Awami League 103, 108, 110, 113, 114, 115, 120–1, 122
Azam, Ghulam 114

Bahromov, Mufti Abdurashid qori 6, 97

Bangladesh 8, 11, 12, 102–23, 170–1
  Islam 102–13, 118–21
  Islam, military rule and legitimacy 111–13
  Islamic militancy 118–21
  Islamic movements 104
  Islamists 104–8
  Jamaat-i Islami 105, 110, 112, 113–15
  nationalism 108–11
  secularism 108–10
  village community 116–18
Bangladesh Nationalist Party (BNP) 113
Bangladesh Peasants' and Workers' Awami League (BKSAL) 108, 110
Bangladeshi Muslims 102, 113, 118
Basic Principles Committee (BPC) 74
Bazargan, Mehdi 54
Bhashani, Mawlana 109
Bhutto, Benazir 80, 82
Bhutto, Zulfikar Ali 7, 75, 76, 77
Bin Laden, Osama 44–5, 89, 119, 120
Bowring, Philip 121

caliphal authority 20–1
Central Asian Muftiyat 171
Central Asian Muslim Board 94
Chatterjee, Basant 106
Council of Indonesian Ulema (MUI) 157
Council for Islamic Ideology (CII) 75, 77
cultural Islam 7, 12, 89–91, 162

184   Index

din and *dawla* 3–4
divine rule 17–18

East Pakistan 75
Egypt 8
Ershad, General 105, 111–12, 113

fatwa 41, 116–18

Guardian Council 51
Geertz, Clifford 152
Golkar 160, 161, 164
Gulf War 34, 114

Habibie, B.J. 163
Hadith, Ahl-i 77
Hajjarian, Saeed 65
Haq, General Zia ul- 7, 70, 76, 77, 79, 80, 110, 111, 113
Haq, Mawlana Ubaidul 119
Harkatul Mujahedeen 85
Hasina, Sheikh 120, 121
Hasyim Asy'ari 150
Hizb ut-Tahrir (Liberation Party) 89, 95, 96, 99, 172–3
human rights 112
Hussein, Saddam 114

Ibn Abbas 18
Ibn Baz, Shaykh Abd al-Aziz 38–9, 41
Ibn al-Muqaffa' 20
Ibn Taymiyya, Taqy al-Din Ahmad 3, 41, 43
Ibn Uthaymin, Muhammad al-Salih 38
Ibrahim, Anwar 7, 144–5
Indonesia 5, 7, 12–13, 150–66
   Islam 151, 152–7
   Islamic politics, 1945–1980s 158–61
   Islamic reform and political revival 161–5
   State Institute of Islamic Studies (IAIN) 157
Indonesian Muslim Intellectuals Association (ICMI) 163
Indonesian Nationalist Party (PNI) 159
Indo-Pakistan War 75
Iran 1, 4, 7, 8, 11, 50–66, 96, 169
   Islam 53–7
   politics 50–2, 58–64

post-revolutionary authority 57–8
velayat-e faqih 56, 59
Iran–Iraq War 54–5, 56, 172
Islam
   Bangladesh 102–13, 118–21
   cultural 7, 89–91, 162
   Indonesia 151, 152–7
   Iran 53–7
   Malaysia 127–9, 140
   Pakistan 70, 71–6
   political 2, 6, 7–13, 25, 50–1, 60, 89, 98, 166
   Saudi Arabia 30, 31–3
   traditional 6
   Uzbekistan 89–94, 98–9
   Wahhabi 30
Islamic
   activism 6, 25–7, 98
   disciplines 17
   history 27
   law, marginalisation of 22
   liberal 71–2, 73
   militancy 1, 4, 118–21, 123
   political thought 2–4, 6–7
   radicalism 1, 6
   symbolism 1–2
Islamic Movement of Uzbekistan (IMU) 89, 95, 96, 99
Islamic Party (PAS) 128–9, 131, 135, 136, 138, 139–40
Islamic Republican Party (IRP) 54
Islamic Research Institute (IRI) 74
Islamic Resistance Party 94, 99
Islamists 104–8
Israel and Islamic militancy 4

Jaish Muhammad 85
Jamiat Ulama-i Islam 73, 76
Jamaat-i Islami 6, 73, 76, 77, 105, 110, 112, 113–15, 116, 117, 121, 122, 170–1
Jinnah, Mohammad Ali 72

Kadivar, Mohsen 59
Karamat Ali, Jaunpuri 107
Karim, Fazlul 117, 118
Karimov, Islam 7, 88, 91–2, 94, 95, 96, 99
Kashi, Muhammad Javad Gholamreza 55

Kashmir 11, 81, 86
Khaldun, Ibn 31
Khamenei, Seyyed Ali 7, 58, 63
Khan, Ayub 74, 75
Khan, Enayetullah 120
Khatami, Muhammad 11, 52, 58, 59, 60, 61, 63, 64, 65
Khawarij rebellion 2
Khomeini, Ayatollah 6, 54, 56, 58
Kyrgyzstan 95, 96

Lambton, Ann K.S. 2
Lashkar-i Jhangvi (LJ) 83
Lashkar-i Taiba 85
law as a function of power 18–19
Lee Kuan Yew 141
Lintner, Bertil 119, 120

Malaysia 5, 7, 9, 12, 22, 127–46
 Islam 127–9, 140
 issues of political legitimacy 138–46
 state and the ulema 130–1, 135–8
 under Mahathir 133–5, 144–5
 under Tunku and Razak 131–3
Malaysian Muslim Youth Movement (ABIM) 12, 128, 136–7, 144
Masyumi 158, 159–60
Mawdudi, Mawlana Abdul Ala 6, 26, 52, 77, 105, 114, 170
Megawati 150, 164, 165
Montazeri, Ayatollah 50, 52
mosques 23
Mu'awiya 16
Muda, Mohd Asri hj 136
Muhammad 2
Muhammad, Mahathir 7, 129, 133–5, 144–5
Muhammad, Ustaz Ashaari 137
Muhammadiya 153, 154, 164
Muhammadulla, Mawlana 112
Mujahedin 55
Mujib, Sheikh 103, 108, 109, 110–11, 122 *see also* Rahman, Sheikh Mujib ur-
 Government 110, 113
Mujibism 109
Musharraf, Pervez 70, 83, 84, 85, 86
Muslim Brotherhood 26, 41, 170
Muslim societies 4–5, 13, 15, 30, 71–2

Nahdlatul Ulama (NU) 150, 153, 157, 158, 159, 164
Naipaul, V.S. 122
Namangani, Juma 96
Naqshband, Khoja Bahoutdin 92
Nasr, Seyyed Vali Reza 26
Nasrin, Taslima 115, 116, 120
National Socialist Party (JSD) 109, 110
Nizam al-Mulk 18
Nizami, Matiur Raham 114
Nouri, Abdollah 50, 52
Nouri, Ali Akbar Nateq 59
Nurcholish Madjid 161, 162
Nuruzzaman, Colonel 114

Othmani, Mawlana Shabbir Ahmed 73

Pahlavi, Muhammad Reza 51
Pakistan 1, 7, 9, 11, 70–86, 96, 170–1
 democratic experience (1988–99) 80–2
 future of the struggle for 'real' Islam 85–6
 and Islam 70, 71–6
 military regime and state-sponsored Islam 76–83
 military rule and liberal Islam 83–5
 society 76–80
Pakistan National Alliance (PNA) 76
Pakistan People's Party (PPP) 75
Palestinian lands 4, 106
Pancasila 156, 160
Pancasila Muslim Service Foundation (YAMP) 160–1
Peters, May Anne 121
political authority 19–20
political hegemony, theology as an expression of 19
political Islam 2, 6, 7–13, 25, 50–1, 60, 89, 98, 166, 173–4
politics and religion 7–13, 15–21, 33–7
Prophet 15–16, 17

Qader, Kazi 112
Quietism 3
Qutb, Sayyid 6, 26

Rahman, General Zia ur- 7, 102

Index

Rahman, Sheikh Muijb ur- 102 *see also* Mujib, Sheikh
Rahman, Shamsur 120
Rahman, Tunku Abdul 130, 131–3, 139
Rafsanjani, Ali Akbar Hashemi 63
rape 78, 117
Rawa, Haji Yusuf 136
Razak, Tun 131–3, 143
religion and politics 7–13, 15–21, 33–7
religious education in schools 23–4
Roy, Olivier 122

Saghafi, Morad 62
Saud, Abd al-Aziz Ibn 31
Saud, Muhammad ibn 31
Saudi Arabia 1, 7, 9, 24, 29–47, 79–80, 96, 169, 172
  history 31
  Islam, politics and 30, 31–3
  religion and politics 33–7
  society 33, 37–44
Schirazi, Asghar 53
September 11 1, 29, 44, 70, 84
Shabestari, Muhammad Mojtahed 59
Sharif, Ahmed 112
Sharif, Nawaz 80, 82
Sikdar, Siraj 109
Soeharto 12, 151, 160, 163–4
Soroush, Abdolkarim 59
Sukarno 151, 156, 160

Tabligh Jamaat 105
Tajikistan 94, 96
Taliban 1, 81, 83–4, 85, 105, 117, 121
Turajonzoda, Qazi-kalon Akbar 97

ulema 9–10, 14–27
  bureaucratisation 22
  caliphal authority 20–1
  challenge to official 25–7
  control of *awqaf* 24
  control of mosques 23

Islamic disciplines 17
law as a function of power 18–19
and Malaysia 130–1, 135–8
marginalisation of Islamic law 22
notions of divine rule 17–18
political authority 19–20
regulating training 23
religious education in schools 23–4
role, status and legitimacy in the modern period 21–4
separation of religion and politics 15–21
state legitimacy 24–5
theology as an expression of political hegemony 19
Umar b. Abd al-Aziz 17
Umayyads 16, 19
United Development Party (PPP) 160, 163
United Malays National Organisation (UMNO) 128–9, 135, 138–46
Uzbekistan 6, 7, 11, 88–99, 171
  cultural Islam 89–91
  Islam in independent 91–4, 98–9
  policy implications 94–8
  and religion 92–3

Vali, Sheykh Abdul 98
Velayat-e faqih 7, 11, 56, 58, 59

Wahhabi Ikhwan (brethren) 31, 33, 37, 107
Wahid, Abdurrahman 7, 12, 150–1, 161, 162, 165
women 74, 78, 82, 112, 115, 116–17

Yassin, Ahmed 170
Yusuf, Muhammad 93, 94, 97, 99

Zia, Khaleda 113, 120
zina 78, 82

For Product Safety Concerns and Information please contact our EU representative GPSR@taylorandfrancis.com
Taylor & Francis Verlag GmbH, Kaufingerstraße 24, 80331 München, Germany

www.ingramcontent.com/pod-product-compliance
Lightning Source LLC
Chambersburg PA
CBHW021758230426
43669CB00006B/118